The Breeches Bible : considered as the basis for remarks, critical and philological, on the English language

James Gurnhill

James Gurnhill

THE

BREECHES BIBLE,

CONSIDERED AS THE BASIS FOR

Remarks, Critical and Philological,

ON

THE ENGLISH LANGUAGE.

CAMBRIDGE:

H. WALLIS, 24, SIDNEY STREET;

LONDON: BELL & DALDY, 186, FLEET STREET.

1862.

CAMBRIDGE :

PRINTED BY J. WEBB, MARKET PLACE.

AUTHOR'S PREFACE.

UPWARDS of half a century has rolled away since INGRAM, in his Inaugural Lecture before the University of Oxford, pointed out with force and eloquence, the utility of Anglo Saxon Literature. The success which followed his endeavours to arrest the attention of his countrymen, not to speak of others, which have since also failed, affords but a poor precedent for any further attempts which may be made in the same direction. "That the Anglo Saxon language has a peculiar share of importance and interest; that it is capable of elucidating the principles of grammatical science, and of leading us to a philosophical theory of Language," are propositions, which, though none might care to question, but few are found ready to prove.

But this is not all. Though Anglo Saxon is a language pre-eminently qualified by the antiquity of its origin, and the purity of its descent, to instruct in the theory and first principles of human speech, it presents yet another aspect, which, as regarding not the philologist nor the philosopher, so much as the mass of Englishmen generally, has claims of a still more urgent character. It is the only language which can lead us to an intelligent conception of the English tongue. To state in round terms, the conclusion to which this assertion (if correct) must lead, that we are as a people ignorant of the very language we speak, might appear somewhat distasteful, nor is this the place to argue in defence of such an assertion.

Yet the Author feels bold to make the avowal, that only the settled conviction of widely prevalent misconception respecting the English Language, and also an earnest desire, to promote, what seem to him, truer and less contracted views, have induced him to publish this little volume.

If it should be urged, as perhaps with some justice it may, that the title selected is not so characteristic and descriptive as might have been wished, the Author would reply that there was really left him but little room for choice. The BREECHES BIBLE seemed likely, not only to afford an interesting and legitimate field of investigation, but also to possess peculiar advantages as a starting point, and basis of future operations. So that, though the object of the earlier chapters is specific,—namely, to institute a comparison between the English of the present and a past century,— and that of the latter generally—to advocate the claims of Anglo Saxon as a *national* study; yet the nature and mode of investigation pursued is throughout the same, even where the particular propositions sought to be established have differed.

It has ever appeared to the Author a matter for regret, that students of Anglo Saxon, who have hitherto written on the English Language, have striven rather to obviate and lessen the necessity of individual recourse to Anglo Saxon, by borrowing from it a few specious rules or illustrations, than to foster its study amongst Englishmen generally, by shewing how it contains, not only the key to unlock the meaning and logic of words, but that it is itself moreover the soul which animates our language. And, though the labours of such men are by no means to be held in light esteem on this account, it seems pretty certain, that to their neglect in pointing to this conclusion, must be mainly attributed the disregard, which as a nation we still pay to the true and only mother of our Language. We have allowed others to read and interpret for us, where in reality a personal enquiry, and an experimental knowledge ought to have enabled us to read and interpret for ourselves. Yet, slender as may at present be the grounds for entertaining such a hope, and few the indications which point to its realization, the Author feels assured, that the day cannot be very far distant, when the apathy and indifference now displayed to the study of Anglo Saxon, must give place to other and more intelligent views. With this conviction before him he has endeavoured to write, so far as his ability served him, not the page over which the advanced student in English or Anglo Saxon literature may pore with satisfied delight, but that rather on which the honest working bee may rest for an hour or so, and find something to carry away, and something to think about.

Nor is he unconscious of the responsibility which must of necessity attach itself to attempts of this kind—a responsibility, unfortunately, which his own imperfections and shortcomings tend rather to increase than to lessen. In one respect, however, he feels he has some claim to that indulgence which he both needs and asks for. His labours, or his recreations (for they seemed at times to be each,) were commenced, and in the main completed, in the quiet seclusion of a country life—amid the bleating of sheep and the lowing of oxen ;—and, though he is proud to possess there many friends, of whose uniform kindness he entertains the most grateful and abiding remembrance, he had still to regret the absence for a long period on the continent of the only friend to whose judgment and revision he felt willing to submit his opinions and proof-sheets. For the assistance, however, which on his return, though late, that dear friend rendered him, the Author is only too glad to have this opportunity of expressing both his obligation and gratitude.

CAMBRIDGE, *Dec. 9th*, 1861.

TABLE OF CONTENTS.

PAGE.

INDEX OF WORDS.   ix

CHAPTER I.

INTRODUCTORY REMARKS.   1

CHAPTER II.

THE GENEVAN VERSION.   13

CHAPTER III.

EARLIER FORMS OF SPELLING SUGGESTIVE OF ETYMONS.   21

CHAPTER IV.

WORDS ALTER THEIR MEANING.   67

CHAPTER V.

OBSOLETE AND OBSOLESCENT WORDS AND FORMS OF WORDS.   84

CHAPTER VI.

OBSOLETE FORMS OF THE PAST TENSE AND PAST PARTICIPLE.   111

CHAPTER VII.

LITERAL CONTRACTIONS—APOSTROPHAL GENITIVE—REMARKS ON SOME OF THE CHARACTERISTIC FEATURES OF THE GENEVAN TRANSLATION AS COMPARED WITH OUR OWN.   ..   119

CHAPTER VIII.

ON THE MEANING AND CONSTRUCTION OF "THAN".   ..   132

CHAPTER IX

OBSERVATIONS ON THE SPELLING IN THE BREECHES BIBLE:—
TENDENCY OF ENGLISH AS ILLUSTRATED THEREBY.   ..   147

CHAPTER X

COMPARATIVE PHILOLOGY—INDO-GERMANIC FAMILY—LATIN AND
GREEK; THEIR ORIGIN AND AFFINITY WITH THE GERMAN
FAMILY—PEDIGREE OF ENGLISH—THE ROMANCE WALLON—
ITS INFLUENCE—THE CLAIMS OF LATIN AND ANGLO SAXON
COMPARED.   167

CHAPTER XI.

THE VALUE OF ANGLO SAXON: FIRST, AS ILLUSTRATING THE
FORMATION OF LANGUAGE GENERALLY, AND OF ENGLISH IN
PARTICULAR; SECONDLY, AS DISCOVERING THE TRUE MEAN-
ING OF ENGLISH WORDS—EXAMPLES—CONCLUSION.   ..   189

APPENDICES.   215

INDEX OF WORDS.

A.

WORD.	PAGE.
Agreeable	165
Ale	54
Ancre, (note)	157
Aught	222
Avoyded	76

B.

WORD.	PAGE.
Backe, Bat	50
Banket	63
Barley, Bere	219
Barm	ib.
Barn	ib.
Baron	ib.
Barton	ib.
Base	71
Beadle	89
Bearn	219
Beech	209
Beer	219
Bene, &c.	160
Bern	36
Berry	219
Bier	ib.
Bird	ib.
Birth	ib.
Bivouac	50
Book	209
Bread } Broth }	216
Bundle	89
Burnt	37

C.

WORD.	PAGE.
Car, Cart	22
Cause	67
Char } Chair }	24

[continued]

WORD.	PAGE.
Chariot	22
Cheap	39
Church	118
Claw, (note)	58
Cleave	57
Clerk	118
Clout	57
Clover, Club, &c., (note)	58
Commoditie	72
Corn	213
Cornwall, (note)	184
Creeple	62
Cress	38
Crime	68
Cyrnel	203

D.

WORD.	PAGE.
-d	194-5
Dangerous, (note)	103
Deed	80
Dettes	163
Disdaine	70
Disease	69
-dom	190
Dung, (note)	94

E.

WORD.	PAGE.
Earnest	202
Ed-	92
Endeavor, (note)	154
-er	192
Evêque	180

F.

WORD.	PAGE.
Facion	157
Faith } Fang }	203

WORD.	PAGE.
Fardel	87
Farm	210
Farthing	32
Fauchin	157
Fet	63, 113
Fiend } Finger }	203
Fornace	162
Forth	48
Foughten	115
Fraile	85
-ful	197

G.

WORD.	PAGE.
Garb	97
Gard	104
Garden	ib.
Garland	ib.
Garter	ib.
Gaunt	78
Gear	95
Ghest	105
Ginn	98
Girder	104
Glain	26
Gome	221
Grenn	94
Grices	90
Groom	221

H.

WORD.	PAGE.
Hand	203
Handle	205
Harberous	101
Harbinger	103
Harbour	101
Harneis	157
Haulm	218
Hee, &c.	161
Hell	218
Helm	ib.
Herbergage	102
Herring	206
Hole } Hollow } Holme }	218
Holpe	113
Holster	218
Holt	ib.
-hood	191
Hornet	209
Hostler. (note)	101

WORD.	PAGE.
Hound	205
Hull	218
Hundreth, (note)	205
Hunter	ib.
Hurted	115

I.

WORD.	PAGE.
Jakes	93
Improve	73
Incontinently	ib.

L.

WORD.	PAGE.
Last	206
Latch	66
Learn } Lere }	206
Lewd, (note)	100
Lore	206
Ludgate, (note)	217
-ly	196

M.

WORD.	PAGE.
Malt	52
Mead	80
Mew	117
Middest	161
Mite	33
Moe, Most } More }	79—81
Mould	52, 220
Mouldiwarp	57
Mowle	50
Morn } Morrow }	34

N.

WORD.	PAGE.
-n	194
Naught } Need }	91

O.

WORD.	PAGE.
Orchard, (note)	194
Ordeal	89
Ought	113
Owe, (note)	ib.
Own	114
Overthwart	161

P.

WORD.	PAGE.
Passe	71
Perfite	156
Pestilences	71
Pight	104
Pile, Pill, Pillage, Pillory	100
Plant	61
Prease	161
Profit	76
Puissant	158

R.

WORD.	PAGE.
Renowm, Reproch	155
-ric	190
Roume	27
Rudder	201

S.

WORD.	PAGE.
Seed	80
Sell, To	36
Sew	116
Shire	191
-ship	192
Shamefast	30
Slouth	45
-some	195
Sore, Sorry, Sorrow, Sour	29
Soul	107
Sparse	104
Stairs	202
Stale	115
Stee	202
Sterope	ib.
Stile	ib.
Strength, Strong	220
Strook, Stroke	111

T.

WORD.	PAGE.
Stretch, (note)	112
Surly	29
Swomme	115
-t	194-5
Term	73
-th	49, 193
Than, Then	ch. viii. and p. 222
The, To, (note)	92
There	199
Threshold	209

V.

WORD.	PAGE.
Vent	61
Vineger	161
Vir	181

W.

WORD.	PAGE.
Wanne	112
Waits, (note)	50
Wan, Wand, Want	76
Wedlock, Welkin,	210
Werwolf	201
Wiers	161
Win, (note)	112
Witchcraft	190
Woman	201

Y.

WORD.	PAGE.
Yard	95, 104
Yarn, Yare	95
Yawn, (note)	98
Yeere	161
Yes	202
Yule	209

ERRATA.

Page   1, line 21, for "Þ, þ," read "Ð, ð."
Page 17, line 3, for "*superintendance,*" read "*superintendence.*"
Page 34, lines 9 and 25, for "*subandition,*" read "*subaudition*"
Page 44, line 5, for "*metalic,*" read "*metallic.*"
Page 89, lines 5 and 9, for "*radicle,*" read "*radical.*"
Page 94, line 4, for "*jacto,*" read "*jacio.*"
Page 106, line 17, for "*hive,*" read "*hire.*"
Page 108, line 9, for "*lays,*" read "*lies.*"
Page 141, line 23, omit "*of*" before "*than,*" and line 17, for "*sover,*" read "*soever.*"

CHAPTER I.

INTRODUCTORY REMARKS.

I KNOW, and can deeply appreciate the antipathy which every Englishman feels to reading a book he cannot fairly be expected to understand. In order thoroughly to investigate many of the examples of the following chapters, I have been driven to that mother of our language, the Anglo Saxon, where, alone, a rational explanation was to be found. My reader is probably aware that the Anglo Saxon characters differ very considerably from our own, and that some little patience and perseverance would be necessary to render them intelligible to his eye. In order to avoid this necessity, however, for, saving two exceptions, there is really no reason why they should be retained, I have taken the liberty of dispensing with them, and in their place substituting the letters of our own alphabet. Had I not adopted this course, one, be it known, sanctioned by the highest authority, I should have had but little hope of finding any but Anglo Saxon scholars among my readers. The two exceptions are the two Anglo Saxon characters which are used to denote the hard and soft sounds of *th*. Þ, þ, denote the hard or rough pronunciation which *th* has in *thin,* and Ð, ð, the soft pronunciation as in *thine.* These, then, are the only two characters, besides those of our own alphabet, which will be met with in the following pages. And even the obligation for retaining these is apparent rather than real, since both sounds are expressed in English by the same symbol. But, as modern Anglo

B

Saxon scholars have thought it advisable to retain them, and the eye rapidly becomes accustomed to them, I have not thought it worth while to depart from the plan usually adopted in this case.

With regard to the rejection of the Anglo Saxon characters, Dr. Bosworth says, that, after mature consideration, and careful weighing of the respective advantages on each side, he is convinced that the balance is in favour of using our own characters. And indeed, it would be otherwise if the Anglo Saxon characters could not be fully represented by our own, that is, by the Roman characters. But with the single exception of *th* they can. And if in reality the Anglo Saxon is the base of the English language it would be absurd to suppose the contrary. The question seems not unnaturally to arise; why, since the structure of English, so far, that is, as it has survived the violent shocks it has had to sustain, is still Anglo Saxon, and since, no less than, out of the thirty-eight thousand words which our language is said to contain, twenty-three thousand—nearly five-eighths—are still Saxon; why, in the face of all this, the Anglo Saxon characters were ever relinquished. The following facts may tend to explain this apparent anomaly.

About the year A.D. 1100 is generally supposed to represent the period when the change from Anglo Saxon to Anglo Norman[1] took place.

---

[1] I use both these expressions, Anglo Saxon and Anglo Norman, under protest, and for the following reasons:—

Of the eight colonies, if so they may be called, which constituted the Saxon Octarchy, one is Jute, three are Saxon, and four only out of the eight are Anglian (from Anglen in Sleswick). The Anglians occupied the North and East of England. The Saxons proper, but called by way of distinction the West Saxons, occupied the South and West parts. In A.D. 827 Egbert king of the West Saxons defeated or made tributary all the other Saxon kingdoms, and united them all in his own person. Egbert was eventually succeeded by Alfred the Great, who expelled the Danes and

This at least is the opinion maintained by Professor Rask in his Anglo Saxon Grammar. The change of course cannot be said to have taken place at any precise date, since it would necessarily be very gradual and extended over many years: but this is the nearest approximation that can be made.

The language spoken at the court of William the Conqueror and his successors was Norman. Each Baron introduced Norman at his castle, and, refusing to learn, what he considered, the barbarous Saxon dialect, compelled those Saxons who lived under him as vassels to learn it also. All property being now in the hands of the Normans, the laws regulating its transfer and tenure were made in the Norman language. Thus the Norman took possession of the Court, the Hall, and the Forum, while the Saxon had to put up with such an asylum as the humble cot of the serf could afford. There is an anecdote told that when Henry the Second, about the middle of the twelfth century was passing through Pembrokeshire he was addressed by the English title of "Good olde Kynge," so ignorant, however, was that monarch of the Saxon tongue that he had to ask of one of his courtiers what was the meaning of "Kynge."

A knowledge of the Norman tongue was at this time an indispensable acquirement for every one who aspired to the rank of a gentleman. Little wonder, then, that, under these circumstances, the Saxon characters

encouraged literature. He translated into his own language the works of Boethius, Orosius, and Bede, thus giving a great stimulus to the *West Saxon* over the *other* Saxon dialects, which caused it eventually to be spoken over the whole of England.

And if *Anglo* cannot with justice be applied to Saxon to designate the language ultimately spoken by our fore-fathers, with how much less propriety can it be applied to Norman, to designate that compound which was formed by the mixture of Saxon and Norman French, and which is now the fabric of the English Language.

should have fallen into disuse. There was in fact
no use for them. This being the case, the Saxon
letters disappeared rapidly and gave place to the
Roman or Italic letters used by the Normans. Power
was wrested from the hands of the conquered Saxons,
who, henceforth, seem to have lost all control over
their literature. Yet, when at last the two classes—
the conquerors and the conquered found themselves compelled to amalgamate[1] the concessions were not all on
one side. On the one hand the Normans were compelled to acknowledge the abortiveness of their attempts
to foist their language on the people they had subdued;
while, on the other hand, the people had lost irre-
trievably the art of writing, in their own characters,
that language, which their conquerors had failed to
deprive them of. Is not this a triumph of nature over
art. Time and adverse circumstances had, indeed,
snatched away the artificial forms of the written language; but the language itself, as it lived on the
tongue, animated the mind, and sanctified many a time
honoured association, required a stronger will than that
of man to displace it.

Many of us have read with a strange curiosity, of
the discoveries which have been made during the last
few years by Layard and other travellers in the East.
We have read of cities, whose very sites had almost
been forgotten; of the palaces and sepulchres of kings,
sepulchres on whose marble walls were delineated the
memorable acts of those whose ashes they contain. We
are told that so far as these drawings or hieroglyphics
have been interpreted and compared with other—principally sacred—records, left us relative to the same
supposed events, they afford a very striking testimony
to the truth of Sacred Historic Narrative. So, then,
in the following pages I have endeavoured to throw a

---

[1] This amalgamation took place in effect about A.D. 1258, in the reign
of Henry III. What was written after this period may be called English.

taper light on one of those sepulchral tablets, which lie, mouldering and forgotten, in the dank catacombs of the past, and will, mayhap, reveal an inscription not altogether uninteresting or uninstructive to repay the toil of deciphering it. Such at least I hope will be the case. What I have done, I have done in good faith, and with the desire not so much to make any new discovery, as to call attention to that most important of all a nation's studies, the study of its own language. I have already alluded to this subject in my preface, though briefly. Permit me, before going further, to revert to it in a more explicit manner. I will begin by relating my own experience so far as it bears on this subject.

I was educated at one of our largest schools, which, though not public in the strict sense of the word, is, yet, I am well assured, inferior to none of those which are, until it was time for me to enter upon my academic course at Cambridge. I am bound to confess, and in doing so I feel convinced I shall not in the least degree be disparaging, in comparison with other public schools, an institution which has claims on my affection, second only to those of Alma Mater, that not till long after I had assumed the "toga virilis" did I obtain any adequate conception of the nature and constitution of my mother tongue.

I do not believe mine is by any means a solitary example; for I do not know of a single school in this kingdom where any attempt is made to impart a fundamental knowledge of English Classics. English Classics! What do they mean? The notion of a classic knowledge of English seems absurd. Greek and Latin form the only classics which come within the range of School-boy[1] experience. As for English, it

---

[1] It will be understood that by School-boys I refer principally to that large and important (prospectively important) class who fill the upper benches at our large Public Schools.

will do for the forms of the lower School, but is
beneath the notice of those of the upper. Indeed, so
long as the Iambics and Latin prose are forthcoming
at due time, it is no concern of the scholastic economy
to look after English grammar. I do not speak with
regard to English composition; for it is impossible to
have better preceptors than the Greek and Latin
authors; but with regard to the anatomy, and constitution of English. How strange it seems that we
should so ignore our own language, while a little
life-time is devoted ungrudgingly to the acquirement of
Latin and Greek.

Is it that there is really nothing in English to
learn but what every body knows; and, that what there
is to learn can best be learned,—nay some would even
say, can only be learned—by studying the Greek and
Latin languages?

It is to afford an answer to these two important
questions that I have written the following pages.

I should be sorry to assert that there is a great
lack of means necessary for acquiring the information I
speak of. On the contrary, there are several excellent
books on this subject, written by men in every way
fitted for their task. Still one swallow does not make
summer; nor do one or two volumes, accessible only
to the means and education of the wealthy, unknown
in our public, much more in our private schools, suffice
to disseminate that knowledge of English, which, it is
not too much to say, every man of even moderate education ought to possess. Better far would it be to lay
no claim to the teaching of the English language than
make it the subject of such a miserable burlesque as is
the case at present. Let us hope the time is not far
distant when we shall awake from our torpor, and Englishmen will remove the stigma, that they know and can
learn all languages but their own.

The investigations of some of the following chapters are I hope calculated to shew, not by mere ipse dixits, or random asseverations, but by the irrefrangible proof of fact the validity and justice of the foregoing remarks.

I have not yet given my reasons for taking the Breeches, or Genevan version of the bible, as my pioneer. I will now do so.

I am unable to regard it otherwise than as a strange coincidence, that a Bible which belonged to my family, probably two centuries ago, should after an exile of a hundred and fifty years find its way back again. Such however has been the case. How this came to pass, it will excite no surprise, that I do not feel entirely at liberty to state, any further than that it appeared to be in the most fortuitous manner possible.

To borrow a simile from antiquity; picture to yourself the heathen who had omitted to insert in the mouth of his deceased parent the small coin necessary to secure him a passage across the Styx, and avert the calamity of wandering for ever and ever up and down its muddy shores; picture the joy which such a son, were he a pious one, would learn that Charon had at length consented to exert his kindly office, and convey the weary shade to the House of Hades. Such a joy was mine in being able to welcome back the old family Bible to its own rightful resting place, after long years of weary travail up and down this wide world.

The remarks of Dean Trench respecting our present version of the Bible are, I conceive, no less applicable to the Genevan version. The following are his words: he is speaking of the composite nature of the English language.

"I do not know where we could find a happier example of the preservation of the golden mean in this matter than in our authorized version of the Bible. One of the chief among the minor and secondary blessings which that version has conferred on the nation, or nations drawing spiritual life from it—a blessing not small in itself, but only small by comparison with the infinitely higher blessings whereof it is the vehicle to them, —is the happy wisdom, the instinctive tact, with which its authors have steered between any futile mischievous attempts to ignore the full rights of the Latin part of the language on the one side, and on the other, any burdening of their version with such a multitude of learned Latin terms as should cause it to forfeit its homely character, and shut up great portions of it from the understanding of plain and unlearned men."[1]

And I think this testimony is applicable to the Genevan version no less than our own, because it was the same spirit, the same thirsting after the word of God by the people of England, that called both the versions, especially the former, into existence.

It was essentially the demand of the people that called forth the Genevan Translation; and it was undertaken by men who knew, that to succeed in their work, they must have, not only learning and piety, but also be actuated by a firm determination to put the result of their labours in such a form as to be within the reach of the humblest reader. On this account I think the Genevan version of the Bible is peculiarly fitted to become the exponent of the English language at the time it was written. We shall do well to recollect that it would then recommend itself to every peasant in the land; to him it would present no difficulties in English; and all those words and phrases which old father Time has somewhat caricatured to us, would be simple and intelligible enough to him. I would observe that we have here no obscure author, or antiquated poet, in whose pages the occurrence of strange words and phrases to us, might, or might not, be indicative of the then condition of the language; but the Book of Life itself, that Book which beside being the only source of true wisdom and happiness here, and our sole guide to heaven hereafter, was for a long time

---

[1] "English, Past and Present," p. 31.

the cherished and favourite version in many a humble cot, and has, therefore, peculiar claims to our affectionate regard. Nor must it be supposed that the difference existing between the Genevan and our present one is very wide. The Text as a whole so nearly resembles our own, that a cursory glance might fail to detect the difference.

It is only here and there; now perhaps, by the antique spelling, by a curious contraction; or, now, by a word that does not seem to fit the eye, or suggest a meaning to the mind, that this difference is forced upon us. The staple is the same as our own version; a fact which will be the more easily credited, when I say that I read through the whole Book of the Prophet Jeremiah without finding above two or three instances of material alteration, either with regard to spelling, in the words themselves, or in general diction. Indeed, so much was this the case that for a time I questioned whether my somewhat laborious task would not in the end prove a fruitless one. I think, therefore, not to speak of internal evidence, the remarks of Dean Trench quoted above are as applicable to the Genevan or Breeches version as our own.

For the information of those who are not already aware of it, I will state the reason why the Genevan version came to be called the Breeches Bible. If we turn to the third chapter of the Book of Genesis, verse 7, we read as follows: "Then the eyes of them both were opened, and they knew that they were naked, and they sewed figge tree leaves together, and made themselves *breeches*."

Such then is the simple reason why this version came to receive the forcible, rather than elegant, epithet of the "Breeches Bible."

The next chapter I have devoted to the brief consideration of the historic records respecting this Book; to that I refer my reader for further particulars. It will be seen there, that the translation was completed in A. D. 1560; my copy however bears the date of 1608, so that it would not be an early edition. I have not had an opportunity of consulting one of the earliest copies published, and, therefore, I cannot say whether any material alterations had taken place between 1560 and 1608. I do not think it is likely, judging at least from my copy. However, such are the facts of the case. For enquirers who can approach their task with a spirit of reverence, I imagine it would be difficult to find any single book whose claims to represent, fully and impartially, our written and spoken language, rest on a more substantial foundation than the Bible, and this on account of the ample scope it affords for the play of language.

In no other is the relationship to time and circumstance so varied, and, consequently, in no other is there so great a demand for variety of style and diction. All phases of life; all classes and conditions of men; all aspects of society, and forms of government, are there, more or less fully, represented.

We have the terse sentences of the annalist; the plain and simple directions of the lawgiver; the calm reflection, the ecstatic fervour of the moralist and poet: and, above all, the thrilling accents of Him who spake as never man spake.

At one time, we enter with the train of kings into palaces of the utmost magnificence, and view with dazzled eyes the fabled splendor of the east; at another we behold the beggar who lies at the gate of the rich man desiring to be fed with the crumbs which fall from his table. Now we listen to the triumphal pœans of a victorious army; again we are called to mourn over a dismantled city, or watch the gaunt forms of its inhabitants as they sorrowfully commence their journey to a foreign land. Such are some of the scenes depicted. Surely these, and there are many others like them, afford scope enough for language. Nor is the opportunity for pourtraying and preserving the colloquial scarcely less than that for registering the written portion of the language :—that portion which lived from day to day in the domestic scenes and the familiar intercourse of man with man. May we not listen to the dialogues of our master as he disputed with learned doctors of the law; or to his precepts as He taught his humble followers, only Himself more humble, the simple elements of that Divine philosophy whose very foolishness was to confound the wise? Or we may even attend them as they "sit at meat," and almost, as it were, enter with them into their varied discourse.

By tracing a river from its confluence with the ocean we may, if we are patient enough, at length discover its source. Or, should the difficulties which oppose the investigation prove insurmountable, and not permit us to ascend further than the mountain torrent, or the subterraneous exit, yet we shall, in all probability, be able to trace it far enough to have our conceptions of its origin and natural history widely enlarged. Language, then, I would compare to such a river, whose source, or sources, it is our wish to investigate;—a poor and thread-bare simile enough, I am ready to admit; yet, sufficient for my purpose, if it assist in explaining my meaning. As, in the case of the natural stream, by carefully following its course, as it winds along the foot of the distant hills, we shall at length reach the mountain pass, whence we may behold the little streamlet, swollen by successive contributions, winding its way through the sloping valleys beneath; so, by tracing the course of language up to the distant hills behind us, and following its banks as they become narrower, and the waters they contain more precipitate, we gain an insight into its origin and nature, which this laborious method alone can afford.

Not that I have, in the following chapters, conducted you, reader, to these hills,—those peaks which loom in undefined outline through the surrounding mists of the past,—nay, we shall scarcely leave the plain, or rather, we shall but mount another step. The river will still flow in mighty span at our feet, though its waters may be somewhat more turgid. Here and there we may perceive a whirling eddy indicative of some antagonistic and inharmonious agency; some inequality, it may be, in the river-bed; or, some tributary stream whose waters have not yet blended with those that receive them.

This is not the place to offer any remarks upon the character of the spelling at the time we are about to consider: they will be found in their proper place. Still there is one conclusion, which I think it will not be amiss here to anticipate. It is the apparent absence of all fixed rules to determine the orthography of words.

On this account alone, would it have been unadvisable to take an earlier version of the Bible. As it is, I have not entirely escaped the inconvenience arising from extreme laxity of spelling; and I have sometimes fancied I have seen an etymology shadowed forth in a peculiar mode of spelling, which, on further investigation, has proved a mere ignis fatuus. So that sometimes a word has given rise to two questions; first, does the spelling indicate anything, or is it to be attributed to the caprice (if that can be called caprice where there is apparently no design) of the age; secondly, if it does suggest anything, what is it? I hope, however, I shall not be found guilty of making capital on this score, or of disturbing my neighbours by the false alarm of " Fire, Fire."

CHAPTER II.

THE GENEVAN VERSION.

THE short respite which the Reformed Church of England enjoyed during the reign of Edward VI. was like the calm which preludes the storm. Scarcely had Mary ascended the throne before she issued a proclamation, which materially altered the condition, and blighted the hopes of the Protestants of this country.

This act, which was passed in the October of 1553, suppressed King Edward's Liturgy and, in effect, restored ecclesiastical matters to pretty much the same state they were in during the latter part of the reign of Henry VIII., when the Scriptures seem almost to have been denied to the people by the prohibition of both Coverdale's and Tyndale's versions.

It was the reinforcement of this Act, and conformity to the injunction of their great Master, who told them, when persecuted in one city to flee unto another, that many of those, who had taken an active part in promoting the Reformation in England, sought to escape the impending storm by voluntary exile.

Germany and Switzerland, that land of classic liberty, afforded a temporary home for these pious men. Frankfort appears to have been chosen at first; and here they might have settled down in peaceful enjoyment of their religion, had not internal dissentions respecting the English Liturgy and other matters of ritual, arisen to disturb that unity. But alas! how often are a man's bitterest foes they of his own household. Here, in common with the French Protestant Refugees, they had the use of one of the city churches for the performance of their services; but party feeling at length became so strong, that the Puritans found it necessary to seek a fresh home. This they did in the city of Geneva, and here it was that the Breeches Bible, or the Genevan version was compiled.

Whatever may have been the faults of the Puritan party, and doubtless there were faults on both sides, there is no doubt it was composed of men of strictly conscientious views; and it is very pleasant to picture to ourselves these poor exiles from their native country for the sake of religion, finding a peaceful retreat on the shores of the beautiful lake Leman. We can imagine how they would rejoice, that at last, even on earth, they had found an asylum, where the hand of persecution could not reach them, and where above all they could sweetly meditate on the words of their Master.

Still, in this their peaceful retreat, they were not unmindful of the spiritual wants of their brethren. They saw the urgent demand there was for a new and entire version of the Scriptures; and, like men actuated by holy purpose, they set to work at once to supply the want of their age.

Surely we cannot wonder, that under such circumstances, the blessing of God richly attended their labours, or that the result of them was to furnish a Bible which would be disseminated through the length and breadth of England, leavening the people, as it were, with its spirit, and, finally, in a great measure, reproducing itself in the very Bible which is now the precious treasure of many an English heart. During the reign of Queen Elizabeth, from 1560 to 1603, no less than one hundred and thirty distinct issues of the Bible were made; and of these ninety were of the Genevan version. This fact affords sufficient evidence of the favour and popularity it enjoyed.

The men principally engaged in making the Genevan version were, William Whittingham, Thomas Sampson an Oxford man, and Anthony Gilly a Cambridge man, who sought refuge on the continent at the commencement of Mary's reign. It is not certain that Coverdale assisted in the work of translation. If he did, it could but have been for a very short time; as he was at Geneva only during parts of the years 1558 and 1559, while it was being made.

William Whittingham, who, it must not be forgotten, had previously, in 1557, published alone a translation of the New Testament, called the Genevan Testament, was educated at Brasenose College, Oxford, and was appointed to a fellowship at All Souls' in 1545. He took part in the Frankfort controversies, and adhering to the Puritan side, accompanied those who held the same opinions to the city of Geneva, and became the minister of the congregation that was presently formed there. The Genevan Bible was completed in April, 1560, and, hence, and from the preface it will appear, it must have been commenced in 1558. Let us listen for a moment while these pious earnest men tell us of their labours.

"Now, forasmuch as God's glory is chiefly attained by the knowledge and practising of the worde of God (which is the light to our pathes, the key of the kingdome of heaven, our comfort in affliction, our shield and sword against Satan, the school of all wisdome, the glasse wherein we beholde God's face, the testimony of his favour, and the onely foode and nourishment of our soules) we thought we could bestowe our labours and studie in nothing, which could bee more acceptable to God, and comfortable to his Church, than in the translating of the holy Scriptures into our native tongue, the which thing, albeit that divers heretofore have indeavoured to atcheive : yet considering the infancy of those times and imperfect knowledge of the tongues, in respect of this ripe age and cleare light which God hath now reveiled, the translations required greatly to be perused and reformed. Not that we vendicate anything to ourselves above the least of our brethren (for God knoweth with what feare and trembling we have bene for the space of *two yeeres and more*, day

and night, occupied herein) but being earnestly desired, and
by divers whose learning and godlines we reverence, exhorted,
and also incouraged by the ready willes of such, whose hearts
God likewise touched, not to spare any charges for the further-
ance of such a benefit and favour of God toward his church
(though the time then was most dangerous, and the persecution
sharpe and furious) we submitted ourselves at length to their
godly judgements, and seeing the great opportunitie and
occasions which God presented to us in his church, by reason
of so many godly and learned men, and such diversities of
translations in divers tongues : we undertooke this great and
wonderful worke (as in the presence of God, as intreating the
worde of God, whereunto we think ourselves insufficient) which
now God, according to his divine providence and mercy hath
directed to a most prosperous end."

We may feel somewhat inclined to smile, when we
hear these good and simple hearted men talk of their
"own ripe age and cleare light:" yet, we shall do
well to bear in mind that each age is only ripe in
comparison with those which have preceded it, and
the time will probably come when the boasted enlight-
enment of the present generation will appear equally
ridiculous and vain. We cannot well over-estimate, not
only the candour and self denial, but also the learning
and piety of these men. We ourselves are reaping the
fruits of their labours, and can ill afford to jest at
their expense. But indeed this was no idle boast, after
all on their part, for the age in which they were living
presented a remarkable contrast to those which preceded
it. The minds of Englishmen were now being eman-
cipated from the galling chains of religious despotism;
awaking to a sense of their degraded position, they
became clamorous for the restoration of their invaded
rights and privileges. Literature and science, too, were
making rapid progress, and, hand in hand with religion,
fast putting to flight the dark shade of ignorance and
superstition, which had brooded, like a foul nightmare,
for centuries past over Europe at large.

The thirst for knowledge of all kinds—of religious
knowledge in particular—had been excited, and now no
barriers were able to repress it. Version after version

testify to the impatience which men felt to obtain for themselves the Book of Life. The Great Bible, under the superintendance of Coverdale and the patronage of Cromwell, Earl of Essex, was printed at Paris in 1538-39, in spite of the opposition manifested by the Inquisition,[1] which caused those who were engaged in this work to delay their labours for a time.

This Bible—the Great Bible—was a revision of Matthew's, or Tyndale's version. In the following year, 1540, another version was issued, which goes by the name of Cranmer's Bible, because it has a preface by Cranmer.

In 1541 appeared another edition, "oversene and perused at the commandemet of the Kynges hyghnes, by the right reverend Fathers in God, Cuthbert, Bysshop of Duresme, and Nicholas, Bishop of Rochester."

The year previous to his decease, Henry VIII. prohibited both Coverdale's and Tyndale's versions. Death however annulled the decree, and opened out the bible again to its anxious enquirers. During the short reign of Edward VI. embracing a period of only six years and a half, no less than fifty editions of the bible were published, and all by the people themselves. Still, no new entire translation was made, till we come to the Genevan version, though at one time it appears to have been in contemplation. Men were now at liberty to exercise their own judgment, and were left to their own consciences as a guide. And, indeed, so good was their will that there was little need of any coercive

---

[1] Coverdale and his party were summoned to appear before the Inquisition, but, knowing the partiality and religious intolerance of that tribunal, they preferred to secure their safety by flight. In doing so they were compelled to leave a large portion of their work behind them, consisting of sheets already printed. These sheets were seized by the Inquisition and some of them were burned. How any of them escaped appears little short of a miracle, yet, we are told that "four great dry flats full" were sold to a haberdasher "to lap his caps in." They were afterwards recovered by Grafton.

influence. They had at last obtained the boon they had longed for, and with a keen appetite they were regaling themselves to the full on the rich repast. But Mary succeeded to the throne, and this brings us to the subject we are more particularly considering, and from which we started.

The style of the Genevan Bible is purely English throughout; so far, that is, as English can ever be called pure: by which I mean, that there is no attempt, as in the Rheimish version, to introduce words which would not be understood by every English reader. In the Rheimish version, which, we must recollect, was prepared in self defence by the popish exiles, we find such words as *"pasche," "azymes," "neophyte,"* and others, the only object of which could be to obscure the true meaning of the text, and, so virtually, render it useless. A similar attempt was made even in Henry's reign by Gardiner, to revise the New Testament, that certain *majestic* words which are found in the Latin Vulgate[1] might be transferred to the New version. His mean design was frustrated by Cranmer.

In the Genevan version, however, we have a faithful portrait of the English language as written and understood at this time. Indeed, when we consider the disadvantages it had to contend with, the obstacles which stood in the way of its ever becoming the popular version in this country, as we know it did, the conclusion forces itself upon us, that there must have been some secret chords of sympathy to knit it so closely to the hearts of our forefathers.

We have already observed that the translation was completed in 1560; still for fifteen years after no edition

[1] Fuller says "Gardiner's design plainly appeared in stickling for the preserving of so many Latin words to obscure the Scripture, who, though wanting power to keep the light of the Word from shining, sought out of policy to put it into a dark lantern, contrary to the constant practice of God in Scripture, levelling high hard expressions to the capacity of the meanest." *Our Eng. Bible.* p. 116.

of this version was published in England. What was the real cause of this, it is difficult now to determine. By some it is supposed that Archbishop Parker opposed the obstacle by wishing to exercise a control over its publication, to which Bodley, who had obtained from Queen Elizabeth the patent for printing the same for seven years, would not submit. Whatever may have been the cause, there is no doubt that, in spite of the difficulty, this version speedily became the favourite with the common people of England.

The "Bible of the greatest volume" which would in all probability be the Great Bible, was that specified in the Queen's injunction, to be provided for every parish church. Still, we are assured that the Genevan version was the one preferred for private and family use.

We must guard against the error of supposing that our Translation was the result of a single well-organized attempt. On the contrary, we may safely look upon it as but a revision, with some corrections and amendments it is true, of all the previous versions. At the time we are considering, it is probable that the people and the clergy were conscious they did not yet possess any single version worthy of their entire confidence.

On this account it was not deemed advisable to stereotype any that had yet appeared by the royal assent; but, rather to allow each person a discretionary power of his own. This fact seems further borne out by Queen Elizabeth granting to Bodley, the father of the celebrated Sir Thomas Bodley, who founded the magnificent library at Oxford, which bears his name, the patent for printing the Genevan version for seven years.

As Archbishop Parker was either unable, or unwilling to countenance the Genevan version, prejudiced perhaps by the Calvinistic principles of its compilers, he set about producing a new one, which, on account of its being the joint work of several of his episcopal brethren, he called the Bishops' Bible. This Bible was published in

1568. Whatever may have been its merits, one thing is certain, that it never enjoyed the popularity of the Genevan version.

At the time of the compilation of our present Bible the Bishops' Bible was that used in churches, and appointed to be generally followed. Still in cases where the superiority of other versions, as Tyndale's, Coverdale's, Matthew's, Whitchurch's, the Genevan, was manifest, the latter were to be followed by our translators: and I cannot but think, from a careful perusal of the Genevan version, that our translators must have derived material assistance from it.

It is remarkable, that long after the publication of our authorized version, which did not take place till 1611, the Genevan version had rooted itself so strongly in England, that it refused for some time to give way. I believe I have good authority for stating that it continued to be printed so late as the year 1641.[1]

But now having exceeded the limits which I originally marked out for this portion of my subject, and having said more than my reader had any right to expect, my book shall henceforth speak for itself.

[1] I will here relate an incident which occurred to me some little time ago, which, though trivial, is, still, in my mind indicative of the esteem in which the Breeches Bible is held. I happened to be looking over some old books in a stationer's shop when the bookseller shewed me a veritable Breeches Bible, which, as he said, he laid great store by. Having examined it, he brought me another, to all appearance, of still greater antiquity. In haste I turned to see if it were also a Breeches Bible, when to my surprise I found the first three chapters of the Book of Genesis missing. On further examination, it turned out to be merely an early copy of our present version, and of little more value, in an antiquarian point of view, than a tenpenny Bible. I have little doubt, that it had been thus mutilated for the purpose of being palmed off on some unwary individual as a Breeches Bible.

CHAPTER III.

EARLIER FORMS OF SPELLING SUGGESTIVE OF ETYMONS.[1]

How the meanings of words may frequently be arrived at by merely tracing them a step or two backwards, nearer their origin, has already been indicated.

Proceeding, then, in conformity with this theory, I have collected in this chapter such words as appear to support it. It is the pride of a mere curiosity seeker, hardly deserving the name of Antiquary, to drag to the light of day relics of the past, which can in no way serve the uses of the present and future. Such, however, is not my intention, in this place at least. It would be quite possible, I doubt not, for any one, who felt so inclined, to string together a number of words entirely strange to men of the present age. I hope, however, the examples adduced in the following pages will not be of barren character, but will contain some lesson, expressed, or understood, that will admit of application to our own wants, and our own times. In this way alone can the exploration of the past be of any service. Words, indeed, unlike the men whose deeds they chronicle, need no historians; they are their own annalists, and tell a story incapable either of falsification, or misconstruction. It needs but that we treat them fairly; that we summon them before us in their natural costume, to learn from them all they can teach us. They will tell their tale in a manner not the less eloquent because silent, nor convincing because brief.

-----

[1] An Etymon is the true origin of a word.

Before entering, however, on the consideration of the following chapters, there is one remark I wish to make; applicable, not to them alone, but to the wide subject of etymology generally: namely, that on no person does a dogmatic spirit sit with so ill a grace as the etymologist; because, in no other subject is there such wide room for difference of opinion.

For the explanations which the following pages contain I lay claim to little merit. If I have found a difficulty I could not myself solve, I have had recourse, in all cases, to the best authorities I could procure. On further perusal, my reader will find to how great an extent I have availed myself of the previous labours of Mr. Horne Took, not that in all cases I have adopted his views, but because his explanations are, I think, on the whole, the most rational and trustworthy.

CHARET.

"And hee said, this shall bee the maner of the King that shall reigne ouer you: hee will take your sonnes, and appoint them to his *charets*, and to be his horsemen, and some shall runne before his *charet*."—1 *Samuel*, VIII. 11.

I am not sure whether our modern form chariot occurs at all in the Breeches Bible; certainly *charet* is by far the more common. It appears almost impossible to see this older form, evidently connected with the more modern one now in use, without asking the question, what does this close resemblance, and yet this difference, intimate? Why is there any difference at all? Horne Took says:

"Car, Cart, Chariot, &c. and the Latin Carrus are the past participle Cy'ren of the Anglo Saxon verb Cy'r-an, to turn. This word was first introduced into the Roman language by Cæsar, who learned it in his war with the Germans."

But this is a very bold assertion; for, in the first place, it is more likely that Cæsar first met with the word among the Gauls, than among the Germans; in which case the word would be Celtic; and, in the second place, the absence of several of these words, *chariot* for instance, from the Anglo Saxon, renders it next to impossible that they should be derived from, or even through, it by immediate descent.

The passage above affords a suggestion we shall do well to notice. Who could see the two words *charet* and *charette*, the one English and the other French, without being at once convinced that they are the same word;—the former the Anglicised counterpart of the latter. The resemblance is so striking; the foreigner had at this time altered his appearance and dress so little, that it is impossible not to distinguish him.

But with our present form *chariot*, the resemblance is not nearly so striking, and a doubt might reasonably be entertained respecting the parentage of the word. It is clear, the word was French before it was English, and this remark is also applicable to some others, which have been deduced in too great haste from the Anglo Saxon. Our word *car* is undoubtedly a French word. Though, it is not impossible that *cart* may be nothing more than the Anglo Saxon word *cræt*, a cart, so altered by transposition. Not only is *char*, a good French word to this day, but we have evidence to shew that this was the exact form in which it first appeared in our language.

> "And as the guise was in his contree,
> Full high upon a *char* of gold stood hee,
> With four white bolles in the trais.
> Instede of cote-armure on his harnais,
> With nayles yelwe, and bright as any gold,
> He had a beres skin, cole-blake for old."
>
> *Canterbury Tales*, 2138.

But whatever may be the root of the words *car* and *chariot*, whether it be Celtic[1] or Teutonic, for it

---

[1] Having insinuated a doubt as to the truth of Mr. Horne Took's assertion, that the word *carrus* was introduced into the Latin language by Cæsar, who learned it in his war with the Germans, I feel bound to say something in support of this opinion.

In the First Book of Cæsar's Commentaries, De Bello Gallico, and at the beginning of the third section, the following passage occurs:

is almost impossible now to ascertain, there is no
doubt that the Saxon verb Cyr-an has bequeathed to
posterity a large and valuable legacy. Thus *char* with
its compounds charcoal, charwoman, churworm; *chair*,
with its compound chairman; churn, cardinal, perhaps
cart, and the verb to jar, as well as ajar, may all be
referred to this root. In each the radical meaning of the
verb is implied.

A *char* means any odd job to which a person may
turn for a short time; and in the Anglo Saxon it
signified exactly what we mean when we use such expressions as "doing a man a good turn," "one good

"His rebus adducti, et auctoritate Orgetorigis permoti, constituerunt,
ea, quæ ad proficiscendum pertinerent, comparare; jumentorum et *car-
rorum* quam maximum numerum coemere; sementes quam maximas
facere, ut in itinere copia frumenti suppeteret; cum proximis civitatibus
pacem et amicitiam confirmare."

Again section 26:

"Alteri ad impedimenta et carros suos se contulerunt."

Now it is very evident, from the context of these passages, that it was
not the Germans with whom Cæsar was now carrying on war. It was
in fact the Helvetii of whom Cæsar himself tells us "they excel the
rest of the Gauls in valour because they are engaged in almost daily
conflicts with the Germans, whether it be in warning them from their
own territory, or making warlike incursions on theirs." So far, then, from
Cæsar borrowing this word from the Germans, the above passages would
prove the exact reverse; namely, that it was a nation which waged continual warfare with the Germans, amongst whom he first found it;
granting this to be the first time. Evidence therefore would point, rather
to a Celtic, than a Teutonic origin. But the fact is, that in nothing more
than in questions of this kind, ought we to be mindful of the maxim
"Est quadam prodire tenus si non datur ultra." Was Mr. Horne Took
aware of the Greek κάρρον, which signified a chariot or car, when he
referred all these words to the Anglo Saxon verb Cyr-an?

It is an error into which we are perhaps too apt to fall, to suppose
that, beyond the pale which separates the great families of language from
each other, we must not expect to find the traces of affinity. We should
rather remember that, even the great branches of language themselves
are all related to one great prototype; all ascend from one common stock;
and that, it is pure speculation to attempt to define the limits of that
confusion, which was the sufficient cause of the dispersion of men at the
tower of Babel.

turn deserves another," &c. It also signified a *choice*, a *will*, because the thing, on which a choice was to be made, was turned over and over in the mind. A churn is a vessel in which milk is turned until the butter is separated. "A chair" says Horne Took "is a species of seat," "turned about, and returned at pleasure." To set a door ajar, or, as it was formerly written, *on char*, is to place it so that it may be turned quite open, or returned shut.

Some have supposed that the char fish is so called because it turns itself very rapidly in the water, though this, to be sure, might be said with equal truth of many other kinds of fish.

It is not unworthy of notice, that the Latin word *carruca*, which would, perhaps, resemble a basket carriage of the present day, was also a foreign word borrowed, probably, from the Celts or Gauls. The different uses, which this word has been made to serve, are also curious. If we are right in supposing the French word *charrue*, a plough, to be the word which the Romans altered into *carruca*, it is then difficult to see how it came to signify a carriage for ladies to ride in; and, probably, could we but know it, there is some little episode connected with this singular circumstance, to account for it.

But *carruca* in Domesday Book has a signification very different to the former, and tending rather to confirm the conjecture, we have hazarded as to its etymology. It seems to have been equivalent to the old ploughland. "The ploughland or carrucate[1] in

[1] Habet O....VI. boves in dominio et villani aliam terram et II. boves. Supp. 224—Ibi est I. carruca G. D. 124.

Les dames de Caen attelaient 8 bêtes à chacune de leurs charrues d' outre-mer: ainsi, elles avaient à Avelingues, 8 *charrues* chacune de 8 bœufs. M. Delisle, 304, 204.—*Eng. under the Normans, Note to* p. 30.

An oxgange, or an oxgate of land, was as much as an ox could till. In Domesday, from 10 to 15 acres make an oxgange; therefore eight oxen would till from 80 to 120 acres; a quantity which may easily have corresponded to the ploughland.

Domesday is called 40, 60, 80, or 95 acres: and so in other documents we meet with ploughlands 60, 72, or 80 acres."—*England under the Normans*, p. 33.

GLAIN.

"And the Israelites *glained* of them by the way five thousand men, and pursued after them unto Gidom and slew two thousand men of them."—*Judges* xx. 45.

Beyond that, the passage here presented to us affords a sort of connecting link between our English verb *glean*, and the French verb *glaner*, I do not know that it contains anything worthy of notice in a philological point of view. It does this, however, and therefore I thought it not unworthy of notice. In some parts of England the custom of picking up the loose ears of corn is not called gleaning, but leasing. In Shropshire, I believe, this is the case. It is a curious explanation which is given of this fact: curious because, if true, it shews how words, springing from the same source, and each flowing, as it were, for a long period through a separate channel, may, at length, so nearly converge as to become in a language strange to both, synonymous in meaning.

Both *glean* and *lease,* are supposed to spring from the Gothic verb *galisan;* the first form being perpetuated by some of the Teutonic tribes, the Visigoths, the Burgundians, and the Franks,[1] who, with the exception of the Normans, were the last settlers in France; and the second form *lease*, being perpetuated by the Saxons, who invaded England, and introduced it into this country.

To lease[2] is an English verb because it was a

[1] See chapter on the "Norman Element."

[2] At the bottom of page 136, "Diversions of Purley" there is the following note:

"Leasing, *i.e.* loosing, *i.e.* picking up that which is loose, separate or detached from the sheaf."

There is surely no occasion for such straining after an explanation, when Dr. Bosworth gives the verb Les-an, signifying even in the Saxon itself, be it observed, to gather, choose, lease.

Saxon one first; but, To glean which has almost supplanted it, is, properly speaking, a French verb, though both are descendants from a common parent, transplanted to different soils. How truly have they preserved the family likeness!

In the vision of Pierce Ploughman, when Perkyn determines to "apparaille" himself "in pilgrymes wise" and set out on a search after Truth, he says:

"A busshel of bred corn
Brynge me therinnee
For I wol sowe it myself,
And sithenes wol I wende
To pilgrymage, as palmeres doon,
Pardon for to have.
And who so helpeth me to erie
And sowen here er I wende,
Shall have leve by our Lorde!
To *lese* here in hervest,
And make hem murie thermyd,
Maugree who so bi-gruccheth it."

Pierce Ploughman, 3919.

ROUME.

This mode of spelling *Room* appears to have been quite common at this time. It occurs very frequently, and is found also in Chaucer in his Legend of Ariadne.

"For in the prison, here as he shall discend,
Ye wote well, that the beast is in a place
That is not derke, and hath *roume* and eke space
To weld an axe or swerde, staffe or knife,
So that me thinketh he should save his life,
If that he be a man, he shall do so."

Chaucer, 1995.

The nearer we trace words to their origin, the nearer does their resemblance to that origin become. Our word Room is the Saxon Rúm, connected with the verb Rý'man, to increase, to enlarge, from which, it is not improbable, that we derive the substantives Rim, Brim, Brink, Brow.

CARKEIS.

I do not adduce this old form of spelling carcass as more correct than our own: for, indeed, the reverse is the case, but simply because it seems to say to us What am I? and what is my history? Let us try to find out. There is no doubt that it is the French word carcasse; but what is the French word carcasse? It is most probable a Latin compound (caro cassa) signifying useless flesh.[1] The French borrowed it, or manufactured it, from the Latin, and we have borrowed it from the French; as has been the case with such a number of other words, now passing for English.

SOWRE.

"Who put darknes for light and light for darknesse, that put bitter for sweet and sweet for *sowre*."—*Isaiah* v. 20.

This method of spelling, instanced in the word *sowre*, is one which much prevailed at this time. Thus we find, Powre for Pour; Flowre for Flour; Towre for Tower, and many others of a similar kind.

Let us just transpose the *r* and the *w* in the word here spelt *sowre*, and compare it, then, with the word printed in italics in the following quotation:

"And I thanked hym tho,
And siththe I hym tolde
How that Feith fleigh awey,
And Spes his fellawe bothe,
For sighte of that *sorweful* man
That robbed was with theves."
Vision of Pierce Ploughman, 11542.

Now, the metathesis, of which this is an example, is common enough. In fact, my reader has already had the opportunity of seeing one other instance of

[1] Lumine cassus, in Virgil, means a deceased person, one deprived of the light of day. Taken in this sense, carcass becomes peculiarly expressive: caro cassa lumine, a body deprived of the light—of day, or of life.

it, in *yelwe* written for *yellow*, though, in that case, the consonant was *l* instead of *r*. Similarly

Sparrow was written Sparwe.
Arrow „ „ Arwe.
Sorrow „ „ Sorwe.
&c. &c.

Sowre has undergone another alteration, and is now written *sour*. Whence, then, do we derive all these words?

Sorrow ⎫
Sorry ⎪
Sore ⎬ They are all derived from the Anglo
Sour ⎪ Saxon Substantive and Adjective (for it
Surly ⎭ is both) Sár, a wound.

The word Sár, very variously written and pronounced, signified a wound, sore, pain, sorrow, grief. It is connected with the verb *sargian*, to give pain.[1]

---

[1] Mr. Horne Took refers this family of words to syrwan, which he says made for its past participle sorw; how this could be I cannot understand, for neither syrw-an nor Sarg-ian could possibly make a past participle sorw, or anything the least resembling it. I do not think we are one iota nearer the root of a word, when we have traced it to a verb, than we are when we have traced it to a noun, which, in all probability, is the root of the verb itself. It is a great mistake to suppose that, nouns must be parts of verbs and formed from them; because it is well-known that verbs in numberless cases are formed from nouns, which in fact, constitute, and are still clearly distinguished in, the roots of those verbs. On this point I will quote Sharon Turner's words in his history of the Anglo Saxons, vol. II. p. 424, he says:

" *Gan* is the verb of motion to go, or the verb ágan to possess, and -an seems to be (I) give, from unnan to give. Thus Deágan, Deágian to tinge, appears to be from Deág, a colour, and -an (I) give; Dæl-an, to divide; Dæl-an, I give a part. Blóstmian to blossom, is Blóstmágan, to have a flower: Byan, to inhabit, is By'-ágan, to have a habitation."

Now let us apply this simple rule to the two verbs Syrwan and Sargian, in the first the root is Syrw, which is clearly nothing more or less than the substantive Syru, with the last vowel reduplicated for the sake of euphony, and signifies a snare; giving us, as we should expect when made into a verb by the addition of the verbal termination -an, the verb Syrwan, to ensnare, to *entrap*, but not to vex or molest, as Mr. Took affirms.

In the second verb Sargian, the root is clearly sár, a *wound*, a *sore*, and thus, when made into a verb by the addition of the verbal termination,

Thus, one little Saxon monosyllable have we managed to split up into no less than four words, distinct from each other, both in spelling and signification; though, it must not be forgotten, that the form corresponding to *sorry* is also found in the Anglo Saxon.

Sorrow and *sorry*, had formerly a meaning somewhat different to that which they have now acquired; that is, they had reference more to the outward *sore* on the body, than to its corroding effect on the mind.

Thus, in an old translation of the New Testament we find the following passage:

"And Ihesu enuyrownyde al Galilee, techynge in the synagogis of hem the gospel of the rewme, and heeling al *sorewe*, ether ache, and sikenesse in the peple."

This meaning still survives in such expressions as "a sorry fellow," "a sorry case," &c.

SHAMEFASTNESSE.

"Likewise also the women that they aray themselves in comely apparel, with *shamefastnes* and modesty, not with broyded haire, or gold, or pearles, or costly apparell."

1 *Tim.* II. 9.

Shamefast is one of those words noticed by Dean Trench in his " English past and present." There will, therefore, be the less occasion for me to dwell on it, to any great length. I cannot do better, than quote what he says on this subject.

"Least of all should our modern editors have given in to the corruption of *shamefastness* (1 *Tim.* II. 9.) and printed *shamefacedness*, as now they do, changing the word which meant once

---

Agan, gives us Sargian, which signifies to have a wound, or *sore*, and, therefore, to be in pain or *sorrow*, which, when long continued, *sours* the temper of the unhappy sufferer.

I think, however, Mr. Took may be right in supposing *shrew* and *shrewd* to come from the verb Syrwan, as they easily may, though it requires a powerful stretch of imagination to believe, that they can come from the same root as sorrow, and its kindred words do.

a being established firmly and *fast* in honorable shame, into the mere wearing of the blush of *shame* upon the *face;* cf. *Ecclus.* XXVI. 15. 25; XXXII. 10; XLI. 16, 24; in all which passages the later editions have departed from that which ought to have been exemplary to them. *Shamefast* is one of a group and family of words, in all which *fast* constitutes the second syllable, thus *steadfast* [A. S. Staðolfæst] *wordfast;* and those good old words *rootfast* and *rootfastness*, which we have now let go." *Page* 245, *note.*

What says the great arbiter of our language on this point? Surely his word must be law. Can it be that the word does not exist in his vocabulary! No, it is not to be found; the nearest approach is *shamefaced*, which he tells us, and truly too, is compounded of *shame* and *face*, and signifies "modest, bashful, easily put out of countenance." Who, we would ask, is responsible for this gross perversion? It would be hard to saddle the great Doctor with it, though it is difficult to excuse him, for not having entered a protest against such a barbarism, even, while compelled, let us hope against his will, to sanction it. Little wonder the error should be perpetuated, since the great lexicographer, from whom there is no appeal to a higher tribunal, has affixed his imprimatur to it.

QUADRIN.

"And there came a certaine poore widow, and she threw in two mites which make a *quadrin*."—*Mark* XII. 42.

I am not aware the quadrin was ever an English coin; nor does its appearance here, in an English translation, at all imply the necessity of thinking it was. The word in the original Greek was borrowed from the Romans, and the very fact of its appearance there affords an undesigned coincidence, that the Jews had at this time passed under the Roman yoke, and become to some extent familiarized with Roman coins, and Roman customs.[1]

[1] Instances of Latin words taking a place in the Greek are by no means rare.

Σουδάριον is simply the Hellenistic form of the Latin *sudarium*, a

The Roman *Quadrans,* or *Teruncius,* was equivalent to about three fourths of our farthing, but like our farthing signified, not only the fourth part of a *coin* (the As) but also, the fourth part of many other things.[1] Indeed, this range of meanings, running, as it were, parallel to each other in the two languages, is rather striking. Thus in both was it used to signify a portion of land ; though, how much, it is not perhaps so easy to determine. In Domesday Book the Ferding is the Farthing, or fourth part of the Virgate. " In Cornwall thirty acres made a farthing land, and nine farthings, on the average, made one Cornish acre[2] or entire field of 270 common acres."—*England under the Normans,* p. 40.

Indeed, in both languages, it is only the fourth part that is signified, without any reference to the thing to be divided. It is scarcely necessary to caution any-one against supposing, that the word Farthing is com-pounded of *Fourth* and *thing.* This would be, really, as great an error in itself, though not perhaps quite so serious in its results, as that we lately observed in the word *shamefaced.* The Saxon had not only the form which has given us farthing, but also, that which would have given us farth*ling.*[3]

As there was formerly a farthing[4] of land, as well as of money, so was there a minute of money, as well as a minute of time, and its value was about half

---

towel ; so also κεντυριών κῆνσος, δηνάριον are words of Latin origin, intro-duced by the Romans, and permanent witnesses of their dominion.

[1] As a coin it was the price of a bath among the Romans. No wonder they were so fond of bathing, when they could indulge in the luxury at so moderate a cost.

[2] " It must be borne in mind that in the Cornish Domesdays *acra* and *ager* mean a large field."—*England under the Normans.*

[3] The Saxon word for farmer is Eorðling, Earthling.

[4] In our antient Law Books, a Farding-deale of land means the fourth part of an acre, the rent of which was in Richard the Second's time so restrained, that for a Farding-deale of land they paid no more than one penny.—*Walsingham,* p. 270.

a farthing. The existence of the Anglo Saxon word *mite* forbids us supposing, that the English word *mite* is but a contraction of this old word minute.

" Ihesu sitting agens the tresorie bihelde how the company castide money into the tresorie, and many riche men castiden manye thinges ; sotheli whanne o pore widewe hadde come, she sent twey *Mynutis*, that is a Farthing."—*Mark* XII. 42.

MURTHERER.

" But let none of you suffer as a *murtherer*, or as a thieffe, or an evill doer, or a busibody in other mens matters."
1 *Pet.* IV. 15.

" For-thi God of his goodnesse
The first gome (man) Adam
Sette hym in solace,
And in sovereign *murthe;*
And siththe he suffred hym synne,
Sorwe to feel,
To wite what well was
Kyndeliche and know it."
Vision of Pierce Ploughman, p. 382.

" And as the weke (wick) and fir,
Wol maken a warm flaumbe, (flame)
For to *murthen* men myd, (with)
That in the derke sitten :
So wole Crist of his curteisie,
And men cry hym mercy,
Both forgive and forgete, (forget)
And yet bidde (pray) for us
To the Fader of hevene
Forgifness to have."
Ibid, p. 362.

My reader will have the kindness to observe the words written in italics in the above passages. We have *murtherer, murthe* and *murthen.* How comes it to pass that there is such a hateful likeness between these words? Is it all chance; the casual effect of mere caprice, or is there something besides this; something which has its seat in the deep recesses of human feeling and human experience? Can these two children, like Cain and Abel, so different in disposition, claim descent from common parents? Apparently so.

D

"Mirth" says Horne Took "that which dissipateth: viz. care, sorrow, melancholy, the third person singular of the indicative of Myrran."—*Div. Pur.* p. 614.

"The Anglo Saxons," he goes on to say, "likewise used morð, morðe, mors, (death), *i. e.* that which dissipateth (*life* understood); the third person of the same verb myrr-an, to mar, &c., and having itself the same meaning as mirth; but a different application and subandition. Hence from morðe, *murther*, the French meurtre, and the Latin mors."

This explanation leaves but little to be said. Reasoning from analogy, there is good ground for supposing that the Anglo Saxon words, myrð, mirth, morð, death, and myrðra, a murderer, are all connected with the verb myrr-an; whether or not, we agree with Mr. Horne Took in supposing that morn, morning, morrow,[1] are to be referred to the same root.

---

[1] For the benefit of those who are not able to refer to the original, I have here inserted, without comment, what Mr. Horne Took has written on the etymology of these words:

"*Morrow*, therefore, and *morn*, the former being the past tense of myrr-an without the participial termination en; and the latter being the same past tense, with the addition of the participial termination en) have both the same meaning, viz., dissipated, dispersed. And, whenever either of these words is used by us, Clouds or Darkness are *suband.* Whose dispersion (for the time when they are dispersed) it expresses."
"*Myrrende* is the regular present participle of myrr-an: for which we had formerly morewende. The present participial termination *ende* is in modern English, always converted to *ing*. Hence morewing, morwing, (and by an easy corruption) *morning*."—*Div. Pur.* p. 462.

"And if the night,
Have gathered aught of evil or concealed,
Disperse it, as now light dispels the dark!"
Milton's Paradise Lost, Book 5.

"To Flandres wol I go to-*morwe* at day,
And come again as soon as ever I may:
For which, my dere wif, I thee beseke
To be to every wight buxom and meke,
And for to kepe our good be curious,
And honestly governe wel our hous."
Cant. Tales.—The Shipmannes' Tale.

So murrain, Anglo Saxon myrring, is a wasting [disease understood] which squanders or dissipates life. The formation of verbal substantives will be again alluded to in the Appendix.

Yet, from the way in which murderer and mirth are at present spelt, who might not well be excused, if he failed to see any connection between the two? There is, apparently, no cause to be assigned for the change, which has so altered their appearance beyond that slow and silent one, the course of time.

CHAPMAN. CHEAP.

"Who have decreed this against Tyrus, (that crowneth men) whose marchants are princes? Whose *chapmen* are the nobles of the world?"—*Isaiah* XXIII. 8.

If I am not mistaken, we have a word here which is fast becoming obsolete. True, on completing a bargain we receive, what is still called, in some parts of the country, "chapman luck," yet the word is evidently not in vogue as it used to be, when the chapman, in Chaucer, tells his "wif,"

> "Thee lacketh non array ne no vitaille;
> Of silver in thy purse shalt thou not faille,
> And with that word his contour[1] dore he shette,
> And down he goth; ne lenger wold he lette;
> And hastily a masse was ther saide,
> And spedily the tables were ylaide,
> And to the dinner faste they hem spedde,
> And richly this monk the *chapman* fedde."
>
> *Canterbury Tales*, 13141.

> "Both my gees and my grys,[2]
> His gadelynges[3] feccheth,
> I dare noght for fere of hem
> Fight ne chide.
> He *borwed* of me Bayard,
> He brought him hom nevere,
> Ne no ferthying therefore,
> For ought I koude plede.
> He maynteneth hise men,
> To *murthere* myne hewen[4],
> Forstalleth my feires (fairs),

[1] What we now call a "counting-house," from the French *comptoir;* from the Latin *computare;* whence also comes our word *accounts,* formerly spelled *accompts.*

[2] Pigs.

[3] Vagabonds.

[4] Workmen.

> And fighteth in my *chepyng*,
> And breketh up my bernes[1] dore,
> And bereth awey my whete,
> And taketh me but a taillé,
> For ten quarters of otes."
>
> *Vision of Pierce Ploughman*, p. 68.

It is true, the family of words springing from the Anglo Saxon verb, cyp-an, *To sell*, has, in one form or another, taken too firm a hold on our language, ever to become totally extinct; yet, not only are some of these words falling into disuse, but others of them, though still used, have undergone material changes in their acquired meaning. We shall best understand this by following the radicle, from its earliest point of view.

Cyp, in Anglo Saxon, signified a measure; thence, by the process of verbal formation, comes Cy′p-an, *To sell,* because things are sold by measure. From the verb thus formed, or perhaps from the original Cyp, the Saxons formed the following substantives:

> *Cy′pcman,* A merchant, a chapman.
> *Cy′ping,* A bargaining.
> *Cy′p-inga,* A market, still surviving in Chipping-Nor-ton, Chipping-Barnard, Chippenham, and others.
> *Cea′p,* A bargain, anything for sale, a price; whence, from conjunction with *Stow,* (a place) comes
> *Cea′p-stow,* A market-place, which is still preserved in the name Chep-stowe; Cheap-side, East-cheap, &c., are all connected with this word.

Now, where, I would ask, in this list, embodying the principal uses and meanings of *cheap* and its compounds, have we the faintest indication of its present signification? The truth is, that the word *cheap* has now lost nearly all trace of its original meaning, and, instead thereof, has assumed one which is but as an adjunct to its former self. Let us not forget that there were influences to account for this degradation.

---

[1] On the derivation of this word, see Appendix.

Yet this change was not made all at once; the step was too great to be taken at a single bound; and, therefore, we find a kind of half-way house, where the word seems to have halted for a time in its downward course.

Formerly, the expressions *good-cheap* and *bad-cheap*, were used to characterize good and bad bargains.

"The sack that thou hast drunk me, would have bought me lights as *good cheap*, at the dearest chandlers in Europe."
1st Part Henry 4th, Act 3, *sc.* 3.

Bad-cheap is now entirely disused, and *cheap* has come to mean what was formerly meant by good-cheap.

"Chap" is sometimes used for "chapman." The use of the verb *Cy'pan* still exists in the expression, "*To chop and change.*" The verb *To cheapen* formerly signified, To attempt to buy, To bid for a thing.

"She slipt sometimes to Mrs. Thody's,
To cheapen tea."—*Prior*.

BRAST.

"Rejoice yee heauens: for the Lord hath done it: showt, ye lower parts of the earth: *brast* foorth into praises yee mountaines, O forest and every tree therein."—*Isaiah* xlvi. 23.

It does not always follow, that the older form, or forms of a word, must necessarily be the more correct. An instance of this fact is afforded us by the above passage. *Brast* is certainly a very powerful word, but it is not so correct as our more modern and weaker word burst. The Anglo Saxon verb, of which they are only metathesized forms, is Berstan, *To burst*. But this liberty of metathesis is one extensively indulged in, not only in Anglo Saxon, but in language generally. There seems to be a peculiar pleasure in doing so, and, only by a knowledge of this habit, can the etymology of many words be explained.

Our English word *Burnt* was formerly written *Brent:* and this earlier, and more correct form, is still retained in the words brown, brand, brandy, bronze, brunt. *Brown* is the colour produced by burning, and *brunt* is the *burnt*, and, therefore, the hot part of anything.

> "For smoke and smolder,
> Smyteth in hise eighen,
> Til he be bler-eighed, or blynd,
> And hoors in the throte,
> Cogheth, and curseth,
> That Crist gyve hem sorwe,
> That sholde bringe in bettre wode,
> Or blow it till it *brende*."
>
> *Vision of Pierce Ploughman*, 12014.

> "The fires brenne upon the auter clere,
> While Emelie was thus in hire praiere:
> But sodenly she saw a sight queinte,[1]
> For right anon on of the fires queinte,[2]
> And quiked again, and after that anon,
> The other fire was queinte, and all agon:
> And as it queinte it made a whisteling,
> As don these brondes[3] wet in hir brenning,
> And at the brondes end outran anon,
> As it were blody dropes many on:
> For which so sore agast was Emelie,
> That she was wel neigh mad, and gan to cry,
> For she ne wiste what it signified."
>
> *Canterbury Tales*, 2335.

In like manner:

> Bird was formerly written Brid.
> Grass   „   „   Gers.
> Cress   „   „   Cerse or Kerse.
> Nostril   „   „   Neisthyrl.
> &c.   &c.

> "Wisdom and wit now,
> Is noght worth a *kerse*,
> But if[4] it be carded with coveitise,
> As clotheres kemben hir wolle."
>
> *Vision of Pierce Ploughman*, 5628.

The ignorant abuse of this harmless word *kerse*, or cress, in the above expression, which, in fact, is pretty much the same as "I don't care a straw," "nought worth

---

[1] Strange.   [2] Vanished.   [3] Torches.   [4] Except.

a pease," *Spens. Shep. Cal. Oct.*, has given rise to the corruption, now so common, "I don't care a curse," which has, in its turn, been also changed into the still more objectionable form, "I don't care a damn."

But, to return to the word *brast*, it should be observed, that, though it cannot be called correct, there is the testimony of antiquity in its favour.

> "He buffeted the Bretoner
> About the chekes,
> That he looked like a lanterne,
> Al his lif after.
> He bette hem so bothe,
> He *brast* ner hire guttes."
> *Vision of Pierce Ploughman*, 4147.

So that, at this time, *brast* may be said to have been good English, because usuage had made it so. The time, however, was now fast approaching, when it was destined to lose its place, at least, in the written language. It still survives in the somewhat altered form *brust*, a great favourite with the agricultural labourers of some parts of England, though, entirely scouted by all those who wish to talk what they consider correct English. The word is, perhaps, worthy of a better place, like many others, which have retired to drag out the remainder of their days in the humble cottage of the peasant, previous to their total extinction, as members of the living tongue. But this we must expect. As in animated nature, the processes of secretion and excretion are continually going forward, so neither does language, the vehicle of thought, form an exception to nature's general law.

HURLYBURLY.

"And as they(c) cried and cast off their clothes and threw dust into the aire."

"The chief captaine commanded him to be led into the castle, that he might know wherefore they cried so on him."

(c) "The description of a seditious hurlyburly, and of an hare-brained and mad multitude."

Acts XXII. 23, 24, *and note.*

The word *hurlyburly*, though now rarely met with, in this exact form at least, has been rendered immortal by a place in Shakespeare's celebrated Witches' scene.

First Witch. " When shall we three meet again?
Second Witch. When the hurlyburly 's done,
When the battle 's lost and won.
Third Witch. That will be ere th' set of sun."

Had it not been for this passage, it is difficult to say what might have been the fate of the word. Macbeth has snatched it from oblivion.

It may be asked, what object I have in noticing this word? I have two reasons. The first is, to shew that so late as the beginning of the 17th century, the word was in familiar use; the second is, that it will afford me a pretext for enquiring into its real meaning and etymology, so far as this is possible. It will be observed, that the word does not occur in the text of the Breeches Bible, but in one of the marginal[1] notes. This, however, does not in the least affect its authenticity. It is, indeed, possible, that a word in the original, which happened to have no exact counterpart in English, might be represented by some conventional compromise, some foreign word, or fictitious coinage, (as was probably the case with *quadrin ;*) but, in the case of an explanatory note, such a thing is, to say the least, highly improbable, if not altogether impossible. We may, then, I think, fairly conclude, that the word *hurlyburly* was at this time a perfectly familiar one.

But what then is the meaning of the word? I mean its intrinsic meaning, for, of course, every one knows that, its acquired meaning is a *tumult* or *riot*.

It is, in fact, a French word, which exists at this day, though, of course, spelt and pronounced somewhat

[1] It is not certain that these marginal notes, which are very copious, and, generally speaking, valuable, were not one of the offending causes, which ultimately prejudiced the minds of those who desired a new version.

differently in French, to what it is in English. It becomes, therefore, a question of French, rather than English etymology. The French word is *hurluberlue*, which, it is necessary to observe, is not only a noun substantive, but also a noun adjective; in which latter sense, it signifies *abruptly, bluntly.*

The following, then, I take to be the composition of the word: *hurler*, to *howl*, or *roar;* and *berlue*, a *glare.*

"Avoir la berlue," is to have a dimness of sight, to see double. Hence *hurluberlue* would appear, as composed of these elements, to mean a "hare-brained" fellow, to whom excitement, and tumults make things appear in one continual glare of bewilderment. It appears that the word, in passing over from the French, has undergone a material change. In the French it is used to designate a person, but when it becomes English, it designates, no longer a person, but a thing. It is not impossible, that it may have acquired its meaning from having, at first, signified collectively, what the French word does individually; meaning a collection of "harebrained" fellows; and thence, as a natural consequence, a riot, or tumult.

The French word *hurler*, and the English words *howl*, owl, and yell, are in all probability connected with the Anglo Saxon *gyll-an*, to yell.

And now comes the question, has the word really seceded from our spoken language? We think not. There is a word sometimes met with on the outskirts of society, for the mention of which, it might be expected, I should make an apology, but which, however, I do not intend to do; a word, which, like a decayed old gentleman, who, is no longer able to keep up appearances, has slunk away into the filthy alleys and narrow bye-ways of society, there, if possible, to bury past recollections, as well as to lose sight of present degradation. The word to which I refer is pronounced as though it were spelt *hullabaloo*. I do not recollect ever to have

seen the word in print; though I have frequently
heard it used. It would but little surprise me to be
told, the word is merely slang, unworthy of consideration,
and beneath the notice of good society and good
breeding. There are some slang words, of which it
may with absolute truth be affirmed, that they have
no etymology whatever, and, were it desirable, it would
be easy to afford examples enough. But, I think the
word hullabaloo is not one of these words. I believe
it to be a corruption of hurlyburly; and in this
conjecture I am, I think, strengthened by the existence
in the Swedish tongue of the word *hullerbuller*, which,
I am told, is used in precisely the same sense.
If this conjecture is a correct one, then, the instance
of corruption, which this word affords us, is only one
more added to an already long list, imported like
slippings, from abroad, and grafted on to the old
stock at home: words, which analogy should teach
us, must undergo serious modification, before they can
become acclimatized.

Not unfrequently, they become misshapen and twisted,
in such a way, that their original meaning and derivation
is, either obscured, or entirely lost. If men do not
see the meaning of a strange word, which, either by
custom or convention, or for convenience, they find
themselves compelled to use, they will presently alter
it, so as to bear a meaning, of their own, or if not
a meaning, at least a national sound. Nor is this a
trait by any means peculiar to one race of people:
it is common to all nations, whose language admits
into its texture words of foreign growth. We know
it was so amongst both the Greeks and Romans;
several instances of which have been already noticed by
Dean Trench, in his " English, past and present."[1]

---

[1] " Thus βούτυρον, from which, through the Latin, our 'butter' has
descended to us, is borrowed, as Pliny (*Hist. Nat.* XXVIII. 9.) tells us,
from a Scythian word, now to us unknown; yet, it is plain that the Greeks

There is a strong intolerance of foreigners amongst us, and unless they quickly become naturalized, and settle down quietly, adopting our dress and customs, the probability is, their sojourn will be short. We know to how great an extent certain writers of the present day, love to interlard their periods with French words, as though the English language were incapable of doing justice to their sentiments. Yet, how very few of these words ever get any farther than the page of the novelist, or succeed in making a permanent settlement amongst us. One cannot fail to be struck with the remarkable contrast, in this respect, which occurs between words which have now long since become part and parcel of our spoken, and written language, and words of recent importation. While, in the first instance, a word is intolerable until it can speak for itself, and lay aside its foreign costume; as time advances, it looses its need of intrinsic meaning, lives no longer by sufferance, but, as it were, by virtue of citizenship, acquired through long continued residence amongst us. Such words are *metœcs*.

If we detect a bright coin amongst the pieces that are paid us, our first impulse is carefully to examine the stranger, and the date and impress it bears. Our friend, the grocer, would strike it down on his counter, while our other friend, the grazier, would toss it from his finger and thumb into the air, to ascertain its " ring." But if, instead of being a new coin, with a finely chiseled bust, and the date of last year struck upon it, it happen to be an old silver sixpence, bald and smooth with age, no curiosity is then excited, nor any doubts expressed of its being current money

---

so shaped it, and spelt it, as to contain apparent allusion to cow and cheese; there is in βούτυρον an evident feeling after βοῦς and τύρον."

So *bozra*, meaning *a citadel*, in Hebrew, becomes βύρσα, in Greek. The Syrian goddess Astarte becomes 'Αστροάρχη, the Star-ruler, &c.

Page 230, note.

with the merchants. And so it is with words, which are but the coins whereby the social intercourse,—the mental and intellectual bartering,—is carried on between man and man. After they have passed through their first ordeal, and lost a trifle of their metalic gloss, the distinctive marks, which were at first necessary to ensure their acceptance with the public, are gradually worn away, till at last, their very guarantee becomes their lack of all internal signification whatever.

Nor is this the case with foreign words only; but, in the main, with words essentially English also, which, owing to their every day usage, have failed any longer to suggest the origin whence they sprang. The meaning of such words is felt, rather than understood. They have acquired a kind of passport of their own through the mind; and the mind seems to grasp them rather by instinct and usage, than by any intellectual effort. In this respect, words are degraded from their honorable office, as mediators between the mental faculties of the human brain, and become mere sounds, expressive of certain trains of ideas, but nothing farther: approaching, indeed, more nearly to the office and function of the calls of animals to each other, than the rational interchange of human thought.

Take, for example, the numerous class of English nouns, derived directly from Anglo Saxon verbs, whether from the past participle, or from the present tense. Even in cases where both noun and verb are still in use, the connexion is frequently not recognized. How much less then, may we expect anything different in cases where the verb is no longer extant to suggest the derivation. It may be said, that words become so altered in their pronunciation and spelling, as to render this oversight excusable. Yet, this is but a lame excuse, as a little careful consideration could not fail to point out the relationship, wherever it exists.

The connexion between the noun *truth*, and the verb, *to trow;* between *birth* and *to bear; health* and *to heal,*

and very many other parallel instances, is surely evident
enough to any one, who gives any attention at all to
the meaning of words.   But when we come to such
examples as girth, strength, month, meat, sloth, ruth,
&c., the connexion is of a less obvious nature, and
more frequently escapes detection.   In many instances,
the spelling alone is sufficient to disguise a word, and
obscure its etymology, which a glance at the word as
it was formerly spelt, could not fail immediately to
indicate.   Take, for instance, the word

SLOUTHFUL.

The connexion between the noun *sloth* and the verb
(now almost obsolete) *to slow, i. e., to retard,* is not of
the most patent character; yet, who could see the
word as it is spelt in the following passage without at
once observing it ?

"A *slouthful* man maketh poor, but the hand of the diligent
maketh rich."   *Prov.* x. 4.

In "*Pierce Ploughman,*" the word is written *sleuth.*[1]

"Among these other of *sloutes* kind
Which all labour set behinde,
And hateth all besines;
There is yet one, which Idelnes
Is cleped.
In wynter doth he nought for cold,
In summer may he nought for hete,
So, whether that he frese or swete,
Or be he in, or be he out,
He woll ben ydell all about:
For he ne woll no tranaile take
To ride for his ladies sake."

Gower, Lib. 3, *Fol.* 69, *p.*1. *Col.* 1.

We may notice, by the way, that, from the time
of Gower, till the beginning of the 17th century, the
spelling of this word appears to have undergone but
little change.

The class of substantives formed on this model is
a large and important one; too large, indeed, to admit

[1] The exact Anglo Saxon word Sleuð.

of mention here. There are, however, two or three I will take the liberty of considering, after we have done with that one already in hand.

From the same root, the Anglo Saxon verb *slawian*, to be slow, from which we derive *sloth*, also come

Slack
Sloven
Slut
Slouch
Slough
Slug

the second and third of which are but different forms of the past participle; the first with the ending *en*, the second *ed*. From this it would appear that they are both equally applicable to either males, or females. Both Chaucer, and Gower, as in the quotation above, seem to apply the word *slut*, or *sloute*, as it was spelt, without any restriction to sex.

The following passage seems peculiarly rich in these verbal nouns:

"For the children are come to the *birth*, and there is not *strength* to bring *foorth*."—2 *Kings* xxxix. 3.

About the first there can be no difficulty. "Strong," Mr. Took says, "is the past participle of the verb *to string*. A strong man, is a man well strung."

"Orpheus, whose sweet harp so musically *strong*,
Inticed trees and rocks to follow him along."
Poly-olbion, Song 21.

And of *strength* he says,

"That which *stringeth*, or maketh one *strong*; Anglo Saxon *streng*." [1]

But what is *foorth?* Is this also a verbal substantive? Scarcely. The following is Mr. Took's opinion respecting it:

---

[1] It seems singular Mr. Horne Took should have referred *strength* to streng, while there is the exact word in the Anglo Saxon; namely, strengx. For the Anglo Saxon streng, as a noun, is a string, a sinew, or chord; and as an adjective, is the same as strong: but in neither acceptation does it signify *strength*. It is highly probable however that the verb Strang-ian, from which *strength* is derived, is formed from the substantive streng. See Appendix.

"From the Latin fores foris (out of doors) the French had fors, (their modern hors).[1] And, of the French fors, our ancestors (by their favourite pronunciation of th), made forð, forth ; as from the French *asses*, or *assez*, they made asseth, *i. e.*, enough, sufficient."

But this must be received with caution. For if, as Mr. Took asserts, our ancestors received it from the French, and, therefore, not before the middle of the eleventh century, how does he account for the presence of the word in Anglo Saxon writings, long previous to that period? The Anglo Saxon poet, Cædmon, died about the year A.D. 680, yet the word occurs in his metrical paraphrase. Aldred, about the year A.D. 900, translated the celebrated "Durham Book" into Anglo Saxon, and the word also is used by him. It cannot be pretended that these men borrowed the word from the French ; so that Mr. Took's conjecture is scarcely tenable. And, even, if there were not proof of its previous existence in the Anglo Saxon tongue, it would be very improbable, to say the least of it, that the Anglo Saxons should have adopted into their own language (for forð is strictly Anglo Saxon) a word from those, whose coming they had such bitter cause to remember. Besides *asseth* never was a Saxon word. It occurs in Chaucer, in the following passage :

"And though on heapes that lye him by,
    Yet never shall make richesse,
    Asseth unto his greedinesse."

Romaunt of the Rose, 5600.

So that it is not a case in point.

The derivation, then of *foorth* must be sought elsewhere.

Now, strictly speaking, I do not see, that either Mr. Horne Took, or any one else, is in any way bound,

---

[1] Well-known to us by the expression "hors de combat," *i. e.* disabled. The Fauxbourg, in Paris, is supposed to be compounded of the word *fors.* It was formerly written *Forsbourg,* by Froissart and others ; "La Bourg de Four n'estoit anciennement qu' un Fauxbourg, qu' on appelloit en Savoyard Bourg de Feur, c' est à dire, Bourg de Dehors."

Histoire de la Ville de Génève.

For a similar reason, perhaps part of the town of Reading is called the Forbery.

while treating of the etymology of English words, to explain also the etymology of Anglo Saxon words. To pursue the subject beyond the Anglo Saxon, seems but a matter of curiosity, and one little likely to be attended with any beneficial results. However, as we have cast imputations on Mr. Took's etymology of the word *forth*, we are morally bound to offer another in its place.

From the Anglo Saxon verb far-an, To go, we are supposed to derive the following words :

1st. The verb to *fare :* "How does he fare?" "Fare-well."

2nd. The substantive *fare, i. e.,* sustenance; passage-money; and in compounds, where it has the force of *going,* as warfare, welfare, wayfare.

3rd. The substantive *ford :* a passage across a stream; and perhaps

4th. The substantive *fardel.*

Now, this verb faran makes the third person singular of the indefinite tense, færð, which seems to me, to bear a very close resemblance, in outward appearance, as well as internal signification, to the word, (call it what you will), forð. Forth, as derived from this source, would embody the signification of *departure :* and hence, would arise the meaning it now bears, of distance, or separation.

> "Look out of lond thou be not *fore,*[1]
> And if such cause thou have that thee
> Behoveth to gone out of countree,
> Leave hole thine herte in hostage,
> Till thou again make thy passage;
> Think long to see the swete thing
> That hath thine herte in her keeping."
> *Romaunt of the Rose,* 2641.

> "Againe the knight tho olde wife gan arise,
> And said; Sir Knight, here *forth* lyeth no way."
> *Chaucer, Wife of Bathe's Tale.*

[1] There is the following note on this very word: *Div. Pur.* p. 275, "*fore, i. e.,* fors, or forth." [Rather the past participle of *fare,* To go.—*Ed.*]

But this is only conjecture, and each one is at liberty to receive, or reject it, according to his own judgment.[1] I certainly know not to what other source we can look for an explanation of the word than this, be it right, or wrong.

[1] I have here subjoined some of the verbal nouns in *th*, the whole of which are to be found in Part II., Chapter 5, of the *Diversions of Purley.*

Truth :—That which a man *troweth,* 3rd person singular indicative of *treowian,* To trust, To trow.

Filth :—Whatsoever *fileth;* anciently used where we now use *defileth.*

Wealth :—That which *enricheth :* from Anglo Saxon *Welegian,* To enrich.

Dearth :—That which *dereth, hurtheth,* or *doth mischief;* from Anglo Saxon *derian,* To injure. *To dere,* is an old English word:

"No deuil shal you *dere,*
Ne fere you in your doing."
Vision of Pierce Ploughman, p. 140.

Mirth :—Has been already noticed.

Mouth, moth :—The same word differently spelt, and pronounced; from *metian,* To eat.

Tooth :—That which *tuggeth;* from Anglo Saxon, *teogan,* To tug.

Earth :—That which one *ereth,* or *eareth; i.e.* plougheth: from Anglo Saxon *erian,* To plough.

"He that *erith,* owith to *ere* in hope."
1 *Corinthies* ch. ix. v. 10.

I feel that I am doing a great injustice to Mr. Took's delightful volume, in thus hashing up a portion of it; were it not to show his theory to those who have not yet had the pleasure of making its acquaintance, I would not have done it.

It has frequently struck me as very strange, that Mr. Took never, so far as I am aware, told us what was his opinion respecting the word *cloth,* or rather the Anglo Saxon word claꝸ. It is impossible that it can have escaped his attention. *Cloth* and *clad,* seem to connect themselves together in the mind, and mutually to suggest each other.

Now, there seems very little doubt, that the Anglo Saxon adjective, *claded,* whence comes our word *clad,* is simply the past participle of *hlid-an,* To cover, and spelt *gehlidad,* or *gehlyd:* and claꝸ, in the same way, I think, must be only a more convenient form, sanctioned by custom and usage, of the word gehliꝸ, a covering; evidently connected with the same verb, *hlidan.* Unfortunately, the verb *hlidan* would

E

BACKE.

"The storke also, the heron after his kinde, and the lapwing, and the *backe*."—*Leviticus* XI. 19.

"At that day shall man cast away his silver idoles, and his golden idoles, to the *mowles*, and to the *backes*."
Isaiah II. 20.

I think a person might well be excused, if he failed to recognize, in this so dusky and obscure a form, that night-loving little creature, the *bat*. He might naturally be inclined to think, that this must surely be a typographical error of the printer, and no genuine English word. But this cannot be the case, since it occurs in three separate places, even if there were no other evidence to adduce in favour of its authenticity. The following seems to be the true *linage* of the word: it springs from a Gothic word, *vauka*, signifying to *watch*.[1] In Swedish, the corresponding word is *natt-baka;* in Danish, *bake;* a form very closely resembling the above; and in Scottish, or Lowland Scotch, it is *bak.* Now, it will be observed, by reference to the philological chart, which I have copied from Dr. Bosworth's Anglo Saxon Dictionary, and inserted at the end of this book, that all these languages, the Swedish, the Danish, and the Lowland Scotch, all belong to the Scandinavian branch; I do not know that the word occurs at all in the Anglo Saxon; at least, I have not observed it, if it does. It would appear, then, from this, that we have borrowed the word from the Scotch; or, otherwise, that it was introduced by the Danes.

There is another word, very closely allied to the

not form its 3rd person singular in ð, like the other verbs. Nevertheless, it would be bold to assert that the terminal letter ð of all these nouns must necessarily be found in the verb. *Cloth*, if derived from this verb, would signify that which covereth. Hloða, in Anglo Saxon, signifies a blanket, or covering. The following words are referred by Mr. Took to this verb, hlidan:

Lid. Blot.
Lot. Glade. Cloud.

[1] For this explanation I am indebted to Thompson's "*English Etymons.*"

word *backe*, both in pronunciation and spelling, which should not be overlooked. It is the word *bivouac*.

At the bottom of page 573, "Diversions of Purley," there is the following editorial note :—

[*Qu.* Bivouac, be-wachten? *Ed.*]

But, if the editor intends this as a suggestion for the Anglo Saxon root, it is unfortunate for his purpose, that no such word is to be found. It would, indeed, be far more convenient if both *backe* and *bivouac* could be traced to some such word in the Anglo Saxon, but the Anglo Saxon verb, which corresponds to the Gothic *vauka*, is *wæcc-an*, and in the form *bewæcc-an*, is not to be found. Indeed, it seems pretty certain, that we cannot trace either of these words to the Anglo Saxon. *Wæccan* has given us the verbs, *To watch*, and *To wake ;*[1] but we must not refer *backe* and *bivouac* to it also.

The Gothic word *vauk*, became in the German, or Teutonic, *bewach*, and in the Swedish, *bewak ;* and the same word, when cast in a French mould, became *bivouac*. Thus did that smooth flowing language avoid the harsh guttural, and turn the word into its present form.

Bivouac is not to be found in Dr. Johnson's Lexicon; from which, it is fair to suppose, that the word is one of comparatively recent introduction from the French. What is the date of its introduction, indeed, I do not know, but it would probably be borrowed, either from French military dispatches, or, when our armies have been allied together. It should not be forgotten, that the strict meaning of *bivouac*, in military language, signifies the whole corps remaining on guard, or *watch*, during the night.

But, to return to our starting point. Is this investigation likely to throw any light on the meaning and origin of the modern word *bat*, whose etymology, says Johnson, is unknown?

---

[1] The "*Waits*," who sing at midnight on Christmas Eve with such solemn effect, are no doubt so called from the fact of their keeping vigil or *watch*.

To assert, that the modern word *bat* is only a corruption, or abbreviation, of the older form, here presented to us, (*backe*) would be simply to affront my reader's judgment. I confess the leap is a large one; yet, it is a tempting one, too. Where, besides, can we look for a meaning, if it is not here? There are not wanting instances, where time has effected changes, in the spelling of words, as great as that we see here; as in the case of *fet* for *fetch*. Still, I prefer leaving the question open to the discretion of each individual, rather than saddling myself with the responsibility of an assertion, which, in the end, may be proved groundless.

But there is yet another word, in the latter quotation, not altogether undeserving of notice. "To the *mowles* and to the *backes*," we are told, shall men cast their idols. Glory to God, this prophecy is fast being fulfilled. The teachings of a divine philosophy are fast dispelling the dark shades of ignorance and superstition: the bright Sun of the glorious Gospel is shedding his rays on every land, and before them the nations of the earth are, verily, casting "to the mowles and to the backes their idoles of silver, and their idoles of gold." Let us rejoice at this change, and endeavour, each of us, as far as in us lies, still further to promote it. It is wonderful, to think how much has been effected since the time we are now considering, when we ourselves had scarcely established our right to the Word of God, and when the translators had to prosecute their arduous task in a foreign land. The work was at this time but commencing.

MOULD.   MOWLE.

"*Mould* and *malt*," says Mr. Took, "though now differently pronounced, written, and applied by us, are one and the same French word, *mouillé*, the past participle of the verb *mouiller*, To wet, or To moisten. *Mouillé*, anglicized, becomes *mouilled*, mould; then moult,

mault, malt.   Wetting, or moistening of the grain, is
the first and necessary part in making what we therefore well term *malt*."

Now *mould* has come to be used in two different
ways.   We make use of it whether we talk of the
"mould[1] of cheese," or the "mould of a garden."

It is at least doubtful, whether Mr. Took's etymology will hold in the first instance, that of *mould*;
in the second, that of *malt*, it certainly will not.

For *malt* was a word well-known to our Saxon ancestors, and, therefore, could not possibly have been
borrowed from the French.

It is difficult to understand, how Mr. Took could
become guilty of the inconsistency he has here betrayed.
In a former part of his delightful book, he animadverts
with some severity on those etymologists, Johnson (his
friend Johnson of course) among the rest, who think,
that etymology consists in finding out parallel words
to those they are considering in other languages.   He
argues in this way: that to trace a word up to its
origin, or parent stock; to shew how it came to be
a word at all, and why, is a very different process
from merely finding a parallel expression in another
language.   To do the latter, is, indeed, nothing more
than reproducing the difficulty, without solving it;   in
short, to borrow a simile from the mathematician, to
endeavour to find the value of two "unknowns" from
two dependent equations.

Every word in the French language needs the etymologist, as much as our own.   When, therefore, Mr. Took
refers us to the French verb *mouiller*, for the explanation
of *malt*, and *mould*, how, to save himself from his own
lash, would he propose to account for *mouiller?*   He
appears as far as ever from throwing any light on
the subject.   It is useless his going to the Latin for
a solution, unless he can go to the Greek also, (for

---

[1] For the probable derivation of *mould* in this acceptation see Appendix to this page.

he is bound by his own rules to trace every word, either to the Greek, or the northern tongues). Again, supposing he could have traced the origin of this word up to the Greek, or where else, I care not, how would he have accounted for the Anglo Saxon *malt*, or *mealt*, which, are the forms whence, beyond question, we derive the word malt; and *molde*, which is as certainly our English word mould, the soil? This must surely be a difficulty. If these words had really descended to us from the French, their presence in the Anglo Saxon tongue would require an explanation that it would be difficult to give; for, of course, every one is aware that the Norman invasion caused the overthrow of the Anglo Saxon tongue. We certainly must not refer to the Norman-French for any solution of Saxon words, since the Teutonic element is pure in the latter, while in the former, as we well know, the Frankish dialect of the Teutonic family has undergone very considerable modifications, through its amalgamation with the Gallic Latin, which was spoken previous to the settlement of the Franks in northern France.[1]

It is evident, then, that we must not look to the French for any solution of the words *malt* and *mould*, if we still require any further than the Anglo Saxon *malt* and *molde* afford. Surely, it can be little short of heresy "grande nefas et morte piandum," to suppose, that to the Normans we are indebted for the cup of nut-brown ale,—the sparkling ealoð[2] of our Saxon grandfathers.

[1] See the chapter on "The Norman Element."

[2] It seems strange that while Mr. Took should have been content to trace the origin of *malt* no further than the French, he should, at the same time, have traced that which is made from malt, namely, *ale*, to an Anglo Saxon root. He says "ale, the Saxon aloð, is the third person singular of the indicative of ælan, To set on fire, To inflame." He then quotes what Skinner, by whom this etymology had been suggested, says "ale may perhaps be derived from the Anglo Saxon ælan, To set on fire, To inflame. Because, when of a more generous nature (*such as was drunk by our ancestors*) it elates the spirits, and warms the blood copiously, often a little too much."

But what, it will be asked, do I propose to substitute for Mr. Took's erroneous derivation; that is, what is the derivation of the Anglo Saxon words *mealt* and *molde?*

Mealt, I think, is unquestionably derived from the Anglo Saxon verb *meltan,* To melt, To dissolve, To cook. The past tense of this verb gives us *mealt,* the precise word we seek; and the past participle is not materially different, except in the ending. It is *molten.* This is the only explanation I am aware of. If my reader thinks it sufficient, it is at his service. Truly, the process of *malting barley,* can scarcely be called *melting* it; yet it may, without doing any great violence to our feelings, be said to be in a manner dissolved; or, we know not how far the process of drying the grain, after it has been steeped, may not have suggested, or answered to, the notion of *cooking.* I believe, indeed, there is a reason to be assigned for every word, could we but discover it. It may not, in every case, be such a reason as to satisfy the rigid demands of advanced science, and yet, may be quite sufficient to have justified the use of a word among our less enlightened ancestors. We know, that in scripture, also, there are many expressions used, as it were, out of condescension to the limited, and, in some cases, erroneous notions of ancient times. But, if it be somewhat of a strain to explain *malt,* by reference to the verb *meltan,* To melt; how is it possible to explain *mould?* The difficulty is one of still greater dimensions,[1] nor

---

[1] The following quotation is extracted from the preface to Thompson's "English Etymons." I do not place any great reliance on it, on account of its extreme vagueness, but give it, as a suggestion, for what it is worth. "To these suggestions, on a very intricate subject, may be added the Gothic mi, mid, med, apparently from the Gothic I, at, in, or between. They correspond with the Latin *medius,* and *medium,* a mean, a half; and, besides, denoted a division and a particle, a mite, or mote; whence Gothic *meida* and *meisa;* Latin *meto,* to cut, divide, mow, mutilate. Compounded with dal, dial, a share, it produced the Gothic *medal,* the *mid deal,* or *middle. Mid, med,* with the Gothic *la* (from laga, To lay, or place), became

do I think there is much good to be derived from speculations, for they can be but little better, on such recondite points as these. It may be some consolation to those who so bitterly complain of the injustice, not to say the national folly, of keeping on the malt tax, while flimsy French wines are admitted duty free, to know, that even our Saxon ancestors were saddled with the *mealtgescot* or malt tax. Surely, then, it is time it was repealed.

But, it will be asked what has this discussion to do with the silky little *mole*, as it is now spelt? It has a good deal, inasmuch, as *mole* is but a mutilated abbreviation of the provincial *mouldiwarp*, the Anglo Saxon molde-wyrp, the mould caster. From this Anglo Saxon word *molde*, then, it seems we derive the following words:

Mould, the soil, and
Mole, by contraction for mouldwarp, the animal which
    burrows under the ground.

In this case, it would appear that the older reading, *mowle*, is not more correct than our modern *mole*, which is itself but an euphonious contraction, even if it can be called that.

midla; Swedish, *medla,* to put between. Medla was contracted into *mella,* which produced the Gothic *mal, mel;* Swedish *măl;* Saxon mal, *mæl;* Teutonic *mal, mahl,* applied in different ways, but invariably denoting intervention, or division. *Mal* was thus a portion of speech, a word, a harangue, a notice, a cause, or action at law, a division of time or space, an interstice, a fragment, a crumb, a spot, speck, painting, delineation, writing, mark, sign, a piece of ground set apart or enclosed, a fixed hour for eating, a moiety of the produce of the soil, as rent, a convention, a contribution, salary, measure, boundary. Our *meal,* time of eating; *meal,* grain reduced to particles, *small:* MOLD, dust; *mole,* a spot on the skin; *mall,* a public walk, the boundary of a town; Scotch, *mail,* rent; and, finally, from the Gothic *mals,* a fixed period for contribution, which has the same root with Teutonic *mas,* a measure, we have Lammas and Christmas: although the word has been generally confounded with *mass,* a religious ceremony. Our *medley,* things intermingled, is the Gothic *medal,* which contracted into *mille,* Swedish *mellan,* is our *mell,* a mixture." p. 24.

But what does the provincial *mouldiwarp* express? For a lengthy word, without an understood signification, is certainly worse than a short one? Mouldiwarp, however, is not one of these. It is compounded of the word *mould,* which we have just been considering, and part of the Anglo-Saxon verb *weorpan,* to throw or cast; and the word mouldwarp, as thus compounded, expresses that habit of the animal, whereby alone its presence is detected: namely, that of *throwing* up to the surface the *mould* of its excavation.

Nor is this the only word we derive from this Anglo Saxon verb, *weorpan,* To cast. The following words spring from it:

Warp,—1st, The gritty, pulverized matter, *thrown* up on the banks of rivers. 2nd, The thread connected with the shuttle, which crosses, or is thrown across, the woof. 3rd, The verb *to warp,*[1] which perhaps, from the metaphor of a river, *warping* up its banks, and so perverting its course; perhaps, from the *warp,* in weaving, being turned across, (though I think the former is the more probable) comes to signify the act of perverting, or biassing the opinion.

CLOUT.

"Thou wast not salted with salt, nor swaddled in *clouts.*"
Ezekiel XVI. 4.

Respecting the word *clout,* Mr. Horne Took says:

"Clout, \ as well as cleeve, cleft, cliff, clift, and cloven, Clough, \ are the past participle of the Anglo Saxon verb cliofian,[2] To cleave."

And he afterwards proceeds to shew how they assumed their present form.

"Clouve, clough, cleaved, or divided into small pieces. Clouved, clow'd, clout."

[1] "Not warped by passion, aw'd by rumour,
Not grave thro' pride, nor gay thro' folly,
An equal mixture of good humour,
And sensible soft melancholy."—*Swift.*

[2] I cannot but think the more correct form would be cleofan, or clufan, for according to Dr. Bosworth, there are three verbs, all closely resembling each other in form, though quite distinct in meaning.

But, surely, all this is not only extremely fanciful, but quite unnecessary, since both *clough* and *clút* a (clout) are themselves Anglo Saxon words. The process of their formation was not conducted in English, but in Anglo Saxon. The words have descended to us from the pure Anglo Saxon, and have not been manufactured by us from an English verb, as Mr. Took's reasoning would lead us to suppose. I should not find fault with him for referring the Anglo Saxon words *clough* and *clút* (u long) to the verb cliofian,[1] but an endeavour to shew how the words were forged with English hammers, is, at the best, but an ingenious fiction.

Philologists are by no means unanimous as to the exact meaning of the word *clout*.

Mr. Thomas Wright, in his glossary to the Vision and Creed of Pierce Ploughman, says "*clouten* (Anglo Saxon) to patch, mend," and refers us for an example of this meaning, to the following passage:

"And I shall apparaile me" quod Perkyn
In Pilgryme's wise,
And wende with yow I will,
Till we fynde Truthe;
And cast on my clothes
Y-*clouted* and hole,
My cokeres[2] and my coffes,
For cold of my nailes."

Line 3909.

But Mr. Took also refers to this passage in support of his meaning of *torn*. In this dilemma, what must

---

[1] There is first clúfan, or cleofan, which makes the past participle clofen, *To cleave, To split*; from which and not from cliofian, are derived the following words: *cleaver, clevage, cleft, cliff, claw*, the divided or cloven foot, and *clover* (from its divided leaf).

Secondly; clifian, (otherwise spelt cleófian and cliofian) which makes the past tense, clifode, and past participle, clifod, an active verb, *To fasten*, or *stick*, a thing whence, probably, are derived *clay, clog, clot*, and *glue*, perhaps.

Thirdly: clifan, perfect cláf, and past participle clifen, a neuter verb, *To adhere, To cleave to*.

Perhaps *club*, an apportioning or dividing of expenditure, and *clough* a vale between two cliffs, are derived from the first of these verbs, clufan.

[2] A stocking or glove. From the Saxon *cocer*, a quiver, a case.

we do? Let us judge for ourselves of its meaning, by the following passages, in which it occurs:

The first I have given in extenso, not only because of the instance it affords of the verbal use of *clout*, but because of the very graphic description of avarice. It occurs in Chaucer's *Romaunt of the Rose*.

"Another image set saw I,
Next covetise fast by,
And she was cleped[1] Avarice;
Full foul in painting was that vice,
Full sad and caitife was she eke,
And also grene as any leke,
So evil hewed was her colour,
She seemed to have lived in langour,
She was like thing for hunger dead,
That lad her life onely by bread
Kneden with eisell[2] strong and *egre*
And thereto she was leane and megre,
And she was clad full poorely
All in an old torn courtpy[3]
As she were all with dogges torn
And both behind and eke beforne
Clouted was she beggerly."

Line 137.

"She fayned her, as that she must gon
There as ye wote, that euery wight hath nede,
And whan she of this byl hath taken hede,
She rent it all to *cloutes* and at last,
Into the preuy sothly she it cast."

Marchaunt's Tale.

"She ne had on but a straight old sacke
And many a *clout* on it there stack,
This was her cote and her mantele,
No more was there never a dele,
To cloath her with;

Romaunt of the Rose, line 458.

"His garment, nought but many ragged *clouts*
With thornes together pind and patched was."

Faerie Queene, Bk. 1, *cant.* 9, *st.* 36.

TRADE.

"Teach a child in the *trade* of his way, and when he is old he shall not depart from it."—*Proverbs* XXII. 6.

---

[1] Called.   [2] Vinegar.   [3] A short cloak.

Transpose the first clause, and how naturally would it read, "Teach a child in the way of his trade, &c." It would amount simply to the trite and well-worn maxim of the world, and would require no explanation whatever. But, as the passage at present stands, it seems as though the cart were put before the horse. Yet, is it so really, or is it only time which has occasioned the confusion of terms? What is the word *Trade*? whence comes it, and what does it mean? How many of all the thousands, who are busily engaged, from Monday morning to Saturday night, in some of the almost numberless ramifications of that social necessity, ever find leisure to think of its meaning?

Trade! what a curious word! yet how suggestive!—of the dock wharf, and the warehouse, the smooth counter, and the dingy counting-house, and many a merchant-man besides, whose gallant form is well-known on the sea's highway.

But this is the modern meaning, and one which the word has, comparatively speaking, only recently obtained. *Trade*, indeed, is simply the Anglo Saxon *trod*, a path, a track, a pace, and is connected with the Anglo Saxon verb *tredan*, to tread.

But, even in English, the word had only this meaning for a length of time, as the following passages will shew :

"They say they con to heaven the high way,
But by my soul I dare undersaye,
They never sette foote in that same *troad*,
But balk the right way and strayen abroad."
Shepheard's Calendar.

"As shepheards curre that in dark eveninges shade
Hath tracted forth some salvage beastes *trade*."
Faerie Queene, Bk. 2, cant. 6, st. 39.

Thus it appears, that *trade*, for a length of time, signified nothing more than a path, or tract. Indeed, the word still survives in some parts with this meaning, though, in a somewhat different form. It is not long ago since I heard the following expression, which struck me at the time as somewhat unusual, for I did not recollect ever to have heard the word made use of before.

"I wish these garden *trods* of mine were weeded."[1]

I am inclined to think that the word *craft* supplied the place of *trade* till recently. How then would this change take place? A man's *trade*, that is, his *path* in life, his calling, or occupation, was formerly called his craft. St. Paul we are told in my old Bible, (with reverence be it said) abode with Priscilla and Aquila, "because hee was of the same craft, (for their craft was to make tents)."

Craft has somehow got into disgrace, as well as crafty, and *trade*[2] now supplies the place of the former, and *skilful* of the latter. It is difficult to assign a reason ; nor should one be expected, for all the alterations which take place in words, from time to time. Words, like the coats we wear, are subject to a kind of fashionable caprice, which clips, and trims, and shapes the words we speak at pleasure.

There are two other words, which, because they are of analogeous formation to the one we have just been considering, I will take the liberty to notice. They are

PLANT AND VENT.

"I have digged and drunke up the waters of others, and with the *plant* of my feet have I dried all the floods closed in.—2 *Kings* xix. 24.

---

[1] As this was a colloquial observation, I make no apology for its homely character. Indeed, I cannot but think, that slippings from the living stock are far more trustworthy and valuable, as indications of the state of the language, than written extracts.

[2] I am aware that some Etymologists prefer pointing to the Italian *tratta*, (from the Latin *tracto*) as the immediate source whence we derive the word *trade;* and, though this may be true of its commercial acceptation, yet it seems at least probable, that the above is the real origin of the word in its domestic, or civil acceptation, of a man's occupation in life.

In this acceptation, the noun *plant* has become obsolete, and I question if, in having dropped it, our language has not sustained a loss which is still felt.

Went, as a verbal noun, though it is no longer in use, in this exact form, has bequeathed to us the noun, *vent*, a passage.

> "And through the long experience of his dayes,
> Which had in many fortunes tossed beene,
> And passed through many perillous assayes
> He knew the diverse *went* of mortal wayes,
> And in the mindes of men had great insight."
> *Faerie Queene, Bk.* 6, *cant.* 6, *st.* 3.

But I find by my list, that I am rapidly exhausting the stock of words, which are to find a place under the heading of the present chapter. I have but two, or three more to consider; nor is there any reason why they should delay us long, for they almost speak for themselves.

CREEPLE.

"And a certaine man which was a *creeple* from his mothers wombe, was carried, whom they layd daily at the gate of the Temple, called Beautiful, to ask almes of them that entred into the Temple."—*Acts* III. 2.

Dr. Johnson hints, that the modern word *cripple* is, perhaps, only an altered form of *creeple*, from the verb To creep, though he does not bring forward any quotations in support of his suggestion. Does the above passage supply the missing link, which is necessary to make Dr. Johnson's suggestion anything more than a suggestion? What think you, reader? Or[1] do you think the bait is too artificial, and prefer looking to

---

[1] By some Etymologists, Thompson amongst them, *cripple* is referred to the Anglo Saxon *crypel*. But this is simply absurd, for, however the words *cripple* and *crypel* may resemble each other, they are quite distinct in meaning. Crypel, the Anglo Saxon word, is a den or cave; also spelt *cryfele*, and I cannot help thinking, though I have no proof of it, connected with the Greek κρύπτω, To hide, and thence, with our English word Crypt. (κρυφῇ, secretly).

Saxon *crepel?* But, remember, the Anglo Saxon word *crepel,* means a little creeper, or crawfish, and *creopere* is really the Saxon word which corresponds to our word cripple. This being the case, I think we shall not be guilty of a great error, if we accept Dr. Johnson's suggestion, now that we have fortified him with a quotation.

BANKET.

"And his sonnes went and *banketed* in their houses, every one his day, and sent and called their three sisters, to eate and drinke with them."—*Job* I. 4.

The word *banket* does not appear quite well pleased at being aroused from its long slumber, to display its quaint costume of the 16th century. But it is not mere curiosity that invokes the shade.

Banket differs from the more modern *banquet,* inasmuch as, while the former is cast in a Teutonic, or German mould, the latter bears evident tokens of French influence; it is, in short, nothing but a pure French word. Of course, both spring from the same Teutonic root, *bank,* Anglo Saxon *benc,* a bench, a table ; and the changes, that have taken place, are only such as may be attributed to the national pronunciation in each case.

FET.

"For as long as the sonne of Ishai liueth upon the earth, thou shalt not be stablished, nor thy kingdome: wherefore, now send and *fet* him unto me, for he shall surely die."

1 *Samuel* xx. 31.

The word *fet,* which occurs in this passage, and elsewhere, has now fallen into such entire disuse, as scarcely any longer to suggest a meaning to the mind, and almost to make us doubt its right to the parentage of our modern word *fetch.* How many times might the latter form occur to us without once exciting our curiosity; yet, who could meet with the former, without immediately desiring to know more about it?

"Fetch," says Mr. Took, "(Anglo Saxon fæc) is the past tense and past participle of fecc-an, fraude acquirere, adducere, To obtain by stealth."

Does Mr. Took mean by this, to say, that fæc is the past tense and past participle of the Anglo Saxon verb *feccan*, To fetch? Scarcely, I should think; for he must have known that *feahte* is the past tense of that verb. Fæc is no more its past tense, or past participle, than þæc is of the verb þeccan, To thatch, or thack. Verbal substantives 'they may be, yet there is a looseness in Mr. Took's way of putting it, that is very liable to mislead. And again, the Anglo Saxon word *fæc* does not, in either of its meanings, correspond with, however much it may outwardly resemble, our word *fetch*. It signifies, firstly, an interval of space, or time; secondly, suspicion. How the verb *fecc-an* may be connected with either of these, is perhaps too subtle a question for speculation.[1]

Let us first consider *fetch* as a verb, and this, perhaps, will facilitate the consideration of it as a substantive.

> "And cart-sadle the commissarie,
> Oure cart shal he lede
> And *fecchen* us vitailles
> At *fornicatores*."
>
> *Vision of Pierce Ploughman*, 1242.

Here we have a very early form of the word, scarcely differing from the original Saxon.

> "Thaune sikede[2] Sathan
> And seide to hem alle,
> Swich a light ayeins our leve
> Lazar out *fette;*
> Care and encombraunce
> Is comen to us alle!
> If this kyng come in,
> Mankynde wole he *fecche*,
> And lede it ther hym[3] liketh,
> And lightliche me bynde."
>
> *Ibid*, 12608.

---

[1] Fácen, deceit, fraud, is more likely to be the root of *feccan*, To fetch.
[2] Sighed.
[3] It liketh him.

In this passage, *fecche* would certainly convey the notion of deceit, as also in the following, in which Christ is represented as addressing Lucifer:

> "Thow fettest myne in my place
> Ageins alle reson,
> Falsliche and felonliche;
> Good feith me it taughte,
> To recovere hem thorugh raunson,
> And by no reson ellis.
> So that thorugh gile thow gete,
> Thorugh grace it is y-wonne.
> Thow Lucifer in liknesse
> Of a luther[1] addere
> Getest by gile
> Tho[2] that God lovede."
>
> *Ibid*, 12783.

It would seem, then, that our more modern form, *fetch*, is a sort of compromise between the two, *fecche* and *fet*.[3]

The substantive, *fetch*, which still retains the element, and gives the notion, of deceit, and cunning, is extant in such passages as the following:

> "Yet since so obstinate grew their desire,
> On a new *fetch* (t'accord them) he relide."
> *Godfrey of Bulloigne, cant* 5, *st*. 72.

> "With this *fetch* he laughs at the trick he has played me."
> *Stillingfleet.*

> "It is a *fetch* of wit
> You laying these slight sullies on my son,
> As t' were a thing a little soiled i' th' working."
> *Hamlet.*

---

[1] Wicked.

[2] Those.

[3] The following parts of this verb occur in the vision and creed of " *Pierce Ploughman:*"

Present Singular. I fecche, Thou fettest.

Perfect Singular. Fet, fette; this form also occurs in the Breeches Bible.

Perfect Plural. Fetten.

Participle Past. Fet.

F

The following are words of analogous formation:

Thatch }
Thack   } from Anglo Saxon Þecc-an.

Lack   }
Latch   } from Anglo Saxon Læcc-an, Gelæccan.
Clutch }

Speak   }
Speech } from Anglo Saxon Speccan.

"The indifferent pronunciation of *ch*, or *ck*, pervades the whole Anglo-Saxon language."—*Div. Pur.* p. 567.

Of course many other examples, besides those above, might be quoted.

CHAPTER IV.

WORDS ALTER THEIR MEANING.

Not only do words alter as to their external appearance, from time to time, but the signification they bear is likewise modified. While, on the one hand, words, which were originally used to designate an effect, come, insensibly, to denote the cause; so, on the other, words, which at first signified the cause, have, through the lapse of years, come to designate the effect. Words have a metaphysical history, and cannot be rightly considered apart from moral and metaphysical causes. So intimately, indeed, are they connected with the machinery of the mind, that they may be truly considered to form an index of its working;—a mirror, in which are reflected those ever-changing images, with which it is conversant, whether considered as animating the individual, or as they are developed in the more collective form of public opinion.

Indeed, the œconomy of words is not a simple subject, nor one to be comprehended within moderate limits. I shall, therefore, content myself with quoting the examples which the Breeches' Bible has afforded me, and leave my reader himself to follow out the conclusions to which they point.

CAUSE.

"And the title of his *cause* was written above, that King of the Jews."—*Mark* xv. 26.

The primary meaning of *causa*[1] among the Romans, whence, I need not say, comes the English word *cause*,

---

[1] The root, I supppose, of *causor, accuso, causidicus, &c.*

was "a suite at law, a judicial process." From this its original, it soon acquired the additional signification of an indictment or accusation. The use, therefore, of *cause* in the above sense would be quite correct; though it is needless to point out, that it no longer bears this meaning with us.

The following passage is strongly illustrative of the different meanings the same word, used by different people at different times, may come to bear.

CRIME.

"Against whom, when the accusers stood up, they brought no *crime* of such things as I supposed."—*Acts* xxv. 18.

A *crime* is now understood to mean an offence, whether against the law of God, or man. But this meaning is one arrived at by the method of induction, and not an intrinsic one. Now, amongst the Greeks, back to whom we must trace this word, it simply expressed the completion of a judicial process; namely, a sentence, whether of condemnation, or acquittal. The Romans borrowed the word from the Greeks, but modified its meaning; so that with them it no longer signified a sentence, or verdict simply, but, inasmuch as persons are not generally brought to trial, unless there be fair grounds of suspicion on which to found an accusation, it came to signify the accusation, or charge of an offence: and thence, the offence itself, by a logic somewhat similar to that contained in the old adage, "give a dog a bad name and hang him."

But it will be observed, that in the above passage the word *crime* has the more classic meaning of an accusation, and not the superinduced signification—a prejudiced one truly—of the offence itself. In this sense the word is now obsolete; yet we have evidence here, that it has only become so during the last two centuries and a half. It appears, then, that this word, originally springing from Greece, centuries before the commencement of the Christian Era, survives to the present day; that during its existence it has been a Greek, a Latin, and an English word; and has generally borne a different meaning in each. Amongst the Greeks it signified a *judgment*; amongst the Latins an *accusation*; and, finally, amongst ourselves, the *offence* itself. What a strange process is here; what curious reasoning! We start from the *verdict*, next we come to the *accusation*, and finally to the *crime*, which ought to be the root, and origin of all. Yet, so it is.

DISEASE.

"Thy daughter is dead, why *diseasest* thou the master any further?"—*Mark* v. 35.

This use of the verb, *To disease*, is somewhat strange to us. Yet, it is not uninstructive, inasmuch as it reveals the kind of reasoning whereby the word has come to receive its present signification.

As a verb, *disease* is now but rarely used, and, when it is, its meaning is quite different from that which it originally possessed. The past participle, *diseased*, is still common enough, to intimate a condition of ill health, but with this sense only. Now, it will be observed, from its use in the above passage, that, formerly, its meaning was simply the reverse of ease, comfort, or convenience; and thus it seems to have been used, so late as the middle of the 17th century, if not later.

"Though great light be insufferable to our eyes, the highest degree of darkness does not at all *disease* them."[1]
Locke.

---

[1] This observation is certainly incorrect; for intense darkness is extremely painful to the eyes.

Disease, then, up to this time, signified that condition of restlessness, which would be caused by trouble, sorrow, or sickness of any kind: but with reference only to the result, and not to the producing cause. Now, however, the word, instead of designating the effect, has been transferred to denote the cause, and is used, I believe solely, to express a malady in its substantival use; and to affect with a malady in its verbal use.

DISDAINE.

"And when the ten heard it, they begun to *disdaine* at James and John."—*Mark* x. 41.

" Therefore some *disdained* amongst themselves, and said, &c."
Ibid XIII. 4.

These passages, in our present version, read as follows:

"And when the ten heard it, they began to be much displeased with James and John."

"And there were some that had indignation within themselves, and said, &c."[1]

The following passage illustrates the meaning this word bore in Chaucer's time:

"The second cause that ought to make a man to have *disdeigne* of sinne is this, that, as saith Seint Peter, whoso doth sinne is thral to sinne, and sinne putteth a man in gret thraldom. Certes, wel ought a man have *disdeigne* of sinne, and withdraw him fro that thraldom and vilany."
Persone's Tale, Cant. Tales.

What, then, are the changes time has wrought in the meaning of this word? It would appear, that the tendency has been to weaken its original force and vigour. What its meaning is now we all know well enough. By *disdain*, we understand rather that contempt and scorn for a thing,—that loathing, somewhat

---

[1] It should be observed that the word in the original, in both passages, is the same, namely, ἀγανακτεῖν, to be grieved, or indignant, which expresses a more powerful emotion than that of mere contempt or scorn.

akin to pride, whether proper or improper,—which cannot stoop,—than real anger, and indignation, which, resulting from supposed sufficient causes, produces displeasure and aversion to a particular person, or thing. So that, if this be true, the *morale* of the word has suffered depreciation, and the word itself, by this very depreciation, become better adapted to a more artificial state of society.

The use of *pestilences* for wicked men, though it sounds somewhat uncouth in our modern ears, has, nevertheless, a moral force, and vigour about it, which cannot be misunderstood.

PASSE. BASE.

In that most touching of all farewell sermons, which the Apostle St. Paul preached to his converts, at Miletum, previous to his final departure, after telling them, that bonds, and afflictions awaited him in every city, he goes on to say " But I *passe* not at all, neither is my life deare unto myself, so that I may fulfil my course with joy :" thereby intimating, as the Greek has it, " I make no account of any thing;" and our own version " But none of these things move me."

How entirely has this word *pass* changed its meaning : even *passion*, though its old meaning is still, and may it long be, consecrated to us by our Church Liturgy, has in the familiar intercourse of society relinquished its original signification of suffering, and, in its place, come to denote, rather the effect of that suffering, or emotion, as it is manifested by external signs. We still talk of " the passions of the mind ;" of " a passive verb ;" or, of " a person remaining passive ;" where the old meaning still survives ; yet *passion* no longer means suffering, but rather intemperate anger ; and a passionate man, not a suffering man, but one who can ill abide suffering.

There is another instance afforded us in the ancient

use of the word *base*, which strongly illustrates the power of the mind in changing the signification of words.

"Which remembered us in our *base* estate, for his mercy endureth for ever."—*Psalm* CXXXVI. 23.

And again, in that beautiful metaphor of old age:

"And when the doors shall be shut without by the *base* sound of the grinding."—*Ecclesiastes* XII. 4.

From these passages, it is plain to see, that, at this time, the adjective *base* was merely one of position, and had not as yet received the inferential meaning of turpitude, which is now attached to it. This was the work of time. It was only by degrees, that men came to the conclusion, that what is *low* and *degraded* generally, though not universally, indicates a depraved morality. Yet, this has been done effectually enough at last. As an adjective, *base* may be said to have lost its simple original meaning (for the two, *i. e.*, the old and the new, are to a certain degree antagonistic), and have adopted in its place a purely inferential, and moral one. A man formerly might be *base*, either through misfortune, or fault; he can now only be so through the latter.

BENEFICIALL.

"Bring my soule out of prison, that I may praise thy Name: then shall the righteous come about me, when thou art *beneficiall* unto me."—*Psalm* CXLII. 7.

The use of *beneficiall* for merciful is somewhat strange to us, and does not exactly correspond to that which obtains in the present day.

COMMODITIE.

"Cause not your *commoditie* to bee evill spoken of."
Romans XIII. 16.

Modern reading:

"Let not then your good[1] be evill spoken of."

[1] The word in the original, thus rendered, is τὸ ἀγαθὸν.

TERME.

"Thou hast caused thy daies to draw neere; thou art come unto thy *terme.*"

These are the words used by the prophet Ezekiel when uttering his curse against the city of Jerusalem.

There is little need for any remark on the use of *term,* in this passage. My reader will see for himself, that *terme,* at this time, was equivalent to *end;* or, as we should now say, *termination.* The word, *terme,* has lost this meaning—its true, and more correct meaning of limit—and is now used to indicate, not the termination of a thing, but rather its duration.

INCONTINENTLY.

"And al the devils besought him saying, send us into the swine, that we may enter into them.

"And *incontinently* Jesus gave them leave."—*Mark* v. 12, 13.

Incontinently has here the force of immediately. In this sense I do not recollect ever to have heard it used; although, it still finds a place in our dictionaries. It is very rarely met with, now, with any other meaning than that of intemperance, or licentiousness; probably, this change has only recently taken place.

IMPROVE.

"Be instant in season and out of season: *improoue,*[1] rebuke, exhort with all long-suffering and doctrine.—2 *Tim.* iv. 2.

Perhaps, it would be difficult to find a word whose meaning has so entirely changed as the above; for it has not merely adopted some inferential, or side meaning,

[1] The word in the original is ἐλεγξον.

which is pardonable, and easy to be accounted for, but it has come, at length, to signify as nearly the reverse of what it formerly did, as possible.[1]

And, although it is not of so great importance in practice, that is, experience, what the meaning of a word may be, or whether that meaning be the correct one, so long as it is uniformly one, and the same; yet, when the word occurs in old writings, with a meaning very different from its present one, it is then the real difficulty arises. Take for instance the following passage:

> ———"Now, Sir, young Fortinbras,
> Of *unimproved* mettle, hot and full,
> Hath in the skirts of Norway, here and there,
> Shark'd up a list of landless resolutes,
> For food and diet to some enterprise,
> That hath a stomach in it."
>
> *Hamlet, Act* 1, *Scene* 1.

Listen to what poor Shakespeare's commentators say. Warburton takes *unimproved* to mean "unrefined;" Edwards, "improved," and Johnson, with the approbation of Malone, says Mr. Tooke, thinks it means "not regulated, nor guided by knowledge, or experience," whereas, it simply means "unimpeached," or "unblamable." Oh, save me from my friends! I notice this case of misinterpretation, not so much for its own intrinsic value, as because it affords a striking instance of the errors the best are liable to fall into, when they dare to ignore

---

[1] It is perhaps mere useless speculation to try and trace this word beyond the Latin *improbo*, to the Greek πρέπειν, *to be fit*, or *becoming :* sufficient for our present purpose, which is rather that of ascertaining the acquired, than the etymological meaning, that it is derived to us directly from the French verb *improuver*, to disapprove, to blame, a meaning which is still retained.

"Elles croient que le corps et le sang sont vraiment distribués à ceux qui mangent ; et *improuvent* ceux qui enseignent le contraire."

Bossuet des Variat des Eglises, Prot.

"La bourgeoisie de Génève a droit de faire de representations dans toutes les occasions, où elle croit les loix lésées, et où elle *improuve* la conduite de ses magistrats."—*Rousseau*, vol. II. p. 140.

the past, and consult the feelings, and dictates of the present only. Words are far too capricious to be safely investigated by any other guide, than that of experience. Here, even the etymologist finds himself at fault, and though, perhaps he may be able to indicate which way the fox ought to have gone, yet it by no means follows that his suggestions are to be relied on. It is unnecessary to point out that, instead of *improve* in the passage which suggested these remarks, our present Version reads *reprove*. The difference is only that of a syllable, yet how strange it would sound now to hear the old reading " improve, rebuke, exhort."

The following appears the rationale of this singular change in the meaning of the verb *To improve.*

That which is faulty, or vicious, requires to be reproved. (I use the words *advisedly,* with their present meaning); and that which is reproved, ought, if the reproof have its legitimate effect, to be improved. Here again, is the same transposition of cause, and effect; and here, again, is afforded us a glimpse at that mysterious logic, which is ever at work in the secret laboratory of human thought, and human feeling; which, snatching the very words out of our mouths, and recasting them in a new model, reproduces them again, after a time, in such a shape that they can scarcely be recognised.[1]

[1] I am not sure that the verb, *To reprove,* as used by our Bible Translators, in the passage "reprove, rebuke, exhort," had the same meaning as that we now attach to it. I am rather inclined to think the *animus* of the word, as they used it, was *conviction;* which implies, not only impeachment, but also that *bringing of a man's offence home* to him, so as to cause him serious apprehension of punishment, and thus lay him under a greater moral obligation to reform his life. What is the difference in our day, between a *rebuke* and a *reproof?* I doubt if there be any attached difference. Yet, we are bound to accept one of two conclusions: either, that our Bible Translators rendered two essentially different words in the original, ἔλεγξον and ἐπιτίμησον (the former, signifying *to convince,* the latter, literally to set an additional price on a thing, and thence, *to rebuke*), by synonymous words in English; or else, that the words they used, at the time they used them, were not synonymous; which appears to me far the more rational of the two.

PROFIT.

"Now the childe Samuel *profited*, and grew, and was in favor with the Lord, and also with men,"— 1 *Samuel* ii. 26.

The verb, *to profit*, is not now used in the sense of thriving, as it appears by the above passage, and many others that I could mention, to have been formerly.

AVOYDED.

The employment of this word in the sense of *emptying* is somewhat curious. I have, unfortunately, taken down the reference to the passage incorrectly, and must therefore, ask my reader to trust to my fidelity. It is but a fragment, but it is sufficient to shew in what sense the word was formerly used.

"When the priests *avoyded* the ashes."

Void is still used with this meaning of making empty; but not, so far as I am aware, *avoid*.

WANT.

"If he be lost, and *want*, thy life shall go for his life."

1 *Kings* xx. 39.

In the sense in which this word is here used, it is now rarely found; still, there are a few homely phrases where it survives, such for instance as "it wants ten minutes to twelve;" that is *"there are wanting* ten minutes from twelve o'clock."

There is another remarkable usage of the verb *To want*, which we seem to have entirely lost. It occurs in *Clement Ellis's* "Character of the true Gentleman."

"He scorns and is ashamed of nothing but sin. He lives in the world as one that intends to shame the world out of love with itself, and he is, therefore, singular in all his actions, not because he affects (loves) to be so, but because he cannot meet with company like himself, to make him otherwise. In a word, he is such, that (could we *want* him) it were pity but that he were in heaven; and yet, I pity not much his continuance here, because he is already so much in heaven to himself."

What interpretation are we to put upon *want* in this passage? The sense would seem capable of but oue. It appears to be equivalent to *To spare*, To do without. And there is another passage, only a little further on, which seems to confirm this.

"Honours he civilly accepts when paid him, but seldom challenges when delayed or with-held; so far I mean, as they concern his person, not his office. For though it be one honour to deserve, yet it is another contentedly to *want* them."

Clement Ellis lived about the middle of the 17th century, or pretty nearly a century after the Genevan Version was published. It appears, then, that since the beginning of the 17th century the verb, *To want*, has borne no less than three different meanings.

1st, with the sense of *To be wanting.*
2nd, ,, ,, *To spare or do without.*
3rd, ,, ,, *In our own time, To desire.*[1]

With respect to the verbal formation of *want*, it will be prudent to speak cautiously.

The substantive *want*, and *wand*, we know well enough to be the past participle of the Anglo Saxon verb *wanian*, To diminish, To take away, with an active signification: then, To wane, To decrease, To decay, with a

---

[1] The Latin verb, *desidero*, with its derivative, *desiderium*, seems to afford a somewhat parallel instance to the above. The word *desiderium* was originally an astronomical term, used to denote the absence of a particular star from a constellation, without implying any notion of *regret* for that absence. Yet, this word, *desiderium*, being a compound Latin word, and, therefore, as a word, incapable of being traced further back, is the root of the French *desire*, and our English *desire*. But, long previous to this, it had lost its original meaning, even amongst the Romans themselves, and signified, first regret, and thence, as a natural consequence, since we always more or less desire that for which we feel regret, it came to mean desire or longing for a thing; so that the changes, this word has undergone, somewhat resemble those of our English verb *To want*.

neuter signification; as also, from the same verb, with the prefix *ge*, ge-wanian, comes the noun adjective *gaunt*.[1]

But whence comes the verb *To want?*

There seems no alternative but to suppose it is formed from the noun substantive, by simply prefixing the English verbal particle, (if so I may be permitted to call it) *to*, of which more hereafter.

If such be its formation, whether regular or irregular, let us not at present decide, we cannot be surprised, that its meaning has varied from time to time; changing rather in accordance with the prevailing under-current of feeling, than with any rule to be found in the nature of things.

Yet, how many verbs there may be, which are as loose in their construction as this, we shall probably never know. There are two, which occur to me at this time. They are the verbs *To twist*, and *To tilt*.[2]

The former is supposed to be the contracted form of *twiced*, *twic'd*, or, as it was formerly written, *twis'd*, whence *twist*, and the verb *To twist*. The latter is "the past participle of the Anglo Saxon verb *tilian*,[3] *i. e. To raise*, or *To lift up*. *To till* the ground, is to raise it, To turn it up. *Atilt* is well said of a vessel that is raised up; but we ought to say *To till*, and not to tilt a vessel."

This concluding remark of Mr. Tooke's is, I apprehend, equally applicable, *mutatis mutandis*, to the case we are considering: namely, the verb, *To want*. But, to pursue this question further, will be to anticipate the subject of a future chapter.

---

[1] So that from the same part of the same verb we obtain, first a noun substantive *want*; second, a noun adjective *gaunt*; and third, as we shall presently see, in all probability, the verb *to want*. See *Div. Pur.* p. 351.

[2] Perhaps the verb *To hoist* is another.

[3] Whence comes the verb *To till*, and the substantive *tilth*.

MOE. MOST.

"O Lord, my God, thou hast made thy wonderfull workes so many, that none can count in order to thee thy thoughts towards us: I would declare and speak of them, but they are *moe* than I am able to express."—*Psalm* XL. 5.

Mr. Horne Tooke's hypothesis of the meaning, and origin of *more* is ingenious, but, we fear, untenable.

In order that I may not misconstrue Mr. Tooke's meaning he shall speak for himself:

"Though there appears to be, there is in reality no irregularity in *much, more, most;* nor, indeed, *is there any such thing as capricious irregularity in any part of language.* In the Anglo Saxon the verb ma'wan, metere, (*To cut*), makes regularly the præterperfect *mow*, or *mowe*, (as the præterperfect of *slagan* is *sloh*), and the past participle, *mowen*, or Saxon *meowen*, by the addition of the participial termination *en* to the præterperfect. Omit the participial termination *en* (which omission was, and still is, a common practice through the whole language, with the Anglo Saxon writers, the old English writers, and the moderns[1]), and there will remain Saxon *mowe*, or English *mow;* which gives us the Anglo Saxon *mowe*, and our modern English word *mow;* which words mean *simply*,—that which is mowed, or mown. And as the hay, &c., which was *mown*, was put together in a heap; hence *figuratively*, *mowe* was used in Anglo Saxon to denote *any* heap: although, in modern English, we now confine the application of it to country produce, such as *hay-mow, barley-mow*, &c. This participle or substantive, (call it which you please, for, however classed, it is still the same word, and has the same signification), *mow*, or *heap*, was pronounced (and therefore written) with some variety *ma, mœ, mo, mowe, mow*, which regularly compared, give

Saxon, ma ......ma-er, (*i. e. S.* mare) ......ma-est (*i. e. S.* mœst).
Saxon, mœ......mœ-er, (*i. e. S.* mœre) ......mœ-est (*i. e. S.* mœst).
Saxon, mowe...mow-er, (*i. e. S.* more) ......mow-est (*i. e. S.* most).
English mo ......mo-er, (*i. e. E.* more) ......mo-est (*i. e. E.* most)."

But there are serious objections to this process. For, in the first place, the past participle of ma'wan is not

[1] I very much doubt, whether what Mr. Tooke conceives to be the past participle divested of the participial termination (without which it is not a participle at all) is, in reality, anything more than the root of the verb. But Mr. Tooke was not in the habit of looking on verbs in this light.

meowen, but simply ma'wen,[1] just as the past participle of sa'wan, *To sow*, is sa'wen; consequently, if we do reject the participial termination *en*, we have, not *mowe*, but *ma'w*.[2] But this objection is trivial compared with the next: namely, that *ma* and *mœ* never did signify a heap in the Saxon, or, indeed, anything else, besides a comparative degree, which we render in English by the word *more*. So that, in fact, Mr. Tooke starts by comparing a word, which, whatever be its positive, is already in the comparative degree. Had he been content with comparing the substantive *mowe*, and then tried to persuade us that *ma*, *mœ*, (for *mo* has no existence in the Saxon) are contracted forms of this comparative, we should still have dissented, though we should not have felt that so great an outrage on common sense had been committed. No doubt *most* (Saxon *mœst*) is the superlative of the comparative *more*, but what the positive may have been, we dare not hazard a conjecture. Mr. Tooke goes on to say, though I warn my reader to use him cautiously:

" *Mo* (mowe, acervus, heap), which was constantly used by all our old English authors, has with the moderns given place to *much*:[3] which has not (as Ju-

---

[1] Perhaps I ought to state my authority for this assertion: it is Dr. Bosworth's Anglo Saxon Dictionary.

[2] We ought to recollect too, that *mead*, Saxon *mœd*, is, as Mr. Tooke himself asserts, p. 585, a verbal substantive, probably of irregular formation from the same past participle; as also *seed*, Saxon *sœd*, from the past participle sa'wen, of the verb sa'wan To sow; *deed*, Saxon *dœd*, from dón To do, &c. Mowe may perhaps be the root of the verb ma'w-an, To mow, or cut; but I do not see how it can be formed from the past participle: otherwise, where must we look for the root of the verb?

[3] If by *mo* Mr. Tooke means the adjective or adverb *more*, he is certainly wrong.

How would it do to substitute *much* for *mo* in the following passage?

"There was also a reve, and a millere,
A sompnour (apparitor) and a pardoner also,
A manciple, (baker) and myself, ther n'ere no *mo*."
Prologue to Cant. Tales.

nius, Wormius, and Skinner imagined of Mickle) been borrowed from μεγαλος, but is merely the diminutive of *mo*." Let this stand for what it is worth, I do not think it is much.

The fancied victories of a too presumptive boldness are, in my mind, more to be dreaded, than either the apathy of ignorance, or the humbler successes of a more diffident enquiry. Men, who will see difficulties nowhere, and even concoct a solution, if they cannot find one, are dangerous partisans, and render but poor service to the cause they espouse; inasmuch as, by so doing, they lay it open to an undiscriminating suspicion. He who attempts to explain, by some conceit of his own, secrets which lie buried far too deep in the tomb of the past ever to be perfectly investigated now, should, at least, do so in a spirit of modesty, and not attempt to dogmatise over the faith of other men.

If in the Sanscrit *maha*, great, the Persian *mih*, and the Gothic *mar*, much, we see, or fancy we see, the word *more*[1] dimly foreshadowed, then it becomes idle to listen to arguments, which endeavour to fix the date of the word no farther back, than its fancied invention by the Saxons. *Favete linguis.*

MOST.

"Yea they worship beasts also, which are their *most* enemies, and which are the worst, if they be compared unto others, because they have none understanding."

Wisdom of Salomon.

"Yet peinted was a little furthermore,
How Athalante hunted the wild bore,
And Meleagre and many other *mo*
For which Diane wrought hem care and wo."

Knighte's Tale.

[1] Thompson in his "English Etymons," says, *more* is contracted from the Gothic *marer*, as Gothic *mar*, *mer*, signified much or great, and corresponds with Persian *mihtar*, from *mih*, Sanscrit *maha* great.

G

We have here an instance afforded us of the obsolete use of *most*, in the sense of greatest; but until we are better acquainted with the nature and origin of the words *much*, *more*, and *most*, we cannot with propriety discuss the question, as to whether this use be correct. Dr. Johnson tells us, that in his time, *most*, in the sense of *greatest*, had already become obsolete.

But, although *most* is no longer used in this particular sense, its meaning and name are still so ill defined, that, perhaps, a word or two respecting them may not be out out of place.

If we say

"A man is capable of doing *most* good in his own sphere;"

we mean by "most good," the "largest amount of good;" in which case, *most* appears to be a noun substantive, and expresses, as an accident of its nature, the quantity, or degree to which that amount reaches.

Again:

"Men are ready enough to acknowledge that virtue is *most* efficacious to secure true happiness."

In this case, what can we call *most* but a noun adjective?

Again:

"He executed the business *most* faithfully."

What noun is *most* in this case? It is not a noun substantive, nor a noun adjective. Indeed, it is difficult to say what it is, unless it be a noun adverb. "Faithfully" expresses the manner in which the business was executed; and as *most* qualifies *faithfully*, it ought, perhaps, rather to share the nature of that adverb.

Indeed, *most*, as well as *much*, and *more*, seem to be reflexive words, on which are reflected the nature of other words, be they substantive, adverb, or adjective, expressed, or understood, to which they happen to be joined. I do not know that we ought to wonder at this. Indeed, the more we meditate on the accidental condition—I had almost said the nature—of our language—how by artificial, and in some cases *jejune* expedients, we have sought to remedy the losses it has sustained, the less will the ambiguous, and irregular use of such words as the above excite our surprise. We must recollect, that previous to the Norman invasion, the Saxon language was like a stately bark, fully manned, and amply equiped, the discipline good, and containing every resource within itself. Thus did it encounter the tempest which burst over it from the south. But when again, the storm cloud had dispersed, and the bright blue sky appeared, our gallant bark lay motionless on the water, all her delicate tracery gone, her masts splintered and broken, her sails tattered and torn,—a mere wreck of her former self. In a future chapter, I hope to investigate more closely the real amount of damage done, and the manner in which this damage has been repaired.

CHAPTER V.

OBSOLETE AND OBSOLESCENT WORDS, AND FORMS OF WORDS.

THAT department of Philology, whose concern it is that defunct members of Language shall not be entirely forgotten, presents, it may be, as few claims as any to real interest and utility. Still, however, there is a sort of idle curiosity, (pretty much akin, I suppose, to that which is felt in walking through a museum), which is not unpleasantly gratified by gazing for a while on those antiquated forms, which were once living words in the mouths of those who spoke them. They have passed away from this earthly stage; their influence is no longer felt, and other men, and other words, have risen to supply their places. Still, though it may be little more than mere curiosity, which prompts us to dig up, and examine those old fossils, so far, that is, as any direct benefit is to be expected from them; yet, in as much as, while we are thus engaged, we are simultaneously, and almost unconsciously, forming an approximate estimate of the *drift* of our language during the last three centuries, the investigation, as to its result, cannot be called, altogether idle. It is only by thus casting the log, while our ship is in motion, that we can obtain a true estimate of her progress.

I have met with comparatively few words in the Breeches Bible, which, since the time it was written, namely, the middle of the sixteenth century, have entirely died out. They are scarcely worthy of a separate chapter; nevertheless, to avoid confusion, I have given them a small corner to themselves. In the next chapter I have recorded such obsolete forms of past tenses, and past Participles of Verbs, as seemed worthy of notice.

FRAILES.

"Then Abigail made haste, and took two hundred cakes, and two bottles of wine, and five sheep ready dressed, and five measures of parched corn, and an hundred *frailes* of raisins, and two hundred of figs, and laded them on asses."—4 *Samuel* xxv. 18.

Dr. Johnson gives two meanings to the word *frail*. It would not therefore be obsolete in his time. He says it means:

Firstly : A basket made of rushes.
Secondly : A rush for weaving baskets.

In the following passage, we meet with the word in an earlier form:

Piers the Plowman is invited by Conscience to dine with Clergie, where he meets Pacience. While the learned Doctour, however, was eating "mortrews[1] and potages," and drinking wine, Pacience and Piers are put to be *macches* "at the side bord," where, as they can get

---

[1] A kind of soup:—

> "He eet manye sondry metes,
> Mortrews and puddynges,
> Wombe-cloutes and wild brawen,
> And egges y-fryed with grece."

"Wombe-cloutes" was what we now call *tripe*.

The *Coke*, in the prologue to *Chaucer's* "Canterbury Tales," is thus described:

> "A *Coke* they hadden with them for the nones,
> To boile the chickenes and the marie (marrow) bones,
> And poudre marchant, tart and galingale,
> Wel coude he know a draught of London ale.
> He coude roste and seethe and broile and frie,
> Making mortrewes, and wel bake a pie.
> But gret harme was it, as it thoughte me,
> That on his shinne a mormal (cancer) had he
> For blanc manger that made with the best."

nothing to eat, they pass the time by conversing on the disgusting behaviour of the Doctour. At length Pacience says,

> " For now he hath dronken so depe,
> He wole devyne soone,
> And preven (prove) it by hir Pocalips
> And passion of Seint Avereys,
> That neither bacon ne braun,
> Blancmanger[1] ne mortrews,
> Is neither fissh nor flesshe,
> But fode for a penaunt[2]
> And thanne shall he testify to the Trinité,
> And take his felawe to witnesse,
> What he fond (found) in a *frayel*,
> After a freres lyvyng;
> And but he first lyve be lesyng,
> Leve (believe) me nevere after."
>
> *Lines* 8215.

On the word *frayel*, Mr. Thomas Wright has the following note:

> " The second Trinity Coll. M.S. has " in a *forell*." *Forel* is the Low-Latin *forellus*, a bag, sack, or purse: a *frayel* (fraellum) was a little wicker basket, such as were used for carrying figs or grapes."

In the Romance of " Richard Cœur de Lyon," the word also occurs.

> " Richard annswereth with herte free
> Of froyt there is gret plenté;
> Fyggys, raysyns, in *frayel*,
> And notes (nuts) may serve us fol wel."

It is hardly necessary to observe, that *fraile* is only a contraction of the earlier form, *frayel*.

---

[1] It must not be supposed, that the blancmanger, here mentioned, bore any resemblance to the viand which now bears that name. There is a receipt for making it in MS. Harl. *n.* 4016. One of the components is "the brawne of a capon, tesed small."

[2] I know not what this means, unless it be "one who is doing penance." This satire on the luxurious life of the clergy is very severe.

FARDEL.

"And after those days we trussed up our *fardels*, and went up to Hierusalem."—*Acts* xxi. 15.

In our authorized version this passage reads as follows :

"And after those days we took up our carriages and went up to Jerusalem."

I should much like to know, which of these two renderings is most intelligible to the general reader of the present day. Both, I suspect, would be about equally significant. In the first rendering, we have a word, which has now nearly, if not quite, become obsolete; in the second, a word, which, though not obsolete in outward form, is, nevertheless, in the sense which our translators attached to it, namely, that of goods and chattels carried during a journey, unpacked when the traveller stops, and packed, or trussed up, when he again sets out.[1] However, it is not our object, or intention, here at least, to draw comparisons between the renderings of our own and byegone versions. Instances, where this difference of rendering appeared to me deserving of notice, will be found in another portion of this work. At present, we have to consider the word *fardel*.

Dr. Johnson refers us to the Italian *fardello*, and most likely, had it occurred to him, would have traced the word a step higher, to the low, or barbarous Latin, *fartellum*, which, no doubt, sprang from *fartum*, the past participle of the Latin verb *farcio*, To stuff, or cram, and as such, signified that which is stuffed or crammed into anything. But by some the word *fardel* has been referred to a very different origin to the above, and it will be remembered, that on page 48, it was said the substantive *fardel* might,

---

[1] The word in the original is ἀποσκευασάμενοι, literally, "having packed up their goods."

perhaps, be connected with the Anglo Saxon verb *far-an*, To go. Yet, though there is something plausible in supposing *fardel*, like *bundle*, to be compounded of a verb (in the first instance *far-an*, To go, in the second, *bind-an*, To bind) and the Anglo Saxon substantive, still an English one, *dæ'l*, a division, or part, I fear the explanation, admirable on account of the ingenuity it displays, has, nevertheless, no further claims to our credit. But, why must this natural and pleasant hypothesis be rejected? why must our faith in Mr. Tooke, for I scarcely need say that the hypothesis is his, be so rudely shaken? Because, it is not supported by the testimony of facts, nor borne out by the analogy of the language. It is far more pleasant, than safe to speculate in etymology. Indeed, etymology does not even open a field to invention, properly so called, but only to investigation. And it is this misconception, which has already laid the foundation of many blunders, which it is only in the power of a more extended, and fundamental knowledge of the component elements of our language to remove. This is the cause to which we must attribute those remarkable blunders— pleasing from their very ingenuity—which Mr. Horne Tooke has made. He, who so unmercifully castigated the failings and mistakes of other men; so unsparingly tore down the veil, with which they had succeeded in hiding the truth, was himself scarcely more successful than they, when he attempted to finish their task by his own unaided imagination. He preferred rather to solve his difficulties by an ingenious fiction, (take for instance, his explanation of the words *barn*, and *bread*) than to seek for a solution, where a true one could alone be found, namely, in the archives of the language itself. And thus it came to pass, that, while by his labours he has conferred a greater blessing on the literature of his country, than perhaps any man before, or after him, he has by his very ingenuity and independence, introduced not a few errors, which still remain to be dissipated. Not that ingenuity is unnecessary in the pursuit of

etymological enquiry; on the contrary, it is highly necessary. Yet, it is that ingenuity which is of a subordinate
character, which is employed, not so much to assist the
flights of speculation, and conjecture, as in detecting the
radicle formation of words beneath those altered forms,
which, through the course of time, and the agency of other
influences, they have at length assumed. And, such being
its nature, it is needless to observe, how indispensable is
a knowledge of the radicle forms themselves, as well as
of the principles of verbal formation. We have said, that
the formation of *bundle* and *fardel*, as compounded of
parts of verbs, with the Saxon substantive *dæ'l*, a part, or
division, cannot be defended, either by the testimony of
facts, or the analogy of the Saxon. For, if *bundle* be
compounded of a verb (*bind-an*, To bind,) and the Saxon
substantive *dæ'l*, a part, then *girdle*, *beadle*, &c. may be
explained in the same way. But we know that the latter
are verbal substantives, formed by the addition of the
terminal syllable *el*,—a formation very common in the
Saxon language;—and there can be no doubt, that *bundle*,
the Gothic *bindle*, and Saxon *bindele*,[1] is of precisely analogous formation. Indeed, I do not find that the substantive *dæl* is ever compounded with verbs, or parts of
them; though it frequently is with substantives, and
particles, if I may use so vague a term.

It is true that very few of these compounds of *dæl*,
a part, have survived to our time; yet there is one, *ordeal*,
which is still common, though not with precisely the same
meaning as it obtained in the Saxon. The Saxon *ordæl*,
signified "a just judgment," or, "a judgment based on
the true principles of equity;" with us it has come to
signify any trying position in which a man may be placed.

As for the word *fardel*, since it does not occur in
the Saxon, nor, so far as I am aware, in the earlier

---

[1] It should, however, be observed, that the Saxon *bindele*, signifies rather
the act of *tying*, a *binding*; and *bunda* is used to designate *bundles*.

Gothic, there seems no alternative but to accept the explanation of it given above.[1]

GRIECES.

"And when he came into the *grieces*, it was so that he was borne of the souldiers, for the violence of the people.

"And when he had given him licence, Paul stood on the *grieces*, and beckoned with the hand unto the people."

Acts XXI. *v.* 35 and 40.

This word is spelt in almost every possible way. We find in Johnson, *greece, greeze, grieze,* and *grice ;* but which of the four is correct I do not undertake to say. Johnson himself, seems to think *greece* is, for he refers all the other forms to it. He calls "it a neuter substantive, [corrupted from *degrees*] ; a flight of steps. *Obsolete.*"

[1] Words, such as the last two we have been considering, *fardel,* from the Latin *fartellum, fartum,* and *fraile, frayel,* from *fraellum,* &c., suggest a remark of general importance, since it concerns, not them only, but also that large class of words, which are not to be traced to any primitive stock, but are the creation of languages themselves not primary. Most languages have, to a certain extent, a creative power of their own. How many words have we now in use, which are the coinage of the times ! How fond we are of modifying the form of a word which already suggests one idea to the mind, so that it shall, in its altered form, suggest another idea ! Examples of this process are afforded by that numerous class of nouns in *age;* as *windage, leakage,* &c. And, although this creative faculty is principally limited to the modification (sometimes by the addition of terminal syllables) of nouns, already existing, still it is easy to imagine, indeed we know it to have been the case, that during late years, when the arts and manufactures have been making such rapid progress, there have been new words invented to meet the growing necessity. In etymological investigation, the superficial method of merely finding the same word in a cognate language, instead of tracing it to its proper and true source, has been censured; and I make this remark to ward off a charge of inconsistency. It will be understood, now, that there is a class of words, which rightly forms an exception to the general rule; namely, those, which are the creation of the language where they are found, and as entire words, taking their origin thence, albeit the root, as in the case of *fartum,* may have to be sought for much further back. As a further illustration of this creative power, I would refer to that large, and still increasing class of substantives in *ee;* as *trustee, legatee,* and even *payee !*

Thompson, in his "English Etymons," says, respecting it, "a flight of steps : French, *gres*,[1] from the Latin *gradus*."

Johnson's derivation is rather too transparent, and artificial, to be accepted as at all probable. I think the following passage from Chaucer's "Canterbury Tales," which I have taken the liberty to quote at some length, for reasons, which I hope will be sufficiently evident, may do more towards settling the difficulty than pages of discussion about it :

"There n' is no thing[2] in *gree* suprlatif
(As saith Senek) above an humble wif,
Suffer thy wives tong, as Caton bit (biddeth)
She shall command, and thou shalt suffren it,

[1] I am not prepared to deny that the French word *gres*, formerly signified "a flight of steps," and so gave rise to the word *greece*; yet it is unfortunate, that the only meaning, which is given in modern French Dictionaries to the word *grès*, is "a sort of brown free-stone." However, it is fair to observe that *les degrés*, is still used in French to denote "the steps of a public edifice;" and it is just possible that *greece*, may be a corruption of this French word *degres*, though not of the English *degrees*.

[2] Lest the reader should suppose, that here, at least, is a remnant of French negative construction, I have appended the following short passage to shew that the usage of a double negative is strictly in accordance with the rules of Saxon construction. Indeed, to them, as to the Greeks, the rule of our modern English grammarians, that two negatives destroy each other, or make a positive, was unknown.

Mid go'dum mannum nis naʒer ne go'ld ne seolfer wiꝸ go'des mannes freo'ndscipe wiꝸme'ten.

Which rendered literally would read as follows:

"With good men, neither nor gold, nor silver is not to be compared to the friendship of a good man."

Nis in the above passage is simply the contraction of Saxon *ne*, not, and *is*, or *ys*, is. And there are not a few other words, which were formed in the same way in the Saxon ; some of which, we still retain, though perhaps, unconscious of their etymology. Thus *naught* is compounded of the Saxon *ne*, not, and *aht*, anything: neither of *ne*, not, and *aꝸor*, either; *need* of *ne* and *ea'd*. *Ea'd* signifies prosperity, or happiness, and *need* as

And yet she woll obey of curtesie.
A wif is keeper of thin husbondrie:
Wel may the sike man bewaile and wepe,
Ther as ther is no wif the hous to kepe.
I warne thee, if wisely thou wilt werche (work)
Love wel thy wif, as Christ loveth his cherche.
If thou lovest thy self, love thou thy wif.
No man hateth his flesh, but in his lif
He fostreth it, and therefore bid I thee
Cherish thy wif, or thou shalt never the.[1]
Husband and wif, what so men jape or play,
Of worldly folk holden the siker[2] way,
They ben so knit, ther may non harm betide,
And namely upon the wives side.

      *   *   *   *

With face sad, his tale he hath hem told,
He sayde, frendes, I am hore and old
And almost (God wot) on my pittes brinke,
Upon my soul somewhat most (must) I think.
I have my body folily dispended,
Blessed be God that it shal ben[3] amended:
For I wol ben certaine a wedded man
And that anon in all the haste I can."

Marchant's Tale.

compounded of *ne* and *ea'd* signifies the absence, or reverse of prosperity; and hence adversity, or want. *Ea'd* also enters into the composition of the Christian or Baptismal names, Edward (happy keeper), Edmund (happy protection), Edwin (happy in war), &c.

[1] "Cherish thy wif or thou shalt never *the*."

i. e. prosper. The verb *To the*, which appears to have been common enough in Chaucer's time, though it has since died out, is the relic of the Saxon verb þeo'n, *To thrive, To flourish*, or *grow.*

It occurs in several other passages:

> "Because our fire was not made of beche
> That is the cause and non other, *so the ich.*"

i. e. So may I prosper." I may have occasion to refer to this verb hereafter.

[2] Siker, means sure.

[3] "Blessed be God that it shall ben amended." It is impossible to read this line without asking the question, why there are the two forms *be* and *ben*, when, in our time, the former would have been quite sufficient. The fact is, we have here a vestige, not quite obliterated, of Saxon syntax. The Saxons had no future tense to their verbs, neither have we, however sur-

I think there is no doubt, but that the first line affords us the true clue to the word *greece*. It is easy to understand, how the early English word *gree*, signifying a step, in the singular number, would become *grees*, *greeze*, and finally, *greece*, in the plural, to signify a collection, or flight of steps. In the same manner, we have degree, from the French *degré*.

It might be thought mere excess of caution, were I to hesitate to refer the French word, whatever it may have been, which gave us *gree*, to the Latin noun subtantive *gradus* ; and as the subject, to which the question properly belongs, will be considered in a subsequent chapter, I will at present do no more than observe, that there is in the Saxon, a substantive *grad*, signifying a *step*, and offer, as a conjecture, that from this root may possibly be derived the Latin words *gradus*, and *gradior*.

IAKES.

"And the king answered and said to the Caldeans, the thing is gone from me. If ye will not make me understand the dreame with the interpretation thereof, ye shall be drawn in pieces, and your houses shall be made a *iakes*.

Daniel II. 5.

"Therefore, I make a decree, that every people, nation, and language, which speake any blasphemie against the God of Shadrach, Meshach, and Abednego, shall be drawn in pieces, and their houses shall be made a *iakes*, because there is no god that can deliver after this sort."—*Daniel* III. 29.

I have been able to obtain very little trustworthy information respecting this word. I do not know, that it occurs

---

prising the assertion may be, in English. What we call the future tense is in reality the conjunction of two verbs: the first, *shall*, which expresses obligation, or duty, and is really a present tense: the second, that which denotes the action, (as *love*, in "I shall love") and is nothing more than the infinitive mood. *I shall love*, signifies, *I owe*, I must, or am obliged to love; and only by a kind of acquired usage, expresses the intention of loving at some future time. So *ben* in the passage above is the Saxon infinitive (almost unaltered), of the verb *beon*, To be.

in any other passages, than the two already quoted; nor, have I met with it elsewhere. It is properly a corruption of the barbarous, or low Latin word *jactio*, a casting, from the verb *jacto*, To cast, or throw. Consequently, if this be correct, the substantive *iakes*[1] would signify a place where refuse matter of any kind is cast.

GRENNE.

"The proude have laide a snare for me, and spread a net with cordes in my pathway, and set *grennes* for me."—*Psalm* cxl. 5.

"Keep me from the snare, which they have layd for me, and from the *grennes* of the workers of iniquitie."—*Psalm* cxl. 9.

It is needless for me to remark, that for *grennes*, in the above passages, our present version has *gins*. The difference to the eye is not great, and as I had never met with the word *grenn* elsewhere, I thought it not unlikely, taking into consideration the laxity of spelling which still prevailed, that it was a corruption, or misprint for the

---

[1] The word *dunghill*, by which it has been replaced in our version, has the same meaning; in all probability, *dung* being connected with the verb *denegan*, To knock, To ding; whence come the substantives *din, dint*, and the verb *to ding*.

> "Sea-nymphs hourly ring his knell
> Hark, now I hear them,—*ding—dong*, bell."

The following are Mr. Tooke's words:

"Dung (or as it was formerly written *dong*) by the change of the characteristic letter *y* to *o*, or to *u*, is the past tense, and therefore past participle of the verb *dyngan*, dejicere, To cast-down."

But *dyngan* only means To dung, to manure, and is rather a verb formed from the Saxon word *dineg*, (which means not only *dung*, but also *new-broken*, or *fallow-land*) than the verb, whose past tense gives us the substantive *dung*. Still, in a subject like this, the truth of which is buried so deep in the remote ages of the past, it well becomes us to eschew anything that savours of prejudice, or dogmatism, and to bring to its consideration only a spirit of candour and docility, which will thankfully accept so much of the truth as is now within our reach, but not be angry, that a portion is for ever lost.

word *gin*. But a little further investigation quickly shewed me, that this was not the case, though I believe the opinion is still upheld by some.

The word does not occur in Dr. Johnson's dictionary; we may therefore fairly presume, it had in his time already become obsolete. Yet, it is well worthy our notice, if not for its own sake, at least on account of its close relationship to several other words, which are still, and, so long as English continues to be spoken, will be current amongst us. Through the long lapse of time these words have become so altered in appearance and signification—have, as it were, so receded from each other—that the family likeness can no longer be traced in their outward form. They have now, to speak familiarly, set up on their own account, and disclaim all connection with their quondam relations. It may appear somewhat bold to assert, that this old, and now obsolete word, *grenn*, is own brother to the words *yard*, *yarn*, *garb* and many others; yet it is more than probable that such is the case. Indeed, there can be little doubt that

Grenn,
Yarn,
Yard,
Yare,
Garb,
Gear,
To Gar,
Perhaps Yore.

are all closely connected with the old Saxon verb, variously spelt and pronounced, *gearwian*, to make ready; to prepare; to procure; to supply.

I think it will be easy to shew, that in most of these words, if not in all, the vital energy of the verb is still discernible.

Grenn, is the old Saxon word *gryn*, and signifies a contrivance, *prepared* to catch living creatures.

Yarn[1] and *yard* are simply yar-en and yar-ed, the two forms of the past participle.

---

[1] "Diversions of Purley," p. 357.

Yarn is wool, or cotton prepared for weaving; formerly wool only.

Yard. The constant use of this word alone has led us to forget its real meaning of something, anything, *prepared*; and it seems natural to look upon it, not as a participle, but as a substantive proper. Habit has caused this inaccuracy. Our Saxon ancestors avoided it by prefixing the word *mete*, To gyrd; thus producing *metegyrd*,[1] a measuring rod. And, in later times, the participle *yard* was not used alone, but in connection with the virtual, and conventional substantive *wand*; though this is in reality, nothing more than the past participle *wan-ed*, of the Anglo Saxon verb *wanian*, To diminish.[2] Even in our day this use of *yard*, in its more general and less definite sense of anything *prepared*, is, I suppose, preserved in the common word *steelyard*; that is, a steel instrument prepared, not to determine the length in this case, but the weight of any material. So, also, formerly there was the *yard-land*, or *gyrd-landes*, (*lit.* yard of land) which varied in different parts of England, but signified in each place a portion of land marked out by the *gyrd*, or prepared measuring wand.[3] Of course it is impossible to assign a reason why *yard* should now denote a measure of length only, instead of area, weight, capacity, or what not. It would be quite as rational to talk of a yard of beef,[4] as a yard of tape, insomuch as the word contains no reference at all to anything.

Yare, as an English word, is used both as an imperative, and a past participle of the Anglo Saxon verb

---

[1] I am not aware whether the length of the Saxon *mete-gyrd* was the same as our yard wand. The prefixed syllable *mete* is part of the verb *metan*, to measure.

[2] See p. 77.

[3] The *yardland*, or *virgate*, was usually the fourth part of the *hyde*, and would, therefore, contain about thirty acres. In some places, it consisted of seven acres of plough land and pasture for two oxen, one cow, and six sheep.

[4] See Appendix to this page.

gearwian, To prepare. Thus, in " Antony and Cleopatra,"
it occurs as an imperative :

" Yare, yare, good Iras."

while in *Chaucer* and *Gower*, it is frequently used as a
past participle :

" The wind was good the ship was *yare*
Thei toke her leve, and forth thei fare."
Gower, lib. 5, *fol.* 101, *p.* 2, *col.* 1.

" This Tereus let make his shippes *yare*
And unto Greece himself is forth yfare,
Unto his father-in-law gan he pray,
To vouchsafe that for a month or tway
That Philomene his wives suster might
On Progne his wife but ones have a sight,
And she shall come to you again anon,
Myself with her I will both come and gon,
And as my hertes life I will her kepe."
Legend of Fair Women,
Cant. Tales, line 2267.

GARB. GEAR.

Garb, gear, proceed from the same Gothic word *gi-orva ;* Saxon *gearwa,* or *geara.* The reason for the
difference is simply this ; *garb* has descended to us
indirectly, through the French, a fact which sufficiently
accounts for the change it has undergone; while *gear*
is nothing more nor less than the Saxon word itself,
descended directly from the Gothic. Even in French,
the word *garbe,* which is the parent of the English word
garb, does not signify dress, or outward appearance, so
much as the " make and rigging" of a thing, in which
sense it answers more nearly to the English word *gear,*
which signifies an equipment, or outfit. It would, however, be too much to expect, that a word from the French,
could settle down in a strange land without undergoing
some modification in its meaning.

H

But, to return to the word which has suggested these remarks, it may be asked, how it came to pass that the good old Saxon word *gren*, fell into disuse? Exactly for this reason, that there was another word, perhaps a little more euphonious, to supply its place. Indeed, we have at this time, A.D. 1600, two words very much alike in outward form, to express the same idea: the wonder is, that both had survived so long. *Gin*, which is substituted in our version for *gren*, has the same meaning as the latter:

> "The *gins* of the workers of iniquity
> Hell *yawneth* upon them."

> "For Gigas the geaunt
> With a *gyn* hath engyned
> To breke and to bete a-down
> That ben ayiens Ihesus."
> *Vision of Pierce Ploughman, line* 12581.

> "He that it wrought he coud many a *gin;*
> He waited (watched) many a constellation,
> Or (before) he had done this operation,
> And knew ful many a sele and many a bond."
> *Cant. Tales, line* 10442.

Whether the word be called Norman, or Saxon, is merely, I take it, a matter of precedence; for there can be little doubt, that the root of the word *gin* is to be found in the Saxon word "gin,"[1] an *expanse, opening, abyss*. It will be seen that, amongst the Saxons, it had not yet obtained the meaning of *deceit*, or *guile*, which it afterwards came to do amongst the French and ourselves. Dr. Johnson supposes *gin* to be derived from engine. The absurdity of such a conjecture needs no demonstration. It is equivalent to saying, that a simple word may be derived from its compound, and, if this were the case, as well might *trance* be called a derivative of *entrance, wrap* of *enwrap*, &c.

---

[1] Whence comes the Saxon verb *ginan*, which is simply the English verb *To yawn*.

PILL.

" Did I *pill* you by any of them whom I sent vnto you?

" I haue desired Titus, and with him I haue sent a brother did Titus *pill* you of anything?"—2 *Cor.* XII. 17, 18.

It may, perhaps, be questioned, whether the word *pill* is strictly entitled to a place in this chapter; inasmuch as, though it has certainly become obsolete during the last two centuries, there are one or two shoots from the same stock flourishing, even in the present day, of which I may mention *pillage* as one. The following seems the genealogy of the word: The Saxon word *pil*, a pile, or dart (whence the Saxon verb *pi"lan*, to beat with a pestle), gave rise in the Latin to *pilum*, a dart, and, I think, to the verb *pilo*, To plunder. The Latin verb *pilo*, became *piller* in the French, whence arose the substantives *pillage, pillour*,[1] both of which were once English words, though the former of them only has maintained its ground. But, observe, there is in the French not only the verb *piller*, To plunder, but also *piler*, To pound, (exactly corresponding to the Saxon verb above, *pilan*), and the substantives *pilier*, a pillar; *pilon*, a pestle, and *pilori*, whence comes our word *pillory*.

Thus, it seems highly probable that the Saxon *pil*,—nay, let us call it, as it is, the English word *pile* (for the accent in the former, and the affixed *e* in the latter, are only different ways of lengthening the *i*), has given words to the Latin and French independently; and also to the French, and thence again to the English, other words through the medium of the Latin. The following plan may serve to make this more plain :—

---

[1] Also *pillard*, a pilferer; *pillerie*, robbery. One is strongly tempted to think *pilfer* must have some connexion with the same root as the above.

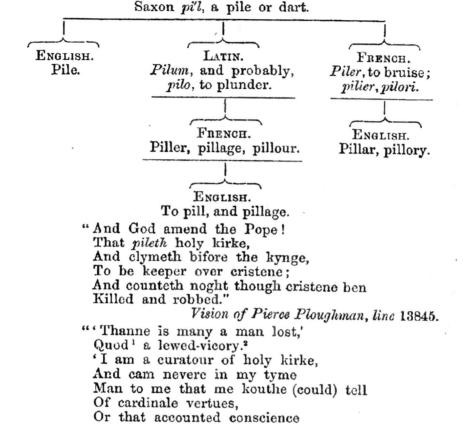

Saxon *pi'l*, a pile or dart.

ENGLISH.
Pile.

LATIN.
Pilum, and probably, *pilo*, to plunder.

FRENCH.
Piler, to bruise; *pilier*, *pilori*.

FRENCH.
Piller, pillage, pillour.

ENGLISH.
Pillar, pillory.

ENGLISH.
To pill, and pillage.

"And God amend the Pope!
That *pileth* holy kirke,
And clymeth bifore the kynge,
To be keeper over cristene;
And counteth noght though cristene ben
Killed and robbed."
Vision of Pierce Ploughman, line 13845.

"'Thanne is many a man lost,'
Quod[1] a lewed-vicory.[2]
'I am a curatour of holy kirke,
And cam nevere in my tyme
Man to me that me kouthe (could) tell
Of cardinale vertues,
Or that accounted conscience
At a cokkes (cock's) fethere, or an hennes.
I knew nevere cardynal,
That he ne came fro the Pope;
And we clerkes whan thei come
For hir (their) communes (commons) paieth
For hir pelure (fur), and hir palfreyes mete,
And *pilours* that hem folweth.'"[3]

[1] Quoth.

[2] A lay-vicar. I do not know that any single passage could give a clearer insight into the ancient meaning of *lewd*, than this. It shews how much the past differed from the present signification, which suggests, not so much simplicity, and ignorance, as vice and licentiousness.

[3] "And pilours who follow them."

Perhaps the reader is not aware, that all the persons in the plural number indefinite tense, indicative mood of Saxon verbs, end in ꝗ or th. At the time when the above quotation was written, about A.D. 1362, this inflection had not been dropped.

HARBEROUS.

"For a Bishop must be unreprouable as Gods steward, not froward............but *harberous*."—*Titus* i. 7, 8.

"Bee ye *harberous* one to another, without grudging."
1 *Pet.* iv. 9.

This word has fallen into disuse from much the same reason, I suppose, as the word *gren*—namely, redundancy. The same idea of the mind requires but one word to express it, provided it is always the same; and as *gren* and *gin* were not both requisite, and consequently the former yielded to the latter, so *harberous* and *hospitable* intimate too nearly the same qualification to require separate expressions; in consequence, *harberous* has disappeared and *hospitable* alone remains on duty. It is remarkable, that in both cases, good old Saxon words have been relinquished for words which, if not newer, would at least be fresher than those they supplanted.

The verb, *To harbour*, and the substantive *Harbour*, were formerly spelt *herberwe*.

> "———
> *Herberued* hym at an hostrie,[1]
> And to the hostiler[2] called,
> And seide 'haue kepe this man
> Til I come fro the justes;
> And lo! here silver,' he seide,
> 'For salve to his woundes.'"
> *Vision of Pierce Ploughman, line* 11514.

> "Befelle, that, in that seson on a day,
> In Southwerk at the *Tabard* as I lay,
> Redy to wenden on my pilgrimage
> To Canterbury with devoute corage,
> At night was come in that hostelrie
> Wel nine and twenty into a compagnie
> Of sondry folk, by aventure yfalle
> In felawship, and pilgrimes were they alle,
> That toward Canterbury wolden ride.

> *   *   *   *

[1] A hostelrie or inn.

[2] The inn-keeper; hence probably comes hostler, a man who has charge of the inn stables.

> Grete chere made oure hoste us everich on
> And to the souper sette he us anon:
> And served us with vitaille of the beste.
> Strong was the wine, and wel to drink us lest[1]
> A semely man our hoste was with alle
> For to han ben a marshal in an halle
> A large man he was with eyen stepe,
> A fairer *burgeis*[2] is there non in Chepe:
> Bold of his speche, and wise and wel ytaught,
> And of manhood him lacketh righte naught.
> Eke therto was he righte a mery man,
> And after souper plaien he began,
> And spake of mirthe amonges other thinges,
> Whan that we hadden made our rekeninges;
> And saide thus; now, lordinges, trewely
> Ye ben to me welcome right hertily:
> For by my *trouthe*, if that I shall not lie,
> I saw nat (not) this yere swiche a compagnie
> At ones in this HERBERWE, as is now."
>
> *Prologue to Cant. Tales.*

But we may make a still nearer approach to the root of this word, which is again to be found in the Saxon.

> "The coke (cook) of London, while the Reve spake,
> For joye (him thought) he clawed him on the bak:
> A ha (quod he) for Cristes passion,
> This miller had a sharp conclusion,
> Upon this argument of *herbergage*."
>
> *Prologue to the Cokes Tale.*

Now *herbergage* is a French word; that is, introduced by the Normans, and signifies a *lodging*. It approaches very nearly to what we must consider the root of this family of words, namely, the Saxon compound *Here-berga*, a station, where an army rested on its march, and thence a harbour. *Here-berga*, a harbour, and *here-bergan*, To harbour, are compounded of

---

[1] "And wel to drink us lest
It pleased us wel to drink."
So "Him lust to ride." "It pleased him to ride." Leste, liste, luste, is an impersonal verb, signifying "it pleaseth," like the Latin *juvat, libet.* It is the Saxon verb *lyst-an*, To wish, (from the root *lyst*, love, admiration, desire), but it does not appear to have been used in a bad sense as it has come to be now.

[2] Hence I suppose, *burgess*, in *burgess-constable.*

the Saxon substantive *Here*, an *army*, and the verb *Beorgan* or *Bergan*, To protect, To shelter, (from the root *beorg*, a hill, a burrow, or barrow).

But, besides this substantive *herbergage*, which does not seem to have been of much use to us, we have to thank our French neighbours for another word of very considerable value.

> "The fame anon thurgout the town is born
> How Alla King shall come on pilgrimage,
> By *herbergeours* that wenten him before."
> *The Man of Lawes Tale, line* 5415.

From the word *herberg*, closely resembling the Saxon *Hereberga*, our ingenious French cousins made two other substantives, *Herbergage*, a lodging; and *Herbergeour*, one who goes before to provide lodging. From the latter of these we are indebted for our pretty word *harbinger*.

It does not appear, that the form *harbour* has been modified by any foreign influence. I believe we have ourselves transformed the Saxon *hereberga* into the English *harbour*. In that pleasing description of a summer garden in *Chaucer's* "Romaunt of the Rose," it is written *herborow*.

> "Into that gardin well yrought,
> Whoso that me coud have brought,
> By ladders or else by degree,
> It would well have liked mee,
> For such solace, such joy, and pleie,
> I trow that never man ne seie,
> As was in that place delicious:
> The gardin was not daungerous,[1]
> To *herborow* birdes many one,
> So rich a yere was never none

[1] "The gardin was not *daungerous*
To herborow birdes."
That is, was not *sparing*. *Daungerous* occurs in one or two other passages in this sense. The construction "daungerous to herborow birdes," seems to remind us of that of the Latin supine "mala tactu vipera." A viper dangerous to handle.

Of birdes song and braunches grene,
Therein were birdes mo (more) I wene,
Than been in all the realme of Fraunce :
Full blisful was the accordaunce,
Of swete pitous song they made,
For all this world it ought glade."

GARD.

"And the imbroidered *gard* of the same ephod, which shall
be upon him, shall be of the selfe same worke and stuffe."

Exodus XXVIII. 8.

Gard is, I suppose, either a contraction of girdle,
Saxon *gyrdel,* or, more probably, the Saxon word *geard,*
an enclosure, itself, which is the root not only of *girdle,*
but also gives us, or enters into the compositon of, the
substantives

Yard.   Garden.
Garter.   Girder.
Garland.   Orchard.[1]

SPARSE.

"As it is written, He hath *sparsed* abroad, and hath given
to the poore: his benevolence remaineth for ever."—2 *Cor.* IX. 9.

The loss we have sustained here is certainly not a
serious one. The verb *To sparse,* besides being very
ill-sounding, would be redundant, while we have the
more euphonious compound *disperse,* and the Saxon
verb *To scatter.*

PIGH.

"*Who*......is a minister of the sanctuary, and of that true
tabernacle which the Lord *pight* and not man."—*Heb.* VIII. 2.

Pight is the past tense of the verb *To pigh,* now
spelt *pitch.* The word occurs under the same form in
Chaucer :—

"Out of the ground a furie infernal sterte,
From Pluto sent at requeste of Saturne,

[1] Orchard is the Saxon *ort-geard,* or *wyrt-geard,* i. e. a *wyrt-yard,*
or enclosed space for the cultivation of herbs; and then secondarily of
fruit trees.

For which his hors for fere gan to turne,
And lept aside and foundred as he lepe :
And˜er that Arcite may take any kepe
He *pight* him on the pomel[1] of his hede,
That in the place he lay as he were ded,
His brest to-brosten with his sadel bow.
As black he lay as any cole or crow
So was the blood grounen in his face."

The Knightes Tale.

The etymology of the verb *To pitch* is somewhat doubtful; nor do I see that this more ancient mode of spelling it affords us any further clue. It is worthy of remark, that this older form was at this time rapidly falling into disuse. Of the many passages in the Bible where it might have occurred, I believe this is the only one where it does.

GHEST.

" But he knoweth not that the dead are there, and that her *ghests* are in the depth of Hell."—*Proverbs* IX. 18.

"So those seruants went out into the highwayes, and gathered together all that euer they found, both good and bad: so the wedding was furnished with *ghests.*

"Then the King came in, to see the *ghests*, and saw there a man which had not on a wedding garment."—*Matth.* XXII. 10, 11.

It was only the spelling of this word which attracted my attention, and induced me to notice it here. Its resemblance to the word *ghost* struck me as remarkable, and suggested a train of ideas, which I hope may not be found altogether impertinent to the general character of my subject. After all, the resemblance between *ghest* and *ghost*—and, to trace them still further back, between the Saxon *gœst* and *ga'st*, whence they respectively spring; a resemblance which to my eye seemed indicative not only of a common parentage, but also of a common animation—may be only fortuitous and imaginary. This, however, I shall leave with my reader to decide.

[1] A *pomel* was anything round. It is now, I believe, used only with reference to *saddle*.

The earliest form in which the word *guest*, Saxon *gœst*, appeared as an English word was *gest*. Thus:

"Antony a dayes
Aboute noon tyme
Hadde a brid (bird) that brought hym breed.
That he by lyvede;
And though the gome[1] hadde a *gest*,
God fond hem bothe."

Vision of Pierce Ploughman, line 10181.

It occurs again in *Chaucer's* touching story of "Patient Grisilde:"

"A few sheep spinning on the field she kept,
She wolde not ben idel til she slept.
And when she homward came she wolde bring
Wortes and other herbes times oft,
The which she shred and sethe for hire living
And made hire bed ful hard and nothing soft:
And aye she kept hive fadres life on loft
With every obeisance and diligence,
That child may don to fadres reverence."

When the noble Markis visits her humble cot, and asks her "fadre" to take him "as his son in lawe," the story goes on to say:

"No wonder is though that she be astonied,
To see so gret a *gest* come in that place,
She never was to non swiche *gestes* woned[2]
For which she loked with ful pale face."

But, indeed, neither *guest* nor *ghost* appear to have been originally spelt with *h*. In the "Vision of Pierce Ploughman," *ghost* is frequently written *goost;* while in *Chaucer* we find repeatedly *gost*, for ghost or spirit.

When the cup of poor "Grisilde's" sorrow was well nigh full to overflowing with the seemingly heartless treatment of her husband, she says to him:

"Ne shall the *gost* within myn herte stent[3]
To love you best with all my trewe intente:

[1] *Gome*, a man. See Appendix to this page.
[2] Accustomed.
[3] Desist.

And with **that** word she gan the hous to dight,
And tables for to sette and beddes make,
And peined her to don all that she might,
Praying the chambereres, for Goddes sake,
To hasten hem, and fast swepe and shake,
And she the most servicable of all,
Hath every chamber arraied, and his hall."

Ibid.

Again:

"It liketh hem to be clene in body and *gost:*
Of min estat I wol not maken bost.
For wel ye know a lord in his household
Ne hath nat every vessell all of gold:
Som ben of tree; and don hir lord service.
God clipeth folk to him in soudry wise,
And everich hath of God a propre gift,
Som this, som that him liketh shift."

The Wif of Bathes Tale.

There is no more reason for spelling *ghost* with *h*, than *guest;* nor, indeed, any reason for either.

As *guest* is the Saxon *gœst,* so *ghost* is the Saxon *ga'st,* signifying first, the breath, and secondly, a spirit, a ghost.

Now, is not the soul or spirit the guest of the body; and may not the body be considered as the earthly house, where a spiritual visitor, or guest is, for a short time, entertained and lodged, before it wings away its flight to its final home—its last abiding place of everlasting joy or misery?

Such a notion would not be strange to, or even unparalleled amongst the Saxons.

The word *sa'wl* (our word *soul*) is a verbal substantive, derived from the verb *sáw-an,* To sow, because the soul is the germ, or seed, sown by the Creator of spirits in the bodies of men.[1] And this metaphor was further prettily carried out by the Saxons in their substantives *sáwl-hórd,*

---

[1] "And the Lord God formed man of the dust of the ground, and breathed into his nostrils the breath of life; and man became a living soul.—*Genesis* II. 7.

sáwl-hús ; both which were used by them to denote the body, as being the repository or chamber of the soul. So that we see the idea of the *ghost* or spirit, as the guest of the body, was familiar to them, whether, or not, there be anything beyond mere conjecture in the external resemblance of *ghest* to *ghost.*

If, indeed, it be that there is, may we not learn a lesson, that our bounden duty is to treat our spiritual guest well, and ensure for it, so far as lays in our power, a better home above—an entrance into a happier abode, when that stern bailiff, Death, shall have laid his distraint on this earthly tenement, and placed our goods in sequestration.[1]

I hope I shall be pardoned for transcribing the following somewhat lengthy dialogue from the " Colloquies of Erasmus." It pursues, and forms, to my idea, no inapt comment to the train of thought which I have alluded to above.

" *Chrysoglottus.* Although the philosophical books of Cicero seem for the most part to breathe a sort of divinity, yet that which he wrote when now an old man, concerning Old Age, certainly seems to me a κύκνειον ᾄσμα (a swan-like song), as the Greek proverb has it. I have been reperusing it to-day, and this passage I committed to memory, because it stands forth pre-eminently beyond the rest: ' But if the Deity should bestow on me the power to become a little child, and utter my baby cradle-notes again, I would certainly refuse the proffered boon: nor, indeed, could I wish, now that my course is as good as run, to be recalled from the goal to the starting place. For what advantage does this life afford which is not rather counteracted by trouble? Or, if not by absolute trouble, at least by a feeling of satiety or disappointment. For I would not bewail my life as many, and they learned men, have often done. Nor does it grieve me to have lived; since I have so lived that I may not think it has been in vain. And I depart this life as it were from an Inn, not as from my Home. For Nature has furnished for us a chamber where we may sojourn for a time, but which we must not look upon as our permanent abode. Oh! for that illustrious day, when I shall set out to join that congregation and assembly

---

[1] Previous to this inspiration the body of man would resemble a new house not yet inhabited.

of spirits, and leave this medley of all kinds of vice.' Thus much Cato. What sentiment more holy than this could have been expressed even by a Christian?   *   *   *   *   *

"*Theophilus.* Probably so; yet permit me to make an observation, which occurred to me while you were reciting that passage. I have often wondered with myself, seeing how all men desire long life, and shrink from death, although scarcely any one is known so happy, I will not say in old age, but in advanced life, who, being asked whether, if he might, he would become young again, knowing that the same good and evil fortune, in every respect, would have to be endured, as had already happened to him in life, would have made the same reply as Cato; especially, were he to consider all the sorrow or joy that had befallen him in the years recalled. For frequently even pleasing recollections are marred by a certain feeling of shame or remorse, and thus become no less painful to the mind than sorrowful ones. This, I imagine, the very best poets have referred to, when they say, that not until the soul has drunk deep at the oblivious stream of Lethe does it feel any regret for the deserted body.

"*Uranius.* That sentiment is certainly a beautiful one; nor does it appear to me to admit of doubt. But how much that expression, 'It does not grieve me that I have lived,' pleased me! Yet how few Christians so regulate this life as to be able to say this of themselves! The majority of men think they have not lived in vain if, when they come to die, they can leave behind them riches heaped together, either honestly or dishonestly, it matters not which. But Cato thinks that he has not been born in vain, because, as an upright and pious citizen, a faithful magistrate, he had lived for the Republic; because he had left to posterity the monuments both of his virtue and industry. What could have been said more beautiful than this, 'I depart as it were from an Inn, not as from my Home.' We may lodge for a time at an inn until the host bid us take our departure. A man is not easily driven from his own house. And yet downfall, or fire, or any other accident whatsoever frequently does effect his expulsion. And, even should none of these ills befall, yet to an old man the collapsing walls of his tenement ought to admonish him that he must presently leave it. Not less elegant is that expression of Socrates in Plato, that the human soul is placed in this body as in a garrison, whence it is unlawful to depart without the permission of the Commander, or to spend any longer time in it than appears good to Him, who appointed us to keep it. The meaning in Plato is more significant, inasmuch as he has used the figure, or simile of the garrison, instead of the house: if, indeed, we do but sojourn for a time in the house, in the garrison we have our proper duties, which our Commander has appointed us to perform : a simile by no means repugnant to Scripture, which, at one time, compares the life of a man to a warfare, at another, to a contest.

"*Uranius.*   But to me at least this speech of Cato's seems beautifully to correspond with that of St. Paul's, who, writing to the Corinthians, calls that heavenly mansion, which we expect after this life οἰκίαν and οἰκητήριον; that is, a house or domicile. But this body he calls a tabernacle, (Græce σκῆνος) a tent.   For we who are in this *tabernacle*, says he, groan, being burdened. And the same figure is carried out by St. Peter, when he says, 'But I think it right as long as I am in this tabernacle to put you in remembrance, knowing that I must speedily lay aside my *tabernacle*.'   But indeed what else is that which Christ himself tells us, when he say, 'that we should so live in watchfulness as those who may be on the point of death; should so be engaged in all virtuous deeds as those who will live for ever.' "

CHAPTER VI.

OBSOLETE FORMS OF THE PAST TENSE AND PAST PARTICIPLE.

EXCEPT that the double forms of the past participle in *en* and *ed,* seem to have been at this time indifferently used, it does not appear that the past three centuries have chronicled many striking alterations in the inflection of verbs. The past tenses which are in use now, were, for the most part, in use at the time we are considering. Still, there are a few noteworthy exceptions to this general rule, which we are bound to notice. They are but few and require but little comment.

STROOK.   STROKE.

The verb *To strike,* which now forms its past tense, and generally its past participle in *struck,* had formerly two other forms, neither of which correspond exactly with our own.

"And always, both night and day, hee cryed in the mountaines and in the graues, and *strook* himself with stones.
Mark v. 5.

"Nevertheless, it satisfieth them not that we are in bitter captiuitie, but they have *stroken* hands with their idols."
Esther (additional portion) ch. XIV. 3.

The past tense, corresponding to *stroken,* would be *stroke.* Possibly our substantive *stroke,* a *blow,* may have originated from this form *stroken*, though we must bear in mind, that the verbs *To strike*, and *To stroke*, *i. e.* to make smooth, were distinct, even in the Saxon.[1]

WAN.

"Thus Antiochus *wan* many strong cities in the land of Egypt, and took away the spoyles of the land of Egypt."

1 Macc. I. 20.

Wanne is also found "Simon *wanne* the citie of Joppa."

Both these forms are more correct than that at present in use. The verb *To win*, if properly conjugated would resemble the verb *To begin*, making the past tense *wan* and the participle *wun*. Why the past participle ever came to be spelt *won* I know not, unless for sake of euphony in spelling.

The Saxon verb *Winn-an* is formed from the root *winn, contention, war, labour, trouble*. It is by a purely inductive method of reasoning, that the verb *To win* has acquired the signification it now implies, namely that of victory, or superiority. And this in the following way :

Winn-an, as formed from the root *winn*, signifies To contend, To make war, To struggle with labour, pain, or anxiety, for a thing : thence, since what is energetically laboured for is in the end generally obtained, it comes to signify To obtain, To acquire, To win, subdue, conquer.[2]

---

[1] The Saxon verb Strecc-an, *To make prostrate*, whence come our verbs *To stretch* :—

"Hee *streched* out his hand to the drinke offering."

Eccles. L. 15.

And *To strike*, is formed from the root *strec*, violence, a stretch ; while Stracian, *To stroke*, is formed from the root strac, *straight*, and therefore signifies "to make straight," or "smooth."

[2] Proper names in -*win* contain this root : as Baldwin, bold in war : Edwin, happy in war, &c. *Winning*, however, in the sense of pleasing, and *winsome* are compounded of the Saxon word *win* or *wyn*, pleasure.

"Shall we never more behold thee ;
Never hear thy winning voice again ?
When the spring-time comes, gentle Annie,
When the wild flowers lie scattered o'er the plain."

Ballad.

FET.

Fet is frequently used as the past tense of the verb *To fet*, or as we now write it, *fetch*.

HOLPE.

"And after he was come thither, he *holpe* them much, which had beleeued through grace."—*Acts* xviii. 27.

This form is still retained in our Church service:

"He remembering his mercy, hath *holpen* his servant Israel."

Holpen is exactly the old Saxon form of the past participle, and it is matter of regret that we have suffered it to fall into disuse.

OUGHT.

This is another instance where time and usage have reconciled us to error; or rather, perverted our eyes till we no longer recognise it as such.

Ought is in reality the past tense of the Saxon verb A'gan,[1] *To own*, or *Have*. It is remarkable, that the signi-

---

[1] The past tense of *ágan* is spelt *a'ht*, which is very correctly denoted in sound by the way in which *ought* is pronounced in English. The *a'* has the broad sound of *a*, somewhat resembling the pronunciation of *o*, in *bone, home, stone;* oa in *broad*, Saxon *bra'd*, *boar*, Saxon *ba'r :* and oe in *foe*, Saxon *fa'*, *doe*, Saxon *da'*, &c.

The following passage, from the Romance of "Sir Guy," may tend to throw some light on the meaning which the verb *To owe* obtained in early English. It will be found, I think, closely to resemble the Saxon verb *ágan*, *To possess*, in the signification it at first bore.

> "To the pallaice he yode (went) anon
> And lyghted down of his steede full soone.
> Through many a chamber yede Raynborne,
> A knight he found in dongeon,
> Raynborne grete hym as a knight courtoise
> 'Who *oweth*' he said 'this fayre pallaice?'"

Indeed, it seems highly probable, that not only the verb *ought*, but also the verb *To own*, are of modern, and when I say modern I mean English, coinage: the first from the past tense *a'ht*, the second from the past participle *ágen* of the Saxon verb *ágan*, *To own*.

On the probable derivation of the noun substantive, see Appendix to this page.

I

fication of duty, *devoir*, &c., does not appear to have belonged to this verb originally, but, that it has acquired it by a kind of inductive reasoning, similar to that noticed above in the case of the verb *To win*.

The past participle of Saxon A'g-an, *To own*, is a'gen; whence comes the possessive adjective *own*, which is affixed to the possessive pronouns *my, thy, his,* &c.

> "Thou sayest, that dropping houses and eke smoke,
> And chiding wives maken men to flee
> Out of hire *owen* hous."
> > *Wife of Bathes Tale.*

"Also we forgive the ouersights, and faults committed vnto this day, and the crown tax that ye *ought* us."
> 1 *Macc.* XIII. 39.

"But when the servant was departed he found one of his fellow-servants which *ought* him an hundred pence, and he layed hands on him, and thratled him, saying, pay me that thou owest."
> *Matt.* XVIII. 28.

Use has seized upon this past tense, and converted it into an independent verb, to signify the obligation, generally moral, by which a man is bound to a certain course of conduct; while, to disguise this perversion, a fresh perfect tense, *owed*, has been coined to supply the place of the missing one. Though no considerations can make that right, which, is radically wrong, still there are reasons which go far in extenuation of this violent procedure. And foremost amongst them would be that need which was felt for such a verb as we now have in *ought*.[1] "I owe to do a thing" sounds awkward, though expressive and correct enough. Even still, our language is somewhat poverty stricken for a substantive to express what is sometimes called "his duty," but which is frequently better expressed by the French word, "*devoir;*" though this word is as much English as, and more right to be so, than many others, which now pass unchallenged amongst us.

---

[1] The verb is only used in those tenses where it is required: namely, the present, and past.

STALE.

" But Jehosheba took Joash, the son of Ahaziah, and *stale* him from among the kinges sonnes, that should be slain, both him and his nource."—2. *Kings* xi. 2.

SWOMME.

" Then the souldiers counsel was to kil the prisoners, lest any of them, when he had *swomme* out, should flee away."
Acts xxvii. 42.

This form of the past participle is undoubtedly more correct than our own: there is no authority, besides that of usage, for *swum*, except in the past tense, and even there, *swam* is more correct.[1]

FOUGHTEN,

As the past participle of the verb *To fight*, is strictly correct; it is found once or twice, 2 *Macc.* xii. 36.

HURTED.

" Thou madest the sun that it *hurted* not them in their honourable journey."—*Wisdom of Salomon*, xviii. 3.

This is the last example I have to notice. It is but fair to inform my reader, that the above forms of the past tense, and past participle, though they do occur, and some of them not unfrequently, in the Breeches Bible, are still the exception rather than the rule. They appear but as the lingering remnants of declining usages,—but as the last descendants of a race, which was rapidly becoming extinct.

It will not have escaped observation, that in almost every case above noticed the change, which time has produced, has been to abolish what are called the strong forms of the past tense, and past participle, and substitute weak forms in their place.[2] This is much to be regretted,

[1] The changes which have taken place in the verb *To win*, noticed on page 112, will occur to my reader.

[2] Weak forms are those where the past tense and past participle are formed by the addition of the syllable *ed* to the present, as *love, loved;* strong forms those, where the past tense and past participle are formed by the change of a radical vowel of the verb: as *drink, drank, drunk.*

inasmuch as the creative power of the language is now gone, and any defection is not only permanent, but does not admit of replacement.

We occasionally hear *sew* used as the past tense of the verb *To sow;* "I *sew* my barley last week." Now I never heard anyone do this, who knew why he did so, or, indeed, for any other reason, than because it seemed an easy natural way of speaking. Nay, further, I have observed men of fair education, who ought to know good English from bad, titter when they heard this word used; and in some instances it has been remarked to me afterwards, in private, "Mr. Mangles must be a very illiterate man, for did you observe he made use of *sew* as the past tense of the verb *To sow.*"[1] Strange, that the man who left school when a boy at fourteen, who has done nothing ever since but ride young horses, and attend the markets, should, as it were by instinct, speak his own language more correctly, than those whose lifetime has been spent in misguided attempts to learn it. Nature, in this case, seems a truer guide than education; because education does not touch the sore, and, therefore, till it does, can never effect a cure. Language is not independent of the *physical* constitution of a people. We are in the main but the descendants of those, who in past time assisted to form the language we speak; and instances like the above are but the voice of nature re-asserting her invaded rights. Already has the study of Saxon—the only language which can give us a thorough acquaintance with English—been too long neglected. Already has this neglect produced evils, which, we fear, it is beyond the power of time to remedy. It remains to be seen, whether Englishmen will at length awake to a sense of their true position, and, though late, take such steps as can alone check the progress of that decay, which, is slowly, but surely undermining the vital energy of our language.

[1] In one of the very early Saxon translations of the Gospels, this past tense occurs in the parable of the Sower, "Behold a man went forth to sow, and as he sowed,"—"and þa he sew, &c."

Another parallel case to the last is afforded in the past tense of the verb *To mow.* He would be a bold man, who would knowingly use *mew* instead of *mowed.* Yet, I have heard it done; not, indeed by men, who know why they did it, but, as before, because it seemed natural. How perfectly arbitrary all this is, will perhaps be rendered more apparent by considering a verb where we have suffered the strong perfect to remain unaltered. The verb *To grow,* is to the point. How harsh would it sound to hear any one use such an expression as "he *growed* very tall;" "the grass *growed* fast after the rain;" and so forth! Yet, this would not be a whit less correct than *sowed,* &c., except that use has established the error in one case, but not in the other. Such corruptions as these can only have had their birth in the grossest ignorance of the grammar of our language, and, if they are to be prevented for the future, it will only be prevented by a simple recurrence to the *only* trust-worthy authority in all points of grammatical inflection, namely the Saxon language.

While we confess the truth of those prophetic words (with which we shall close this chapter) uttered nearly two thousand years ago, by a great arbiter of his own language, we should recollect, that the changes which time produces ought not to run counter to, but in harmony with, the true principles of a nation's language. We willingly acknowledge, not only the necessity, but also the convenience of that power of modifying, altering, or even inventing words adapted to the particular requirments of each successive age, and we shall only be justified in complaining, if, in these changes, the vital energy is found to suffer, or the true and essential principles of our language to be violated, through mere ignorance, and culpable neglect in acquainting ourselves with them.

"It always has been, and always will be, lawful to coin a word, stamped with the impress of the current age. When the woods lose their leaves at the decline of the year, the oldest drop off first: just so is it with regard to words, those of great antiquity perish, and those of more recent date, like young men, flourish and grow strong. Death claims both us and ours: the greatest achievements of mortals will perish, much less may the integrity and grace of their speech escape. Many words, which have already fallen into disuse, will hereafter be revived, and those which are now held in high esteem rejected, if only *usage* shall decree it—*usage* in whose power alone it is to act as arbiter on the laws and forms which regulate our speech."[1]

[1] Hor. Ep. ad. Pisones.

CHAPTER VII.

LITERAL CONTRACTIONS.—APOSTROPHAL GENITIVE.—REMARKS ON SOME OF THE CHARACTERISTIC FEATURES OF THE GENEVAN TRANSLATION AS COMPARED WITH OUR OWN.

Wisdome of Salomon, Chapter IIII.

" But though the righteous be preuented with death, yet fhall he be in reft.

" For the honourable age is not that which is of long time, neither that which is meafured by the number of yeeres.

" But wifdome is the gray haire, and an vndefiled[1] life is the old age.

" He pleafed God and was beloued of him, fo that wheras he liued among finners, he tranflated him.

" He was taken away, left wickednef fhould alter his vnderftanding, or deceit beguile his mind.

" For wickedneffe by bewitching obfcureth the things that are good, and the unftedfaftneffe of concupifcence peruerteth the fimple minde.

" Though he was foone dead, yet fulfilled he much time.

" For his foule pleafed God : therefore hafted he to take him away from wickedneffe.

" Yet the people fee and underftand it not, and confider no fuch things in their hearts, how that grace and mercie is vpon his Saints, and his prouidence ouer the elect.

" Thus the righteous y^t is dead, cõdemneth the vngodly which are liuing : and the youth y^t is foone brought to an end, the long life of ye vnrighteous.

" For they see the end of the wife but they underftand not what God hath deuifed for him, and wherefore the Lord hath preferued him in fafetie.

---

[1] The reader will obferve the transposition of *u* and *v.*

"They fee him and defpife him, but the Lord will laugh them to fcorne.

"So that they fhall fall hereafter without honour, and fhall haue a fhame among the dead, for euer more: for without any voice fhall he burſt them and caſt them down, and fhake them frō the foundations, fo that they fhall be vtterly waſted, and they fhall be in forrow, and their memoriall fhall perifh.

"So they being afraid, fhall remember their finnes, and their owne wickednes fhall come before them to conuince them."

Portion of Chapter VII.

"God hath granted me to fpeake according to my minde, and to iudge worthily of the things that are giuen me: for he is the leader vnto wifdome, and the directer of the wife.

"For in his hand are both we and our words and all wifdom, and the knowledge of the workes.

"For hee hath giuen me the true knowledge of the things that are, so that I knowe how the world was made, and the powers of the elements.

"The beginning and the end and the mids of the times, how yᵉ times alter, and the change of yᵉ feafons.

"The courfe of yᵉ yere, the fituation of the ſtars.

"The nature of liuing things, & the furioufnef of beafts, yᵉ power of yᵉ winds, & the imaginatiōs of men, yᵉ diuerfities of plants, & the vertues of roots.

"And all things both fecret and knowen do I know; for wife-dome the worker of all things, hath taught me it.

"For in her is yᵉ fpirit of vnderſtanding, which is holy, the only begottē, manifold, subtil, moueable, clere, vndefiled, euidēt, not hurtfull, louing the good, fharp which cannot be letted, doing good."

Ezekiel xvi. 9.

"I clothed thee alfo wᵗ broydered worke, and fhod thee with badgers fkin."

Salomon's Song, vi. 3.

"Thou art beautifull, my loue, as Tirzah, comely as Jerufalē, terrible as an army wᵗ banners."

I think the above quotations afford examples of all the contractions, or methods of contraction, which are to be found in the Breeches Bible, and which, consequently, we may fairly presume to have been in general use at this time. There is no need for comment on them, being curious and arbitrary rather than instructive. The custom of dropping the consonants *m* or *n*, after a vowel, (the omission being marked by a hyphen placed over the vowel) sometimes so alters the appearance of a word as almost to prevent our recognizing it. Thus :—

Strãger	for	Stranger,
Womã	for	Woman,
Thẽ	for	Them and then,
Coũsel	for	Counsel,
Amẽd	for	Amend,

and many others which might be named, strike the eye as very strange words.[1]

All these contractions, as they had no root in the fundamental principles of the language, but were the spurious invention of a corrupt age; so, neither have they been able to maintain their ground. The same caprice, which called them into being in one age, swept them away in the following, and they have now entirely disappeared. But not the spirit itself. It still remained behind, one proof of which has, I dare say, already presented itself to my reader. He must have observed, that no instance of the apostrophal, or syncopated form of the possessive or genitive case of nouns substantive has occurred in the quotations I have made so far from the Breeches Bible. In fact there is not one to be found. Thus we learn incidentally, that the apostrophal, or contracted genitive, dates at least no further back than the close of the 16th century; and that, so far from being founded on any fundamental principle of our language, it is, like the contractions noticed above, a mere capricious usage, (not, indeed, without its recommendation), and so liable, like them, to be again

---

[1] What may have given rise to these contractions I am unable to say, unless it may have been the desire for brevity in writing. It is scarcely probable, that they had anything to do with the pronunciation of the words so contracted.

swept away by the whim of posterity.[1] Let us briefly consider the nature and object of this contraction.

THE APOSTROPHAL FORM OF THE POSSESSIVE CASE.

The termination *es*, or *s*, affixed to nouns substantive, to indicate possession, or procession, is a traditional remnant of Anglo Saxon inflexion; a large body of nouns substantive, in that language, forming their genitive, or possessive case in this manner. When, in the confusion which succeeded the Norman Conquest, the distribution of substantives according to their proper declensions was forgotten, the *casual* terminations, which distinguished those declensions, likewise disappeared, with the exception of the genitive case of one of them. And this sole surviving termination of the genitive, or possessive case, from having belonged in the Anglo Saxon, to a certain class of what are now called nouns substantive only, came at length to be applied indiscriminately to all.[2] Thus, it may appear as correct to speak of "a week's suspense," as "a kingdom's wealth:" of "a youth's intemperance," as "a

---

[1] "Fayrest of fayre, O lady min, Venus
Daughter of Jove and spouse of Vulcanus,
Thou glader of the mount of Citheron,
For thilke love thou haddest to Adon
Have pitee on my bitter *teres* smert,
And take myn humble praier to thin herte."
The Knightes Tale, line 2224.

[2] In France, Spain, Portugal, and Italy, where the languages are a compound of the Teutonic and Latin elements principally, the inflexion of nouns has been still more effectually destroyed. Not only are there no oblique cases, but even the nominative case of the noun itself is formed, in many instances, from an oblique case of the Latin noun.

The Italians have, it is true, preserved, in a more or less faithful manner, the Latin nominative. But the Spaniards and Portuguese have adopted the accusative form; while in the Provincal, M. Raynouard has endeavoured to shew, that the nouns were formed from Latin substantives by depriving them of those terminations which marked their cases;

smith's anvil," &c.: and so indeed in English it may be;
yet, from the analogy and teaching of the Anglo Saxon,
it appears, that only the latter, in each of the above comparisons, is correct; the nouns "*week*," and "*youth*," &c.,
never having made their genitive in *s*, or *es*. Nor must we
suppose, that the older and uncontracted forms of the
genitive, such for instance as "smithes," "kingdomes," &c.,
as they would have been written in the Breeches Bible, are
a whit less correct, than our apostrophal form now in use.
For the principal utility of the apostrophe seems to lie in
its enabling *the eye* at once to detect whether the genitive
singular, or *plural*, is intended.[1] It does not appear to
influence the pronunciation, and can, therefore, be of no

that is, from the root. Thus, from *abbat-em* was formed *abbat;* from
infant-em, *infant*, &c. I have no acquaintance with either the Spanish or
Portuguese languages, and am indebted to M. de Sismondi for what I
have said respecting them, as also for the following examples which will
serve as illustrations:

Latin.	Italian.	Spanish.	Portuguese.
Oculi	occhi	ojos (oculos)	oilhos.
Cœli	cieli	cielos	ceos.
Gaudium	gioia	gozo	gozo.

[1] If it could be shewn, that, previous to the introduction of the Apostrophe, the universal and acknowledged form of the genitive had been in
es, and not *s*, then it might have been urged, that the apostrophe was
introduced for the purpose of abbreviation. Thus, if the genitive of *camel*,
&c., had been *cameles*, then certainly it would have been both more
convenient and euphonious to have spoken of "camel's hair," than
"cameles hair." But this was not the case, as the following passage from
the Genevan Version will show:
"And this John had his garment of camels haire, and a girdle of
skinne about his loynes."—*Matt.* III. 4.

Euphony had been consulted long previous to the *invention* of the
apostrophal form of the genitive; its invention therefore did not confer
any advantage in this respect. Where the old genitive in *es* is found, as
in *kingdomes* for *kingdoms*, it is because the nominative case was spelt
with the final *e*, and not because the genitive was formed by adding another
syllable to the noun. The *es* would not be pronounced in *kingdomes* any
more than in our more modern *kingdom's*.

assistance to the ear.[1]   For instance, if we speak of "the Church's Ritual," the syncopated *e* is not the less sounded in the pronunciation of Church's, because it is syncopated; nor, on the other hand, in such instances as these, "a man's actions," "a woman's fidelity," does the apostrophe indicate the omission of *e;* for this simple reason, the *e* was not according to English usage, previous to the introduction of the apostrophe, missing.[2]

The use of the apostrophal genitive is, no doubt after all, of some value as an artificial adjunct to our Language. Alas! that it should require so miserable a shift as this to repair the damage it has sustained.   But, since we have had the ill luck to lose our Donet, let us be thankful, that artifice has in some measure made up for our loss.   Only let us be chary, as well as charitable, in what we say about

---

[1] For example, "the princes power," "his friends advice," would beget an ambiguity as to number, which the apostrophe would at once dispel; since its position before, or after the final *s* at once indicates whether the singular or plural number be intended.

[2] The following is what Mr. Thomas Tyrwhitt says on the use of the apostrophal genitive in some words:—

"As to the present method of expressing the genitive cases of nouns ending in *s*, by adding another *s*, with a mark of syncope, as Peneus's, Theseus's, Venus's, &c. It seems absurd, whether the addition be intended to be pronounced, or not. In the first case, the *e* should not be cut out; in the second, the *s* is quite superfluous.   But the absurdity of this practice is most striking, when the genitives of *monosyllable* nouns are thus written: an ox's horns; an ass's ears; a fish's tail; St. James's Park; notwithstanding that the *e*, which is thus directed to be cut out, is constantly and necessarily to be pronounced, as if the several words were written at length: oxes, asses, fishes, Jameses."

This is quite true; but Mr. Tyrwhitt escapes the question of ambiguity by the preposition of the singular article, or by the nature of his examples otherwise.   Let us reject the indefinite article (in this case definite as to the number of the substantive) and take, either no article, or the article *the:* we shall then see, that an ambiguity arises both to the eye and the ear.   "The asses ears," may mean the ears of one ass, or more. "The fishes (for *fishes* is as correctly the plural of fish as *dishes* of dish) scales," the scales of one fish, or of more.   In these, and similar instances, the utility of the apostrophe is apparent; though, at the same time, I should think it doubtful whether this was the true motive of its introduction into our language.

English Grammar. Let us not be told what is right and wrong in speaking and writing by dogmatic pedagogues, who, having lived only in their own days, have no conscience of better, and would fain have us believe, that usage imparts to their doctrines the sanctity of truth. To usage, indeed, we must and do conform, for it has become our inexorable fate; but let us not take usage for our standard in the investigation of essential truth, nor suffer necessity to assume the garb of reason. Rather like the captain, whose vessel having slipped her cable is now borne by the force of the current he scarce knows whither, let us candidly acknowledge our unfortunate position, but still do our best to keep our craft together, and repair, so far as possible, in the calm the damage it sustained in the storm.

OBSERVATIONS ON THE GENEVAN VERSION IN POINT OF TRANSLATION.

I believe, though I am not quite certain, that I promised my reader some remarks on the comparative merits of the Genevan and our own Version in point of translation. I could well wish to have avoided this invidious task altogether; and that for several reasons. I am not afraid, indeed, that our own Version might suffer from the comparison on the whole; but I think, that anything which tends unnecessarily, or unprofitably, to throw the slighest discredit upon it, and so undermine the reverence and authority it has so justly earned, is a thing of itself to be specially avoided. It would be a mere idle conceit on our part to attempt to add to, or detract from, the reputation our present Version enjoys, either in point of translation, or composition; for the subject is one now beyond the reach of individual criticism. But, in addition to all this, my reader must long ago have detected the real object I have had in view in perusing my old Bible; he must have seen, that it has been rather to draw out a comparison between the English in that day and our own, than between the relative merits of two Bible translations; and that consequently I should be likely to pay but small attention to passages which presented nothing akin to the object of my search.

From the brief and disconnected nature of the extracts I have made from the Genevan Version, it would be too great an assumption to suppose, that any very clear conception of its general character could have been gained. Yet I think the reader cannot fail to have been struck with a clumsiness of style, and a want of finish, from which our Version is nearly, if not quite, free. Nor should this surprise us, when we take into consideration the hurried manner in which the Genevan Version was executed, and the difficulties which attended that execution; that it was the work of a very few men, and they intent rather on supplying spiritual food to the half-famished legions, who had just broken from their necks the slavish yoke of Rome, and were now crying out for the bread of Life, than to produce a translation whose literary merits might stamp it a master-piece of the English language. This being the case, we can be neither surprised nor disappointed, that its style of composition is less elaborate and polished, than that of our own. But leaving this conclusion, which after all is one of trivial importance to us, to be supported by the extracts already given, we turn to consider another point, in which it seems to us the Genevan Version contrasts favourably with our own. It is in point of translation. The passages I intend to bring forward in support of my position, though few, are still, I think, sufficient to support it. I would have them regarded, not so much for their intrinsic importance above others which might be adduced in support of the same argument, as for their generic character, and as typical of that spirit which actuated the labours of the translators.

In the gospel of St. Mark, ch. ix. 47., I find a rendering which seems far less likely to create misunderstanding, I do not say in the minds of educated people, but of the mass of readers generally, than the rendering of the same passage in our own Version. It runs thus:—

"And if thine eie *cause thee to offend*, plucke it out: it is better for thee to goe into the kingdome of God with one eie, than hauing two eies to be cast into hell fire."

No misconception could possibly arise here: while the passage as it reads in our Version "if thine eye offend thee" only yields its true meaning by a wordy explanation, that *to offend* means, *to cause thee to offend.* Some of my readers are doubtless aware, that the word in the original, rendered by "offend," signifies to place a stumbling block in the way, and so to occasion a fall.[1] Now, whatever may have been the acquired meaning of the verb, To offend, when our translators used it, (and from that which it bore in the earlier quotation above, it seems fair to infer, that its meaning did not differ much from the present one) it is at least certain, I think, that neither its classical meaning, nor that of our own day, justifies the use to which it is put in our own Version.

The following instance is one of a similar nature to the last, and seems to me strongly indicative of the different characters of the two translations. I place them in juxta position, that the reader may himself strike the comparison.[2]

Present Rendering.

" Take therefore no thought for the morrow : for the morrow shall take thought for the things of itself. Sufficient unto the day is the evil thereof."—*Matt.* VI. 34.

Genevan Rendering.

" Care not then for the morow for the morow shall care for it felfe : the day hath enough with his owne griefe."—*Ibid.*

---

[1] Σκανδαλίζω, from σκάνδαλον, *a stumbling block,* or *cause of offence,* from σκάζω, *To limp.* Is it possible, that the translators attempted to transfer, for the first time, the rich meaning of the Greek word, to another, which, neither as a Latin word (offendo), nor an English one *To offend,* could legitimately receive it? If so, the attempt was a failure, or at least has become one.

[2] *Orig.* Μὴ οὖν μεριμνήσητε εἰς τὴν αὔριον· ἡ γὰρ αὔριον μεριμνήσει τὰ ἑαυτῆς. ἀρκετὸν τῇ ἡμέρᾳ ἡ κακία αὐτῆς. The reader must judge for himself whether the dative, τῇ ἡμέρᾳ, which has no reference to future time whatever, is appropriately rendered in English by "*unto* the day," which seems naturally to refer the mind to the morrow, τὴν αὔριον, the last mentioned.

I ask first, are the impressions, which these renderings make on the mind, identical? If they are, I have done. If not, let us consider them further.

The whole question turns on the meaning, which is conveyed in our Version by the words "sufficient *unto* the day." Unto what day? the present, or some future day,—or the morrow in short? And to our mind, both the context, and the wording "unto the day," unmistakably suggest some future day. So that the meaning of the whole passage would seem to be as follows: "that provision against a future day of trial is of itself an evil, and, therefore, to be avoided, as constituting an additional trial to the trials of the morrow." Such seems the impression which our rendering leaves on the mind. We have been told, often enough, that the injunction "take no *thought* for the morrow," implies no *anxious thought.* Yet surely, if provision against the trials of the morrow be in itself an evil, it were well to take no thought whatever, but absolutely to leave the morrow to take thought for the things of itself.[1] Happily, the words of the original demand no such construction as this. It is the present day which we are commanded not to burden with the cares of the future.

I would not assert that the passage, as it stands in our own Version, is absolutely incapable of the construction, which it bears in the Original and the Genevan Versions; still less would I say, that our own rendering is not supported by the Original. On the contrary, it would be difficult to imagine a much *closer* imitation of the passage, as it stands in the Greek, than the words, "sufficient unto the day is the evil thereof" afford. So literal, indeed, is the translation, that though written in English characters and

---

[1] The word in the Greek, μεριμνάω, which is rendered in our version by "To take thought," would perhaps, be better expressed by the verb, *To distract;* "do not distract yourselves about the morrow." "Curæ," it has been well said, "animum divorse trahunt," "cares *distract* the mind," and the same feeling, or sentiment is bound up in the composition of the verb μεριμνάω, or rather, perhaps, the noun substantive μερίμνα, which is derived from the verb μείρω, *To divide.* Hence, by etymology, μερίμνα is that, which like anxious care *distracts* the mind.

words, it continues in construction and idiom as much Greek as ever. And the result, as might have been anticipated, has been to introduce into the English an ambiguity, against which the more grammatical, and delicately organized structure of the Greek was alone a sufficient safeguard. The transference of idiom, or a due allowance for the different idiomatic usages of languages, as much requires attention, on the part of translators, as the grammar of the languages itself.

Let us look briefly into the context of the passage, and endeavour to learn what was the lesson our Saviour was endeavouring to inculcate. It is clear, he wished to show his disciples the folly of giving way to anxious thought about the future. "Which of you by taking care," he had said only a short time before, "is able to adde one cubite unto his stature? And why care ye for raiment? Learne how the lilies of the field doe growe: they are not wearied neither spin." And then he adds, "But seeke yee first the kingdome of God and his righteousnesse, and all these (minor) things shall be ministered unto you." In conclusion, he warns them against that anxiety about the future which is the offspring of distrust in their heavenly Father, and tells them, they will find each day bring with it its own load of cares and sorrows, which they must not seek to augment by adding to them the imaginary evils of the future. Such seems the obvious meaning to be gathered from the Genevan rendering; a rendering, which it seems to us is more accordant with the original and the context, than our own; while, at the same time, it makes a more powerful appeal to the feelings and experience of our every day life.[1]

In the following passage, though not in itself of much importance, the balance again seems to favour the freer Genevan translation :—

"Yee have heard of the patience of Job, and have knowen *what end the Lord made."—James* v. 11.

[1] It also brings out the meaning of the injunction, "take no thought," in a very clear and forcible manner.

K

My reader will recollect, that our version reads "the end of the Lord," instead of "what end the Lord made."[1] I think there can be no doubt which of these two readings is the better. Indeed, "the end of the Lord," is not English, and, like another instance we have noticed, requires to be paraphrased before it becomes intelligible.

The passage, Matth. xxiii. 24, which in our version is incorrectly rendered "which strain *at* a gnat and swallow a camel," but more correctly in the Genevan version, by the words, "which straine *out* a gnat, and swallow a camel,"[2] has no direct bearing on my argument. But the examples I have quoted, though they are few in number, are I think, sufficient to justify our arriving at one great and important conclusion, with respect to the different spirits which animated the translators of the Genevan and our own version; namely, that the translators of the former used greater license, and followed the original with less of verbatim accuracy, than those of the latter; that the effect of this has been to render the former more perspicuous, generally speaking, to the mass of readers, and freer from obscurity, than our own rendering, where, by a perhaps too close and timid copying of the original, the translators have not at all times succeeded in emancipating their translation from that ambiguity which Greek idiom will sometimes introduce in English.

It is easy to see, that much might be said on either side of this argument.

What the Genevan translators gained by the transparency, if I may use such a word to express my meaning, of their translation, it is possible they might lose in accuracy: and, on the other hand, what little our own version loses by its occasional obscurity, may be amply

---

[1] *Orig.* τὸ τέλος κυρίου: literally, "the end of the Lord." But, to suppose this a translation, is to suppose the English genitive case as wide in its signification as the Greek.

[2] See this passage discussed in Dean Trench's "English, Past and Present." Note to p. 245.

compensated by its close and truthful resemblance to the original. We shall do well to recollect, too, the different circumstances under which each translation was made. While the Genevan version was the work of but two, or three, men, whose views on religion and theology coincided; our own, on the contrary, engaged the labour of a very much larger body of men, amongst whom, it is absurd to suppose, no diversity of opinion to have existed.[1] And, in cases where this diversity of opinion manifested itself, it is clear, that the readiest way of over-ruling it would be by rigidly adhering to the original. Nor does it appear there was much to be regretted in this method of settling differences; for the error, if any resulted, was in the right direction. No party could feel its own particular views impunged, nor, what was of far greater importance, succeed in wresting any passage in favour of them; while the rendering adopted was throughout so close as almost to constitute it in English a fac-simile of the original Greek. And while we are proud, and justly so, of this spirit of integrity, which characterizes our version, the regret may not be unpardonable, that, owing to it, some few obscure constructions have crept in to puzzle the simple reader.

[1] The number of men engaged in the task was forty-seven. They were divided into six companies; two of which sat at Westminister, two at Cambridge, and two at Oxford. According to rule (9) of the code which regulated their labours, as soon as one company had dispatched a book, they were to "send it to the rest, to be considered of seriously and judiciously."

CHAPTER VIII.

ON THE MEANING AND CONSTRUCTION OF *THAN*.

I am not aware, that any attempt has hitherto been made to explain the meaning and construction of the word THAN. I, therefore, feel somewhat diffident in offering, for the first time, such an explanation to the public. For I am assured, that, if there yet remains amongst us any regard for the accurate determination of the principles of our Language,—any censorship over its integrity,—my observations and arguments will have to pass through the ordeal of rigorous criticism.

But the man whose intentions are honest, and whose motives are sincere, has, after all, but little cause to dread the scrutiny of the critic : for, if his strictures are just and true, they will carry conviction, first to the mind of him whose work is being tested; and if they are false, they lose their sting, and call rather for pity or contempt, than anger or concern. As I am conscious of no personal motive, I may the less anxiously await the trial,—the more contentedly abide the result.

The abstract nature of this enquiry will, I fear, tend to rob it of some of the interest, which it might otherwise possess, and which I feel it deserves. Yet, this objection is one which lies with almost equal weight against all questions relating to the economy of words ; and on this account alone to refuse such questions our attention would argue an indifference to the forms of correct speech, and the rules of true construction, which I should be loath to assume.

There is, perhaps, no word in our daily vocabulary, so frequently used, so little understood, as the word THAN; no word whose original signification has been so entirely obscured by the encrustation of time, and so entirely neglected by the excavators of the English language.

For a length of time before the present solution occurred to me, I felt, that the unsatisfactory state of our knowledge of this word was not only a thing to be deplored, but one, also, which demanded our careful attention. I viewed it in the light of a disgrace, to be constantly using a word most useful, indeed,—nay, indispensable in our daily intercourse,—but which, beyond this, seemed shrouded in inscrutable mystery. The word had become a mere sound significant, whose office was definite, and its effect uniform, producing a fixed idea, (if I may use the word in this sense; perhaps better, operating consistently), in the mind, yet revealing nothing of the mechanism whereby the effect was produced, the impression formed.

Whether, or not, the explanation, I shall presently offer, be sufficient to remove this objection, I must leave to my reader himself to determine. By way of caution, lest he should form too great expectations, I would have him remember the very early period to which it is necessary to revert, for the supply of our materials; a period, since which, it would be strange indeed, judging from the analogy of language in other respects, if no modifications in usage, and construction had taken place.

The following is what Dr. Johnson says respecting the word :—

"THAN. adv. [ðanne, Sax.] a particle placed in comparison after the comparative adjective, or adverb, noting a less degree of the quality compared in the word that follows than."[1]

---

[1] Even this is only conditionally true, as may readily be seen by taking one or two examples, and applying the above test.

Ex. "Wisdom is more precious than rubies."

The quality compared in this example is clearly (pretium) price; and

To inform us that *than* is a particle placed in comparison after the comparative degree of the adjective, or adverb, I suppose amounts to much the same as telling us what we all knew before. A particle, too, is a term more convenient, than explicit; inasmuch as it is useful in the arts and sciences, as well as in supplying a name to some part of speech, in more languages than one, of which nothing is known, and so at the same time affording a fitting pretext to hide our ignorance.

Richardson was not less lucid than Johnson; but he had this advantage, that he expanded his remarks into two or three times the bulk, which had sufficed for his predecessor.

That Mr. Horne Tooke has offered us no remarks on the word, is surprising. It could scarcely have escaped his attention; more especially as he approached very near the heart of the difficulty, when he attempted to explain the origin and meaning of the definite article THE, and the demonstrative pronoun THAT.

And now, since it seems we shall meet with but small help in our difficulty at the hands of those, from whom we have been accustomed to expect it, let us fling aside these artificial supports, and strike out boldly for the shore.

Psalm xix. 9, 10.
"The fear of the Lord is cleane and endureth for ever: the judgments of the Lord are trueth: they are righteous altogether.

"And more to be desired *then* golde, yea, *then* much fine golde: sweeter also *then* hony and the hony combe."

Psalm cxix. 98, 103.
"By thy commãdements thou hast made me wiser thẽ[1] mine enemies: for they are ever with me.

---

it is as clear, that this quality is less in the word *rubies*, which follows *than*, than in the word *wisdom*, which precedes it. But take another example :—

"Solitude is less irksome, than the company of a braggart."

In this case irksomeness is the quality compared: but, instead of being less in the word which follows *than*, it is, on the contrary, greater.

[1] Contraction for *then*.

"How sweete are thy promises unto my mouth! yea, more *then* hony unto my mouth."

It would be easy to multiply quotations, but these will suffice to shew, that, at the time we are now considering, *then* was commonly written where now. we should write *than*. With us *then* and *than* are words of widely different signification: so different, indeed, that we are apt to overlook the fact, that in reality they are the same word, differing only in acquired signification and spelling. In the early days of English literature *thanne*, or *than*, was commonly used for *then*.

> "*Thanne* drough I me among drapiers,
> My *donet*[1] to lerne,
> To draw the liser[2] along,
> The lenger it seemed."
>
> *Vision of Pierce Ploughman, line* 2989.

> "*Thanne* loked up a lunatik
> A leene thyng with-alle,
> And kneeling to the king,
> Clergially[3] he seide,
> ' Crist kepe thee, sire kyng,
> And the kyng-ryche[4]
> And lene[5] thee lede thy lond,
> So leauté thee lovye,
> And for thi rightful rulyng
> Be rewarded in hevene.' "
>
> *Ibid, line* 245.

So also in Chaucer, *than* and *thanne* are used, as we should say, adverbially for *then*.

> "Now was there *than* a justice in that toun,
> That governor was of that regioun."
>
> *Doctoures Tale.*

---

[1] Grammar, or first principles; from Ælius Donatus, a Roman Grammarian, whose elementary work on the Latin language was commonly read in Schools.

[2] Probably the *list*.

[3] Learnedly.

[4] Kingdom. The Saxon word *rice*, signifying *dominion*, still survives in the word *bishopric*.

[5] Literally, "lend thee," *i. e.* "grant thee to lede the lond." *Lene* for *lend*, is still common.

"A lecherous thing is wine, and dronkenesse
Is full of striving and of wretchednesse,
O dronken man, disfigured is thy face,
Sour is thy breth, foul art thou to embrace;
And thurgh thy dronken nose semeth the soun,[1]
As though thou saidest ay, Sampsoun, Sampsoun;
And yet, God wot, Sampsoun drank never no wine,
Thou fallest, as it were a stiked swine:
Thy tonge is lost, and all thine honest cure,
For dronkenesse is veray sepulture
Of mannes wit, and his discretion.
In whom that drink hath domination,
He can no conseil kepe, it is no drede.[2]
Now kepe you fro the white and fro the rede,
And namely fro the white wine of Lepe,
That is to sell in Fish strete, and in Chepe.
This wine of Spaigne crepeth subtilly
In other wines growing fast by.
Of which there riseth swiche fumositee,
That *whan* a man hath dronken draughtes three,
And weneth that he be at home in Chepe,
He is in Spaigne, right at the town of Lepe,
Not at the Rochell, ne at Bardeux town;
And *thanne* wol he say Sampsoun, Sampsoun."

The Pardoneres Tale.

Than was also used in the sense it now has, for the purpose of comparison :—

"For though a widewe hadde but a shoo,
(So pleasant was his In principio)
Yet wold he have a ferthing or he went,
His purchas was wel better *than* his rent.
Somewhat he lisped for his wantonnesse,
To make his English swete upon his tonge;[3]
And in his harping *whan* that he had songe,
His eyen twinkeled in his hed aright,
As don the sterres in a frosty night."

Prologue to Cant. Tales.

[1] "Appeareth the sound."

[2] *Drede* signifies *fear, doubt.* "It is no *drede*," I suppose, means "there is no doubt."

[3] I take this for an undesigned coincidence, to show that, even so late as the 14th century, it was the custom to fill the vacancies, which occurred in the Religious Orders, by Priests invited from Normandy.

The inference to be drawn from these examples is simple, and clear enough. It appears from them, that *than* and *then* have, at different times, borne precisely the same meaning; namely, those which we now attribute to the adverb of time *then*, and to the word *than*, be it what it may. In the time of Chaucer, *than* was used indiscriminately both for *than* and *then*,[1] while, by the middle of the 16th century, *then* had come to be used for the same purposes.

What, then, it becomes our duty to ask, is the origin, or origins, of these words, which seem alternately to have mounted guard for each other? There is but one source to which we can look for any information on this point, and that source, I need not say, is the Anglo Saxon. To the Anglo Saxon, then, we must turn, and I trust the necessity will be a sufficient excuse in the eyes of my reader, for bringing before him one, or two passages in Anglo Saxon, which he may not be able to understand, but which I will do my best to make intelligible to him. For convenience, I have selected the passages from Mr. Barnes's "Anglo Saxon Delectus," with one exception, which, if I mistake not, is to be found in Mr. Thorpe's "Analecta Anglo Saxonica."

"Sume tunglu habbað scyrtran hwyrft þonne sume habbon."

Translation:

Some stars have a shorter revolution *than* others.

"Gebeorhlicre ys me faran to ea mid scype mynum þænne faran mid manegum scypum on huntinge hranas.

"For hwi swa?

"Forþam leofre ys me gefon fisc þæne ic mæg ofslean, &c."

Translation:

It is safer for me to go on the river with my ship, *than* (þænne) to go with many ships hunting whales.

For why so?

Because I would rather take a fish *which* (þæne) I am able to kill, &c.

---

[1] It is worthy of remark, that the *form* "then" is rarely met with, (I dare not say never) either in the "Vision and Creed of Pierce Ploughman," or in Chaucer. Its place is supplied at one time by *than*, at another by *tho*.

There are other uses to which þœnne, or þonne, our English *than,* was put in the Anglo Saxon, but I wish to avoid confusion, and therefore decline to notice them in the text at present.[1]

But now comes the question, what is the Saxon word þœnne, or þonne? for of course no one in his senses will for a moment question, that here we have the etymology of the word THAN.

The Anglo Saxon article is thus declined :—

	Mas.	*Fem.*	*Neut.*
Nominative...	Se	Seo'	þœt.
Genitive	þœs	þœre	þœs.
Dative	þa'm	þœre	þa'm.
Accusative ...	þone or þœne	þa'	þœt.

But the Article se, seo', þœt, was used, not only as we now use the definite article *the,* but also *relatively,* where we should now use the pronouns *who, which,* or *what.*[2] Indeed, the second of the above extracts affords an instance of this relative use of the article.

This is the inflexion usually followed.[3]

Now, referring to the masculine accusative, we find þone, or þœne, which the Saxons slightly altered for the purpose of distinction, by doubling the *n,* and then used in exactly the same manner as we now use *then* and *than.*

---

[1] See Appendix to this page.

[2] "The article or definitive Se, Seo', þœt, are generally used for the relative *who, which.*"—*Dr. Bosworth's Anglo Saxon Grammar,* §. 33.

[3] Professor Rask also gives, what he considers a separate ablative case, "þy seems justly to be received as a proper *ablativus instrumenti,* as it occurs so often in this character, even in the Masculine gender, as mid þy, aþe, with that oath L. In. 53; and in the same place, in the dative, on þœm, aþe in that oath."

	Mas.	*Fem.*	*Neut.*
Ablative....	þy	þœre	þy.

Mr. Thorpe's Translation, §. 147.

It is very clear, therefore, that we must not seek any explanation of the grammatical structure of *than* on English ground solely. The question is now become one of abstract grammatical structure. We have shown, I think, that the word *than* is the same word, used in the same manner, as the Anglo Saxon þœnne, which is the accusative of the relative pronoun se, seo', þœt, answering to our *who* or *which*. We have now to investigate the construction of this *Relative Pronoun*,—the reason why it ever came to be used for the purpose of comparison. It will be observed, that we are not now pursuing an etymological enquiry as to the origin and meaning of þœt, or þœnne, this Mr. Tooke has already attempted, with what success my reader shall presently judge for himself. It is our present object to discover what operation of the human mind it was,—what method of reasoning,—which led to the Relative Pronoun þœnne, and, consequently, our English *than*, being put to the use we find them. And this object, I apprehend, will be best attained by taking some example and operating upon it, in such a manner as the above considerations suggest. I will take the simplest instance I can find to begin with.

Example 1.

Where the relative THAN relates to a substantive :

" *Virtue confers more happiness* THAN *riches.*"

Now let us substitute for *than* (or þœnne as it would have been written in Anglo Saxon) its meaning as a Relative Pronoun. The sentence becomes, if we transpose the clauses,

"Than (*i. e.* which happiness *understood*) riches (confers *understood*) virtue confers more happiness."[1]

Here it will be seen, that the Relative Pronoun *than* agrees with the noun Substantive *happiness,* that being the quality compared, and that both are in the Accusative or Objective case, governed, as it might seem, by the verb

---

[1] In this and the following examples, it will be found, that, on leaving out the words between the brackets, the sentence remains exactly as before, except for the transposition.

confers, which is understood from the other clause. But the example I have taken is one of the simplest, and easiest kind, and it will, perhaps, be objected, that this process of manipulation could not be applied in every case. Before entering on the consideration of other examples, where certainly the construction is less easy, and the applied reasoning less perspicuous, I would say, once for all, that I do not think there is any obligation to account for all those usages, which, like an after or second growth, have sprung up in the course of time from the original stock. We know how arbitrary custom occasionally is; and it ought not to surprise us, that we do not always find in this second offspring the same individuality of character, the precise lineaments, which marked the parent. We know this is the case in the natural world, why should it not be the same in the metaphysical. But we do not say this by way of deprecation; nor do we intend to shirk the question, because it is, in some of its aspects, rather a difficult one. It shall, so far as lies in our power, be faithfully put : the reader himself must use his discretion, and honestly test the weight of our arguments. I do not say, that in every usage of the word *than* the above reasoning is equally applicable, for there are some, where the usage is, we think, incorrect. Such are those where *than* is written for *except,* or *but* (both verbs), for example :—

"Of all his friends he chose none other *than* the man whose friendship had been tested by adversity."

Here *than,* it should seem, is incorrectly[1] written for *but, except,* or *besides.* Yet, generally speaking, I think the same train of reasoning, more or less perfectly conceived, will be found to lie at the bottom of all constructions in which *than* has rightly a place. Of course, it is of essential

[1] By *incorrectly,* I only mean, that in such case the construction does not seem favourable to the use of *than.* In other words, it would be better if *than* were replaced by *except,* or *but;* for then the construction would be perfectly simple. Thus: "Except (*i. e. take out*) the man whose friendship had been tested by adversity, he chose none other of all his friends."

importance, that the objects, or qualities, of comparison be kept clearly in view: otherwise, we shall lose sight of that to which the relative, *than*, has reference; and, if this be the case, the point of the construction is lost. It would, perhaps, be tedious to endeavour to obtain types of all the different forms of speech, in which *than* is found. The examples, I have given below, have been taken at random, from amongst many others, to all of which I found the reasoning no less applicable.

Example 2.

Where the relative THAN, relates to an adjective:

" *The pomp of death is more terrible* THAN *death itself.*"

Bacon's Essays. Of Death.

Here the quality compared, or presented for comparison in the antitheses, "the pomp of death," and "death itself," is, to use a barbarism, *terribleness.* To this quality, then, the relative *than*, relates. We may see this more clearly, if we put it thus:—

Than (*i. e.* how terrible sover, or to *what* þœnne degree terrible is) death itself, the pomp of death is more terrible.

In the following example, the comparison is what might, perhaps, not inaptly, be called a comparison of impersonals.

Example 3.

Where the relative of THAN, relates to an adverb:

" *It were better to have no opinion of God at all,* THAN *such an opinion as is unworthy of Him.*"

Bacon's Essays. Of Superstition.

Here the advantages, or disadvantages, of entertaining certain opinions respecting the Deity are contrasted, and, at the same time, an *assertion* is made with regard to them. Bearing this in mind, and making the requisite subaudition to which THAN (þœnne, þœne, *which,* or *what*) relates, namely advantage, or position, the sentence becomes,

" *Than* (*i. e.* what advantage it would be to have) such an opinion (of God) as is unworthy of Him, it were better to have no opinion of God."

It were easy to multiply examples, but these, I think, are sufficient to serve the purpose of illustration. I leave my reader to amuse himself by applying the same method in other cases, which may occur to him; that so he may test the truth of a theory, which in its application to the more simple constructions of THAN, (such as that afforded in Example 1), cannot admit of doubt; nor, indeed, in others more complicated, if we allow those considerations their due weight, which are concomitants of both the early growth, and more mature developement of language.

But let us turn for a moment to analyse the construction we have attributed to *than* in the preceding examples. Of what does it consist? We shall find, that it divides itself into two separate clauses.

1st. The Absolute Clause.

2nd. The Assertive Clause.

The *Absolute Clause* serves to introduce a certain condition, or position.

The *Assertive Clause*, referring to the *Absolute Clause*, makes an assertion with respect to it.

But this will appear clearer by experimenting on some example. Take the following :—

"The ditties of the ancient poets, had no greater disproportion with their subject, than our songs of famous victories have with theirs; or other passionate ditties, with their composer's affections; albeit, he that hath experience of love, or abundant grief, or joy, will speak in another dialect *than* ordinarily he useth, without any touch of affectation."

Dr. Jackson on " The Sacred Origin and Right Use of Poetry, with the Manner of its Corruption by the later Poets."

Transposing, and substituting as before, the passage becomes,

Than (*i. e.* þœnne, þœne, which or what disproportion, *understood*) our songs of famous victories have with theirs, —ABSOLUTE CLAUSE.

The ditties of the ancient poets had no greater disproportion with their subject.—ASSERTIVE CLAUSE.

And so in other examples, where the relative THAN refers, not to a Substantive, as in this case to disproportion understood from the second clause, but to a noun, Adjective, or Adverb, so introducing a condition of quality or advantage.

It does not affect the above reasoning whether, or not, we accept Mr. Tooke's theory respecting the demonstrative pronoun, and conjunction THAT. As we have before referred to it, our reader may feel some curiosity to know more respecting it. I shall give Mr. Tooke the opportunity of speaking for himself. These are his words:—

"THAT (in the Anglo Saxon, Þœt, *i. e.* Đead, Đeat) means *taken, assumed;* being merely the past participles of the Anglo Saxon verb Đean, Đegan, Đion, Đicgan, Đigian.[1] *To* THE, *To get, To take, To assume."*

> " I'll mote he THE
> That caused me
> To make myself a frere."
> *Sir Thos. More's Workes,* p. 4.

I have no desire to enter on a discussion with Mr. Tooke on a point so abstruse as the derivation of the Saxon þœt, and the English THAT. He may, or may not, be right; though at the same time, I do not see that he shows the slightest grounds on which to support this fiction of his imagination. Nor would I be inclined to deny, that the verbs Đion, and Đicgan, may not originally have sprung from the same root; yet this at least is certain, that they soon acquired in the Anglo Saxon very different meanings; Đion, or Đeón, signifying *To flourish, To thrive;* whence comes the verb *To* THE; and Đicgan, *To take, To receive, To eat,* whence comes our word *Thane,* a nobleman.

But if indeed THAT really mean *taken,* or *assumed,* then THAN must mean the same, and we may, if it be thought worth while, substitute this signification in the above examples or any others.

---

[1] I do not know, that the form Đigian has any existence, and the past participle of the other forms would, since they are verbs of strong formation, end in *en,* and not *ed,* or *od.*

I chanced to enter the cottage of a peasant's wife the other day. A respectable woman she was, and kept a cow. As may readily be imagined of a good housewife, it was not long before she got talking to me about her dairy, and in the course of her conversation she made a remark which struck me, not indeed for its shrewdness, but for the way in which it was worded. "Some kye," said she, "will give as much more butter than other some." Why, thought I, the woman talks Saxon. I turned on my heel, thanked her for her useful information, and jotted down her little speech in my note book, lest I should forget it. Let us operate on this almost Anglo Saxon sentence.[1]

"Than (*i. e.* according to Mr. Tooke, taken or assumed, the butter *understood*) other some (kye will give *understood*) —ABSOLUTE CLAUSE.—Some kye will give as much more.— ASSERTIVE CLAUSE."

It will thus be seen, that whatever credence we may be inclined to give to Mr. Tooke's theory, respecting the meaning and origin of *that*, and consequently of *than*, can in no way invalidate, while it may confirm, the truth of the above conclusions respecting the construction of THAN.

One more example and we have done :—

"Quarrels and divisions about religion were evils unknown to the heathen. The reason was because the religion of the heathen consisted rather (*i. e.* sooner or more) in rites and ceremonies, *than* in any constant belief; for you may imagine what kind of faith theirs was, when the chief doctors and fathers of their church were the poets."—*Bacon's Essays. Of Unity in Religion.*

Transposing and substituting as before :—

Than (*i. e.* taken or assumed, the degree to which the religion of the heathen consisted) in any constant belief,— ABSOLUTE CLAUSE—the religion of the heathen consisted rather (*i. e.* to a greater degree) in rites and ceremonies.— ASSERTIVE CLAUSE.

---

[1] This woman, though she had certainly no English School Mistress to thank for it, spoke a dialect more nearly approaching Anglo Saxon than any thing we ever recollect hearing. So true is it that the real remnants of our Language are to be sought and found amongst our rustic population.

Such, then, is the method whereby we would seek to explain the meaning, and construction of THAN. We are aware, that it is not entirely beyond the reach of cavil; that, specially against the latter examples, it may be urged we introduce THAN in the Accusative, or Objective case, without any verb, or word to govern it in that case, since only in examples of the first class was there anything to account for such an usage. Is, then, this objection one of vital consequence, and, therefore, fatal to the theory we have imperfectly sketched out? To us it would seem not. And, however repugnant our Reader may at first be to admit such irregular constructions, in proof of any theory whatsoever, we think, that a more mature consideration of the whole subject will not fail to remove his objections, and cause him to see in such examples, and apparently irregular constructions as the latter, merely the extension of an idiomatic usage.

He will remember, that there are instances, like Example I, where the position and government of THAN in the objective case, seem sufficiently well accounted for. When, further, he considers, that such examples are of the simplest kind; those which were most likely to have occurred in the early intercourse of man with man, and so, in all probability, to have originated this method of comparing one thing with another; it will not strike him as in any way singular, that a common colloquial expression, though somewhat confined in its application, at first, should hereafter have had its bounds increased, albeit with some loss of its original grammatical accuracy.

We are conscious, that a question, relating, not so much to any particular language, as to an operation of the mind, which must reproduce itself in language generally, ought scarcely to be discussed on grounds so narrow as those on which we have ventured to discuss it.

We know, that by so doing, we lose sight of the arguments from analogy, which are frequently of much importance; but we could not transfer our reasoning to a stage beyond the reach of the general reader without in a measure violating the tacit engagement we had entered upon. In the appendix, however, to this page, we felt ourselves less constrained, and there the reader will find, if he care to consult them, some of the arguments drawn from analogy, as well as a more general view of the entire subject.

CHAPTER IX.

OBSERVATIONS ON THE SPELLING IN THE BREECHES BIBLE:— TENDENCY OF ENGLISH AS ILLUSTRATED THEREBY.

WE have now detailed all those characteristics in the English of the 16th century, as chronicled in the Breeches Bible, which, either on account of the contrast they present to the usages of our own day, or for other reasons, seemed deserving of our attention. The materials now in our possession, for striking a comparison between the English of that and the present day, and for estimating the nature of those changes which have taken place during the intervening period, are, we must admit, of a less general character, than could have been desired. But it was easy to see from the beginning, that this must have been the case, where it was sought from one book alone, albeit the fittest and most comprehensive for the purpose, to obtain general views, and deduce general conclusions as to the nature of the English Language at that time.

Thus much, however, must be allowed, that the comparison, however it may be deficient as to detail, or generality, will be one based, so far as it goes, essentially on facts, and the rigid teaching of past experience. We have purposely abstained, hitherto, from commenting, or attempting to theorize, on the facts which from time to time have been presented to us. We have preferred to let those facts speak for themselves, though, now that we have heard their evidence, it cannot be thought premature to seek out the conclusions to which they point, and the lessons they would teach us. To some extent this has, perhaps, already been done by the reader himself, nor do we at all wish to question his ability to do so as well as ourselves. Yet, there are some conclusions, which, we apprehend, it would be almost presumptuous to suppose he could have arrived at from the mere perusal of the brief and disconnected extracts, such as have alone been submitted to him. And particularly does this remark apply to the spelling—for I will not call it Orthography—of the period we are considering; so far, that is, as we may be guided thereto by the character of the spelling found in our Text Book.

There may be, and have been periods in a nation's history when, from anomalous causes, it becomes necessary to look with distrust, or at least excessive caution, on the form its written language assumes.

At such a time, spelling may, or may not, be a safe guide in investigating the Etymology, and meaning of words. And this evil is still further aggravated when, as was the case with our own, the language has been subjected to foreign influence and modification. Such, to a great extent, seems to have been the period we are considering, and, to a still greater, the century immediately preceding it. Let us explain our meaning more fully.

It is well known, that during the middle ages, both in England and on the Continent, literature, learning, and science found but a poor asylum in the ancient monasteries, and religious houses. Had it not been for the Church, in those dark ages of ignorance, and superstition, answerable though, no doubt, she was to a great extent, for bringing about those very evils which she prevented from lapsing into extremity, it is fearful to think what might even now have been the condition of England.

The only records which have been handed down to us of these ages, seem to have been those which alone were kept; namely, the meagre monastic chronicles, and these written more frequently in Latin than in the mother tongue. Several causes contributed to this dearth of literary productions, amongst which must be specially mentioned the extreme scarcity of writing materials. Parchment was enormously dear, the Egyptian papyrus had ceased to be imported into Europe after the victories of the Arabians, and paper was not yet invented, or had not yet been introduced by commerce into the West.[1] Some idea may be formed of this extreme scarcity from the fact, that in the archives of the Tower of London, in " the Rolls of fines," each contract for sale of lands never occupied more than a single line. But, though the scarcity of writing materials is sufficient to account in a great measure for the low state of literature, and the small progress in civilization which was made during the middle ages, we must carefully bear in mind, what we have already hinted at, that the land was wrapt in ignorance, and its people enslaved by the most degrading superstition ; that priestly intolerance had reduced them to the deepest moral and intellectual degradation, and that very Institution, which, to serve its own purpose, just kept alive the few dying embers, the memorial of past rather than the proof of present learning, was also, in the main, the cause which compelled literature to seek so mean a refuge. It can excite but little surprise, then, that, while such was the condition of the people even up to the time of the Reformation, the art of writing, and, as a natural consequence, that of spelling, suffered severely from neglect. Since the time of the Norman Conquest no opportunity had been afforded Englishmen to remodel their language, and to reduce its incongruous elements to something like harmony.

---

[1] *Literature of the South of Europe : Vol.* I, *p.* 36.

" All the rude chronicles in which passing events were at distant intervals registered, were written in Latin. All contracts of marriage, or of purchase, lending, or exchange, were in the same tongue, or rather in that barbarous jargon as far removed from the written as the spoken language."
Ibid.

" From the eighth to the tenth century, all annals of the Franks, written in the convents, followed the same rule, and, whatever the number, or importance of events, the same annalist was bound not to exceed the line for each year."
Ibid, p. 37, *note.*

It was not the work of a day, nor yet of a generation, to classify all those words, which had now obtained too firm a footing in the Language to be easily displaced, and to regulate the spelling, or orthography of those words according to the rules which obtained in the particular languages whence they sprang. Still more difficult would this task be amongst a people who did not enjoy the facility of writing, and reading, and whose minds, moreover, were crushed with the fetters of Romish priestcraft. But the morning star had already risen, and soon the foul bird which for so long a time, had brooded, like a nightmare over the face of the country, shook its dank plumage, and, winging away its heavy flight before the dawn of day, was soon seen as but a speck in the far distant horizon. And, though from that day dates the birth of intellectual and religious freedom for Englishmen, the progress for some time was slow.

As, when the invalid is recovering from the delirium of a fever, his exhausted frame seems at first unable to put forth its energies, or his baffled mind to collect itself in steady thought; so the people of England, when at length it pleased God they should be recalled from that state of religious delirium into which they had fallen, felt at first incapable of exerting to the full those powers, whose very possession long tyranny had almost rendered them unconscious of. And thus it came to pass, that, when this long-neglected power of writing was restored, we have the singular anomaly presented to us of a people writing a language they but very imperfectly understood. The English Language at this time seems to have been in its embryo state. That extensive class of foreign words, introduced by the means of the Normans, yet retained their own strange accent and costume, and imparted to the language, spoken and written, a motley appearance equally removed from Saxon, and French.

The following extract from a manuscript translation of the Gospel of St. Matthew, and part of that of St. Mark, made by Sir John Cheeke about the middle of the 16th century, and now lying in the library of Corpus Christi College, Cambridge, will further illustrate the unsettled state of spelling at this period.

"When Jesus was boorn in Beethleem, a citi in King Herods dais, lo there the wisards came from the 'est parties to Jerusalem and asked whier the King of Jews was y^t was new boorn. For we saw his sterr in the 'est, and we cam to worship him. When K. Herod herd this, he was trobled, and al Jerusale's with him: and he gatherd together al ye hei priests, and scribes of ye people and asked of them wheer Christ shold be born. And thei answerd in Bethleem of Juda, for so it is written by ye prophet; and thou Bethleem of Juda, thou art no wais ye lest among the princes of Juda, for out of ye schal come a ruler y^t shall feed Isrl mi people."

In this short extract we have *whier* and *wheer, came* and *cam; y^e* for both *the* and *thee; schal* and *shal; Beethleem* and *Bethleem.*

Indeed, from the time of the invention or introduction of printing, about the middle of the 15th century, down to the close of the 16th, may be considered especially the period when the principles of Orthography first began to receive attention.

It is exactly during such transition periods as these, when the written expressions of a nation's language require to be received with caution. For, accustomed only to speak, and not to write their language, the people lose sight of the true origin and parentage of words; and, since Etymology is the only true guide to Orthography, fall into all kinds of fanciful, and phonetic methods of spelling. And thus it will not unfrequently happen, that the spelling of one age will serve but to confuse, if not actually to mislead, the enquirer of the next.

The question, then, which more immediately concerns us, is whether this uncertainty prevails in the Genevan Bible, and, if so, whether to such an extent as to render fallacious any conclusions, etymological or otherwise, which we may fancy ourselves able to draw. Our answer must be a qualified one. For, on the one hand, it is impossible to deny, that the spelling throughout bears most evident marks of the laxity, and entire want of uniformity which at this time prevailed.   Indeed, it is in this respect that we conceive our Text Book to be peculiarly valuable; namely, because it affords us so true an index, not only of the peculiar texture of English at the time, but also of that phase through which it was passing.

And again, on the other hand, it does not appear, that this informity ought to mislead the discriminating enquirer, for as soon as he has become conscious of it his greatest danger is over, and a knowledge of the parent tongues, the Anglo Saxon and French, ought to afford a sufficient safeguard, and enable him to discern at once, whether a particular form of spelling ought to be attributed to corrupt usage, or a closer approximation to one of the superior tongues.

It will be found from the specimens given below, that, at this time, the French element in our language had undergone but slight modification, and still bore a close resemblance to what we find it to have been in Chaucer's time.   It is this constituent element which we purpose now to consider, and also, more particularly, those changes which have assimilated it to the rest of the English Language.   We take our stand, then, at this time, on an eminence, as it were, from which we can look down on the conflict being waged at our feet.   We see before us a written tongue, in which Orthography, if not entirely unknown, resembled but a spar floating on the ocean, and tossed to and fro by every wave of caprice and whim; and we watch till we see, at the commencement of the seventeenth century, and in our own authorized Version, most of these discordant members reduced to harmony and subjection, and our Language presenting for the first time some appearance of uniformity.   Of the extreme uncertainty which still prevailed in spelling, the verb *To weigh*, affords an excellent example.   It occurs in no less than four different forms; namely, *wei, wey, waigh,* and lastly, that to which use has affixed its sanction, *weigh*.[1] Frequently, in the same verse, a word is spelt in two different ways.

SETTLERS FROM FRANCE.

Of words derived to us through the French, those now ending in *y*, formerly ended in *ie*. Thus, we find *glorie* for *glory; envie* for *envy; vanitie* for *vanity; prudencie* and *prudency* for *prudence*, &c., &c. Still the use of *y* for *ie*, in such words as these, was already known, and frequently adopted.

In the class of words, of which *joyne* and *poynte* are examples, the use of *y* for *i*, where even etymology did not require it, should seem to indicate the French pronunciation, which such words still retained.[2] Having been spoken long before they were written, it was not unnatural, that when they came to be expressed in writing, they should exhibit some trace of their pronunciation.

Another important class of words, which we find in the Breeches Bible, is composed of those ending in *our*. Important, we think, as showing *the tendency of the English Language to retrace words back to their Latin roots, in preference to retaining the Gallicized, or French form.* As examples of this class, we may notice the words

Creditour (Fr. *crediteur*,) modern *creditor*, (Lat. *creditor*.)
Oratour, (Fr. *orateur*,) " *orator* (Lat. *orator*.)
Errour (Fr. *erreur*,) " *error* (Lat. *error*.)
Governour (Fr. *gouverneur*,) " *governor* (Lat. *gubernator*.)
&c. &c. &c. &c.

[1] Here we have an instance of the formative process, the birth throes, as it were, of our English verb *To weigh*, from the Anglo Saxon *weg-an*. This verb, derived apparently from the Anglo Saxon substantive *weg*, a way or passage, signifies first *To bear, To carry, To move;* secondly, *To weigh, To weigh anchor.*

[2] But the substitution of *y* for *i* was very common. Thus we find *anoynt* for anoint; *oyntment* for *ointment; yce* for *ice; yles* (French, *ile*) for *isles, gyant, ayre,* &c.

In all these instances, and many others might be noticed, the French, or semi-French termination in -our has given way to the more simple Latin one in -or. This process is not yet universally applied. We still occasionally meet with such words as *honour, labour, endeavour*,[1] &c., where the French termination is still apparent. And there is even one example where the Latin termination -or, having been adopted, the French -our has again been taken up. This is the word *Saviour*, which is found written *Savior*. But here the laws of Euphony have evidently interposed to control the undoubted tendency with regard to words of this class.

The spelling of the following, and like words, shews, not only the source whence they were derived, but also, it

---

[1] This word, in this form occurs two, or three times in the Breeches Bible. I need not say it is in its older meaning, still to be found in the Collect for the second Sunday after Easter: "Give us grace that we may always most thankfully receive that his inestimable benefit, and also daily endeavour ourselves to follow the blessed steps of his most holy life."

Some, perhaps, not aware of the old meaning, and construction of the verb *To endeavour*, may read the latter clause, as though it were written, and meant nothing more than, "may ourselves daily endeavour, &c." So, in the following passage, the use is the same.

"Brethren I count not myself that I have attained to it; but one thing I doe, I forget that which is behinde, and *endeuour* myself vnto that which is before;"—*Phil.* III. 13.

But the old meaning was very different from that which obtains in the present day; and this difference may perhaps be best expressed by saying, that, while in the first instance, *To Endeavour*, was an active verb, derived immediately from the French verb *Endêver*, "to be in a rage," and governing an accusative case of the person, who put himself into a rage; it has now lost its active signification, and bears a kind of neuter signification, (though it may still be said to govern a sort of verbal accusative.) By this change the verb has lost much of its original force, since "to endeavour oneself to do a thing" expresses the act of arousing, or stimulating oneself to a pitch of indomitable determination, for the accomplishment of the object proposed; while "to endeavour to do a thing" only expresses an intention on our part, without at all denoting its intensity. So that the present force of the verb *To endeavour*, is merely equivalent to the verb *To strive*.

should seem, the way in which they were for a length of
time pronounced. We have coupled the old form of
spelling with the French verb, that the connexion may be
more apparent.

Old form.	French.	Modern form.
Reteined.	Retenir.	Retained
Marveil.	Merveille.	Marvel.
Restreined.	Restreindre.	Restrained.
Traveil.	Travail.	Travail.
Reveil.	Révéler.	Reveal.
Ordein.	Ordonner.	Ordain.
Renue.	Renouer.	Renew.
&c.	&c.	&c.

Although in this class of words it can scarcely, in
some cases at least, be said, that the tendency has been
to retrace the form of the Latin root, for the dissimilarity
between the Latin and French is sometimes too great
to permit this, yet the tendency has been clearly to leave
the French form, both in writing and pronunciation.

The following examples are of a more specific nature,
and must be considered by themselves.

RENOWME. REPROCH.

"And (I) will raise up for them a plant of *renowme*, and
they shall be no more consumed with hunger in the land,
neither beare the *reproch* of the heathen any more."

Ezekiel, xxxiiii. 29.

Of the two words in italics in this passage, the latter,
Reproch, is merely the French *reproche*, with the final
e dropped; probably to intimate to an English eye, that
the *o* was to be pronounced short.

The former *Renowme*, requires more careful consideration, because to this word we are indebted for our
substantive *Renown*. *Renowme* was the form which the
French substantive *Renom* (from the verb *Renommer*,
to give repute), assumed when it first began to take its

place in the English language. The remarkable change it has since undergone,—a change, which has produced *Renown*,—affords an example in which Euphony has triumphed over Etymology. *Renown*, though a pleasant word enough to the ear, is, nevertheless, a deformity whose construction will not bear investigation.[1]

PERFITE.

" O Tyrus, thou hast sayd I am of *perfite* beauty."
Ezek. XXVII. 3.

Perfite is evidently the French *parfait*, from the Latin *perfectus*. Here, as in so many other instances, modern usage has shown its *preference to Latin over French forms*. The double forms of spelling French words are sufficiently indicative of the uncertainty which prevailed, as also of the change which was now taking place. And, according to the prevalence of the French, or Latin form over each other, we may form, I apprehend, some just estimate of the progress of that change in particular words.

Thus the French form *domage*, though occasionally found, was rapidly giving way to our present form, *damage*, which leans more to the Latin. The same applies to the French form *marchants* (Fr. *marchand*), *victuals*, were as yet generally written after the French method *vitailes* ;[2] though the Roman form *victuals*, was evidently coming into use.

Virtue was at this time commonly written *vertue*.

Licour (Fr. *liqueur*) had not receded before the Latin form *liquor*.

[1] As, however, *noun* is a contraction of the Latin *nomen*, so some may be content to see in the last syllable of *renown* a similar contraction, rather than be compelled to adopt the above ungrateful conclusion. Notwithstanding, we fear this is not the real clue to its formation.

[2] The French word for victuals is *vivres*, but the above form is still extant in the words *avitailler*, To victual, and *Avitailleur*, a Victualler.

Maister (Fr. *Maître*) still survived in places; though the present form *master*, more nearly approaching the Latin *magister*, was generally used.

Fashion, if possible, shewed a still closer affinity with France, than even in our own day. This word is usually spelt *facion*, from the French *façon*, *façonner*, To form.

"Who received them at their hands and *facioned* it with yͤ grauing toole, and made of it a molten calfe."
Ezekiel xxxii. 4.

Chapiter is found for *chapter*; *roule* for *roll*; *proces* for *process*; *maner* (Fr. *manier*, to handle) for *manner*; and many others, which it would be tedious to notice in detail, but which all appear to support directly, or indirectly, the theory we have advanced of an innate preference in our language of Latin over French forms.

The form *ancre* (Fr. *ancre*) for *anchor*, prompts us to ask the question, why, in retracing the Latin *ancora*, the letter *h* has been inserted, since its insertion cannot be either required by pronunciation, or defended by Etymology?[1]

"And fearing lest they should haue fallen into some rough places, they cast foure *ancres* out of the sterne, and wished that the day were come."—*Acts*. xxvii. 29.

The French word *harnais* had not as yet assumed its modern Anglicised form *harness*, but is found written *harneis*.

"Let not him that girdeth his *harneis* boast himself as he that putteth it off."—1 *Kings*, xx. 11.

Fauchin, the Roman *ensis falcatus*, or curved sword, was still written after the French form, preserved in the words *faucher*, to mow, and *faucheur*, a mower.

"And she came to the post of the bed, which was at Holofernes head, and tooke down his *fauchin* from thence."
Judeth, xiii. 6.

---

[1] We are assuming here, that we have retraced the Latin *Anchora* through the French *ancre*; though there is no necessity for such an assumption since we might derive the word immediately from the Anglo Saxon *Ancor*, an Anchor.

But it is needless to multiply examples; the above will amply suffice to shew how these strangers were being dealt with, and how at length the great mass of French words have become domesticated amongst us. Before, however, dismissing this branch of the subject it may be well to anticipate a question, which may be put, as to whether any large proportion of these French words have disappeared altogether from our language since the time we are considering? In answer to this question, it may be said, that very few of them seem to have so disappeared. Indeed, they had already been copiously thinned. Since Chaucer's time, numbers of them had become obsolete; not even his illustrious sanction was able to enfranchise them. True, those that did remain still retained pretty much of their primitive costume, but, nevertheless, a silent agency was at work; first it thinned the bed of seedlings; then, when this was done, it set to work at training, and trimming the remainder. The first of these operations may be said to have occupied the fifteenth century; the second the sixteenth; while in the seventeenth century the class of words they had been manipulating became kneaded up with the rest of the language, an integral, and, to a certain extent, a homogeneous portion of it.

We recollect to have found but one instance which properly comes under this category; still it is not impossible a few others may exist, which have escaped either our eye or our memory. It is the word

Puissant—" Thou art more bright and *puissant* than the mountaines of pray."—*Ps.* LXXVI. 4.

SPELLING OF SAXON WORDS AND OTHERS.

But we now pass on to consider some of those changes which were taking place in words of a more strictly English, that is, Anglo Saxon, character. Already had this portion of the language, the base as it were of the English tongue, received its present stereotyped form, as regards grammar, and construction. The changes which may be said to have converted Saxon into English, took place in Chaucer's time, about the year 1350, when the declensions of Substantives were reduced from six to one, and the case endings from four to one, or two. Yet, even Chaucer's phraseology differs from that of the Breeches Bible, not only in containing a much larger proportion of French words, but also considerably more of Saxon inflection. By the middle of the 16th century, these remnants of Saxon grammar had entirely disappeared, and given place to that construction, which must now be considered permanent in the English Language. It is, then, with the spelling alone of Saxon words that we are now concerned. For, as soon as a certain set of rules came to be generally recognized,— call those rules grammar if you will,—and the language had received pretty nearly its complement of words, it remained but that some uniform method of writing and pronouncing those words should also be adopted. We have already remarked, the Breeches Bible affords abundant evidence, that no such unanimity as yet existed; though, at the same time, it is clear this subject was receiving attention, which hereafter developed such a code of spelling, or orthography, as, in the main, obtains in our own day.

It is hoped, that the reader has been enabled to form some adequate conception of the manner in which English was written and spelt, about this time, from the examples, which, short and disconnected though they were, have already been adduced. In that case, there will be the less necessity to enter minutely into the investigation of a subject, which, apart from affording us a measure of the changes that have been instrumental in imparting to English words their present form, seems to possess no particular interest. Indeed, the task would have been both a laborious and a tedious one to have attempted a detailed examination of all the grotesque, double, and often triple forms of spelling, which prevailed at this time.

Scarcely a single word is always spelt in the same manner; and even terminating syllables, such for instance as *-ness*, *-ly*, *-full*, &c. follow no general rule. Indeed, such was the want of uniformity, that it is impossible to find out a single rule which seems to have been generally recognized. The most, then, we can do is to specify which of these various forms was the most common; though it is frequently difficult to do even thus much.

The termination *-ness*, is generally written *-nesse*, sometimes *nes*, but very rarely *-ness*. Thus we find *darknesse*, and *darknes; businesse* and *busines*, &c. but not *darkness*, nor *business*.

Monosyllables, whether verbs or substantives, now ending with a consonant, generally doubled the final consonant, and added *e*. Sometimes, however, the present form of spelling such words is found, indicative of the change, which was beginning to take place. Thus, we find, *dogge, warre, wanne, ranne, ramme*, &c.; for *dog, war*, &c.

Words now ending in double *l*, generally, but not always, appear with a single *l*; as *wel* for *well; wel, hel, shal, hil*, &c. for *will, hell, shall, hill*, &c.

S is frequently used for *c*, and *c* for *k*. Thus *twise* for *twice; mise* for *mice; minsing* for *mincing*, &c.; *skout* for *scout; carkeis* for *carcase; patriark* for *patriarch*, &c.

I and *y*, seem to have done duty alternately. Thus we find *eie*, and *eye; syrs* and *sirs*. *Yce* and *Ice*, &c., &c.

Such were some of the peculiarities which affected the language generally. The following examples are of a more specific nature :

Been, that word which has now come to be looked upon as the past participle of the verb *To Be*, though incorrectly so, occurs in no less than three forms, differing from our own, namely, *bin, bene*, and *beene*.

Year appears in four forms; *yere, yeere, yeer,* and *year.*

Prease is commonly found for *press,* and *prest* (*presto* of the conjuror) for *present.*

Mids, middes,[1] and *middest,* apparently a kind of superlative form, at length verged into *midst,* are all found.

"And he made the *middest* barre to shoote through the boardes, from the one side to the other."

Exod. XXXVI. 33.

Hearbs, and *herbs; hundreth,* and *handred,* are both found.

"Then the King of Israel gathered the Prophets *upon a four hundreth* men, &c.—1 *Kings,* XXII. 6.

Utter frequently occurs for *outer.*
Wiers for *wires.*
None for *noon.*
Overthwart (twisted over) for *athwart.*

The personal pronouns *me, he, she, thee, ye,* were generally spelt with the double *e,* as we now spell *thee,* though occasionally with the single *e.* It is difficult now to conjecture, much more to ascertain, what was the cause which led to this method of spelling these words; a method which has since been dropped, excepting in the case of *thee,* where its retention is desirable, if only for the purpose of distinction between it and the definite article *the.*

There are two or three instances of spelling, which, contrary to the principle some time ago laid down, time seems to have altered for the worse.

Vineger, the form constantly found in the Breeches Bible, should seem more correct, as derived from the

---

[1] Anglo Saxon *middes,* the genitive case singular of *midd, middle,* connected probably with the Anglo Saxon verb *Midan,* To hide.

French *Vin aigre,* (sour wine) than our modern form *vinegar.* So also the form *Tentation* seems better than the modern one *Temptation.*

Fornace, as it was commonly spelt, showed a closer affinity to the Latin *fornax,* than our present form *furnace,* which seems rather to resemble the French form *fournaise.*

But the change which has taken place in these words, and, it may be, in one or two others, will, since they are the exceptions, only serve to confirm the general rule which has been applied to the mass of French words, and which abundantly shows the innate preference in our language for the Latin over the French type.

And it is well that such a preference not only manifested itself, but that there was no cause to prevent its being carried into effect. For had either the choice or the opportunity been wanting, it seems tolerably certain, that English, considering the various discordant elements which it would have contained, could never have been written with that exactitude, and almost classic precision, of which it is now capable. Not that the losses it sustained can either be replaced, or ever cease to be deplored, but having been already incurred, this retrograde movement served to restore a character of precision and integrity which must otherwise have been sought for in vain.

Suppose for instance, our language, instead of referring back to their Latin models the extensive class of French words, with which it was formerly inundated, had retained those words in the corrupt and mutilated forms they at first assumed, what would have been the character of English now? Instead of preserving in the roots of many of its words a close resemblance and affinity to the Latin, the Latin element would have undergone a second dilution, and the probable consequence would have been, that this likeness and affinity would have been generally weakened, and sometimes entirely lost. If we now wrote *debts*, as it is commonly written in the Breeches Bible, *dettes*, and as it is even now written in French, how obscure would become the connexion between this word, and the Latin form from which it springs, *debitum*. We are compelled to pronounce the word as before, yet we have done our best to show that we are conscious of its antecedents, as well as of those events which transferred it to English soil. On this account it is that English Orthography presents such difficulties to the foreigner, because, while the pronunciation of French words has undergone but slight change, the retrogression from a French to Latin type, in spelling, has considerably modified the aspect of the written language.

Where there is no law there can be no transgression, consequently we should not be justified in stigmatizing the spelling of Saxon and French words at this time as vicious, or faulty. For, as not even the slightest pretence to any uniformity was made, so was it impossible that anything like uniformity should exist. The language, with regard to its spelling, was in a state of transition and re-formation. Yet, even at this time, there was a class of words whose violated orthography it is difficult to excuse; those words we mean which bear on their surface unmistakeable tokens of their etymology. True, though instances which come under this class are not numerous, yet, as examples of the spelling of this period, they must not be omitted. We have observed

Prophane for *profane*, (Lat. *profanus*).
Preheminence for *pre-eminence*.
Abilliments for *habiliments*, (Fr. *habillement*).
Society for *satiety*, (Lat. *satietas*).
Wain for *wean*, (Anglo Saxon *wenan*).
Prease for *press*, (Lat. *pressus*).
Ballance for *balance*, (Fr. *balance*), &c.

This is the only class of words whose spelling may be termed reprehensible. For here it is no longer possible

to plead those peculiar circumstances, which entirely pro-
hibit hostile criticism in regard to the main body of the
language. Such instances as the above could but have
arisen from ignorance, or forgetfulness, of the roots
whence they sprang, not from any uncertainty or vari-
ableness in the words themselves.

But, while on this topic, we may even ask ourselves,
whether the usage of our own day is in all cases
correct and well informed; for, if not, we should be
cautious how we inculpate that of the past. Is it probable, that in some remote period, when our present
Version shall perhaps have become old and obsolete, like
that which now lies before us, some curious investigator
shall open its yellow worm-eaten pages, and be able to
point out here and there instances, as he will call them,
of faulty spelling; instances which will shew, that the
principles we have observed in the Breeches Bible have
not as yet received their full recognition, nor our
language its greatest polish and information? It should
seem that such an event is not altogether improbable;
for there yet linger amongst us some few words whose
spelling can scarcely be defended. It is no part of our
duty, now, to ransack the English of the day in search
of such examples; yet one, or two, occur to us, which
we may be pardoned for noticing. Those verbs compounded from the Latin verb *cedo*, To go, appearing
again in the French under the form *ceder*, afford us a
case to the point.

It is true, indeed, that each individual compound
formed from this root (to use the term for convenience) is
spelt, not in two, or three, different ways, but uniformly
the same; yet, what amounts to precisely the same
thing, the identical common part, as it enters into
different compounds, is spelt in different ways. Thus
we spell *Proceed*, To go forward, with the double *e*;
while the verb *To recede*, To go backward, differing only
in the prefix *re*, we have thought proper to spell with

a single *e*. Similarly *concede, intercede, precede,* &c. after the French model *céder, précéder,* &c. It is not certainly a matter of much importance, which of these forms we adopt, so long as we consistently abide by the choice we make; but to use one form with one prefix and another with another set of prefixes, argues inconsistency at the least, and is, moreover, apt to mislead as to the identity of the verbal compound in such words. Present custom seems rather in favour of the French form *-cede*, if we may judge from the majority of compounds; if so, why should not *proceed, succeed,* and the rest, conform to usage, and be spelt *procede, succede,* &c.? or else let all such verbs be spelt with the double *e.*

Proffer, we are accustomed to write with the double *f,* while *prefer,* and *defer,* compounds of the same Latin verb, and differing[1] only from the first, in having the prepositions *pre* and *de* instead of *pro* prefixed to the verb *fero,* are rightly written with the single *f.* This, too, seems inconsistent. What would the world think of a man who wrote *agression* instead of *aggression ?* Would it not immediately set him down as ignorant and ill informed ? Yet such a man would be guilty of no error, which is not committed every day by those who write *agreeable* with a single instead of a double *g.* The former, it is true, has the sanction both of the French word *agréable,* and also of long usage; yet, neither the one, nor the other, makes it essentially correct; nor, as it seems to us, affords any satisfactory reason, why the more correct forms, *aggree* and *aggreeable,* should not be restored. Restored, we say, because the earliest form of the word, and that from which the French borrowed theirs, was *aggradevole* in the Italian. For changing this into *agréable,* the French language may have had reasons, the validity of which we are perhaps

---

[1] *Differ* and *difference* are rightly spelt with the double *f,* because the Latin verb, as compounded of *dis* and *fero,* is so written.

scarcely competent to dispute ; but, at any rate, the same reasons cannot be urged in its defence any longer when it became an English word.

It is hoped, that these few general and cursory remarks on English spelling, may serve to throw some light on the steps by which we have at length arrived at the orthography of our own day.

The spectacle we have had presented, it should seem, leaves us but little room for boastful satisfaction. Nay, rather, when we consider how much of what is purely arbitrary, and fortuitous, entered, and still enters, into our standard of right and wrong, we ought to feel humbled, and learn, that bad spelling is reprhehensible, not so much because it implies ignorance of the roots and composition of our language, as because it betokens habits of inattention, and disrepect to the general consent of good society, whose decision, after all, must in the main be final.

Here we bring to a close the remarks which have been suggested to us by the English of the Breeches Bible. In the two remaining chapters we propose to take a brief survey of the European Languages, and more especially to consider the bearing of the Anglo Saxon on the English Language.

CHAPTER X.

COMPARATIVE PHILOLOGY.—INDO-GERMANIC FAMILY.—
LATIN AND GREEK; THEIR ORIGIN AND AFFINITY
WITH THE GERMAN FAMILY.—PEDIGREE OF ENGLISH.
—THE ROMANCE WALLON;—ITS INFLUENCE.—THE
CLAIMS OF LATIN AND ANGLO SAXON COMPARED.

THE analogy which exists between Philology and
Geology is of so striking and patent a character, and
has, moreover, been so frequently insisted on, that we
feel ashamed again to resort to this trite simile for an
illustration. Yet, hackneyed as it has now become, it is
one in which there is a parallelism of truth, extending
even to the primæval world, and embracing in its area
kindred problems, whose solution is of the highest
interest and import to man. Both are studies of
comparatively recent birth, and in both the ground
as yet explored is as nothing to that which remains.
As in Geology we find a volume in which the natural
history of the world has been chronicled, in characters not to be misunderstood; so in Philology we
find a second volume, devoted to the history of the
lord of that world,—God's highest creation, man. The
former is not more definite and intelligible than the
latter, nor more infallible in its teaching. Neither must
be read alone, though each independently; and the
results must be compared not so much with themselves,
as made to throw their combined light on that third
Volume, given to us by that God of nature Himself whose
existence and identity has received such proof in the
person of Jesus Christ, as must compel the assent of
man so long as he is a reasonable creature.

"External probability, arising from the study of comparative Philology," says the most celebrated linguist and philologer that England has ever produced, the late Dr. Donaldson, "leads us to the conclusion, that the varieties we distinguish, as well in the form as in the language of man, must have been produced by some violent dispersion of the human race over the whole surface of the Earth, and by the subsequent operation of the multifarious causes to which the different parts of the separated family would be exposed. The result of investigations of this nature is generally more satisfactory to our inquisitive spirit than any written testimony, however authenticated with regard to the creation and early state of man: for the facts to which such a testimony relate occurred long before the invention of writing; they are traditions handed down by word of mouth from father to son, beginning with the first man, and so going on to the man who wrote them down, and of which even the earliest narrator could have known but little without direct and immediate inspiration."[1]

Again, the same writer says "It is time that some attempt were made to show that the philosophy of language is so far from ministering to materialism and scepticism, that it actually stands forth as the chief confirmation of those systems which form the basis of all that human reason has ventured to contribute to the support of religion and morality."[2]

Such is the pleasing testimony of one, who on this point speaks with an authority which few will care to dispute. At the outset, then, the subject of comparative philology affords the student this pleasing reflection, that he is entering on a study, whose direct tendency hitherto has been to strengthen the claims which the inspired Writings have over his belief. And this, surely, is no trivial consideration in the present day, when a spirit of

[1] "The New Cratylus," p. 43.
[2] Ibid, p. 73.

bold criticism has been set afoot, which has not hesitated to impugn the most sacred objects of our faith. Surely we can afford to lose not one iota of evidence, which tends to the support of Christian Philosophy against the rash, the ill-grounded, and, it is scarcely too much to say, the blasphemous speculations of the present day. Already, within the last half century, the study of comparative philology has done much to impart to our belief, in certain parts of the Scripture narrative, a rationality, which cannot but place that belief on more substantial, because more intellectual grounds, than it has hitherto held.

We are now beginning to recognize the fact of the common parentage of men, and languages, not only because Scripture assures us of it, but because in a multitude of instances we can trace the relationship for ourselves.

Yet, it is, after all, very few who have ability, time, and opportunities, such as to render them capable of becoming original explorers in this wide and rich field of discovery. The great majority of us must be content to enjoy the fruits of others labours, and tread the ground already cleared by such pioneers as Donaldson, and men of similar attainments. But is it not so in other branches of study beside this? How few, compared with the number of those who read mathematics, are able to enlarge the boundary of that science. Yet this is no argument against reading mathematics. And so in like manner should it be with regard to the study of comparative philology.

We may not indeed be able to render our names famous by making fresh discoveries, or pushing our researches into regions as yet unexplored; yet the acquisition of sound and practical information on a subject, which ought at least to be interesting to each of us, the history of our race—and Comparative Philology is nothing less—should afford a sufficient inducement to bestow more attention to the subject than has hitherto been given.   But, beside these general incentives, the very nature and composition of our own language is such as to demand some knowledge of this subject, before we can rightly understand the relative bearing of English to the other languages of Europe.   A few men here and there devote themselves to it, but as yet it has received no public recognition; our public schools, and even our Universities ignore it, nor does there appear at present any symptoms of their awaking to a sense of its importance.   Our surprise may, indeed, be somewhat lessened, when we recollect, that Comparative Philology, like Geology, was, as a separate study, unknown to the Greeks and Romans.   As colonists, in the wider sense of the term, their time was in the early ages of their settlement employed in establishing themselves in their new homes, in organizing their constitutions, and in subduing their enemies.   And when, at length, their institutions had acquired a permanent consistency, their natural genius preferred, and justly so, to soar on the free and unfettered wings of fancy, rather than to tie itself down to the tedious investigation of the past, or, to them, the monotonous study of themselves.   Indeed, to them there would be no past; all would be present and future.   "At the period," says Sismondi,[1] "when nations yet in their infancy are animated by a creative genius, which endows them with a poetry and literature of their own, while it renders them, at the same time, capable of splendid enterprises, susceptible of lofty passions, and disposed to great sacrifices, the literature of other nations is unknown to them.   Each draws from its own bosom that which best harmonizes with its nature."

And thus it was with the nations of ancient Greece and Rome.   Their languages so speedily diverged from those, which, even to this day, betray unmistakable signs

---

[1] "Literature of the South of Europe," vol. 1 p. 25.

of affinity; so soon acquired a character and individuality each of its own, that this very affinity seems to have been ignored; nor does a consciousness of the position they held, relative to the remaining members of the same great family, ever appear to have returned. Besides, a succession of prosperous circumstances, or circumstances calculated to develop their intellectual and warlike capacities, by raising them above the level of the nations by whom they were surrounded, at the same time severed those bonds of sympathy which should have connected them with the rest of mankind. It may be doubted, whether they would not have repelled with disdain the notion, that a common brotherhood, and, in some sort, a common language existed between themselves and the nations who bowed in subjection at their feet, or whose conquered princes served often but to increase the magnificence of a triumphal procession.

And thus, to a great measure, has it been with ourselves hitherto. We have been too deeply engrossed with topics of a religious, political, or civil character, to think much upon ourselves and our language. Yet the time seems now to have arrived when our attention may not unfitly be turned to these and kindred studies, which demand for their consideration, not so much the romantic and impulsive energy of a nation's youth, as the sober thoughtfulness of its manhood. Already, on the continent, have these studies received considerable attention, and Germany more particularly has become famous by the number and ability of her philologers. Of the few in England who have devoted themselves to the subject of comparative philology, there is none to whom it is more indebted than the late Dr. Donaldson, and for the convenience of those who are unable to consult his works for themselves, we have ventured to draw, in rough outline, a sketch of his theory—perhaps better, the results which his labours enabled him to arrive at respecting the great Indo-European family of languages. We simply desire to widen the bed over which the streams of his information flow, or by diverting them into smaller, albeit shallower, channels, bring that information within the reach of those who otherwise would not obtain it.

Dr. Donaldson, then, divides all known languages into three great classes.

1st.   Languages with monosyllabic roots, incapable of composition, and therefore without Grammar, or Organization. To this class belongs the Chinese.

2nd.   Languages with monosyllabic roots capable of composition. To this class belong the Sanscrit family, and all other languages not included under classes 1 and 3, preserved in such a state, that the forms of the words may be resolved into their simplest elements.

3rd.   Languages consisting of dissyllabic verbal roots, and whose grammatical forms are produced, not merely by composition, as in class 2, but also by a simple modification of the roots themselves. This class contains the Semitic Languages only : that is

Hebrew $\begin{cases} \text{Chaldee.} \\ \text{Syriac.} \end{cases}$
Arabic.
Aramaic, &c.

Of these three classes, the second, as embracing all the languages now spoken in Europe, is by far the most important to us, and to this therefore we shall confine our attention. It has been variously called the Sanscrit, Indo-Germanic, or Indo-European. Of these the second, or Indo-Germanic, is the most significant, inasmuch as it implies the connexion existing between the Indian and Teutonic Languages.

The nursery, if not the birthplace of this great family, seems to have been a country in Asia, called Irân, bounded on the North by the Caspian Sea, on the South by the Indian Ocean, on the East by the Indus, and on the West by the Euphrates. The people inhabiting this district appear to have spoken two languages, which bore the same relation to one another as the High and Low German of the present day ; namely, Low Iranian, spoken by those who dwelt in the low countries to the North and East ; and High Iranian, by those on the mountainous districts of the South. When the population of this country became too numerous to be confined any longer within its comparatively narrow limits, the Eastern and Northern tribes sent off migrations to the South-East and North-west, the latter driving before them, as is usually the case, the tribes, and amongst them the Low Iranians, by whom they were hemmed in. Thus, there went forth a band of High Iranians to the South-east, who succeeded in mastering the Northern part of Hindostan, and perhaps some of the Polynesian Islands ; and also a band of emigrants to the North-west who stayed not till they reached the shores of the Atlantic, carrying along with them their Low Iranian dialect, and spreading it over a great portion of Asia, the whole of Europe, even to the Islands of the West. The proof of this colonization of Europe and Northern India, by the inhabitants of Northern and Eastern Irân, rests upon the agreement of the languages spoken by the oldest inhabitants of India and Europe, and on the obvious derivation of the names of the earliest tribes in both, from the country which afterwards became Media.[1]

From these Low Iranian migrations, probably following

---

[1] *New Cratylus*, p. 83. *Again*, p. 84. "The argument from the Language is decisive of the whole question. The resemblances between the old Low German dialects, (Gothic, Saxon, &c.) and the Sanscrit, even after a separation for thousands of years are so striking that an eminent Philologer (Bopp) has said "when I read the Gothic of Ulphilas, I could believe I had Sanscrit before me." On the whole, then, we consider it as nearly certain, that the Hindus in India, and the Low Germans in Europe, are emigrants from the country about the Southern extremity of the Caspian Sea."

each other at widely distant intervals of time, arise, not only those languages called Low German, because spoken in the low countries of Northern Europe, but also, Dr. Donaldson is of opinion, arguing from what he knew of the Etymology and Grammatical structure of those languages, the Low Celtic or Erse, the Lithuanian, and the Sclavonian languages.

It would appear, then, that from the Low Iranian migrations have sprung the following languages :

1.   The Low or Old Celtic, comprising

> The Erse of Ireland.
> The Gaelic of Scotland.
> The Manx of the Isle of Man.

2.   Low German, including three divisions ;

I.   The Scandinavian family ; viz.

> Icelandic.
> Swedish.
> Danish.

II.   The Low German dialects proper ; viz.

> Saxon, and *Anglo Saxon*.
> Frisian.
> Flemish.
> Dutch.

III.   The Old or Mæso-Gothic; or, as Bopp calls it, the German Sanscrit.

3.   The Sclavonic, the most widely extended of the Indo-Germanic family, spoken more or less over that tract of country bounded by the Pacific on the East, the Baltic on the West, the Arctic sea on the North, and the Adriatic on the South ; and in Europe, by the Russians and Rusniaks, the Bulgarians, Servians, Bosnians, Dalmatians, Croats, the Wends and Sorbs in Lusatia and

Saxony, the Slowaks in Hungary, the Bohemians, Moravians, Poles and Silesians.[1]

4. The Lithuanian Languages ; viz.

Lithuanian Proper.
Lettish.
Old Prussian.

Such, according to Dr. Donaldson, are the offspring of the sucessive Low Iranian migrations into Europe. The order in which these migrations took place may be inferred from the present position in Europe of the people who speak their respective languages. The Celts, no doubt connected to some extent with the Finns,[2] were the first emigrants into Europe, and it is thought, that by them the British Isles were peopled so early as B.C. 1200. The Teutonic and Scandinavian family was the next to follow, pressing on the Celtic as closely as possible, and detruding them to the utmost limits of the west. They are supposed to have entered Europe by the Kimmerian Bosphorus, about B.C. 680.

The Sclavonians were the last in order, and consequently occupy the eastern parts of Europe.

But, besides the Low Iranian migrations, Dr. Donaldson is of opinion, that there was another Iranian migration of mixed character, to which he would attribute what he calls the High German, and High or New Celtic dialects. This migration he supposes to have followed, and been caused by, the subjugation of the Medes, a Low Iranian, by the Persians, a High Iranian people.

---

[1] "The different tribes who spoke this language were known to the Ancients under the names Rhoxolani, Krobyzi, Sarmatæ, Sauromatæ, Pannonians, and Venedi, or Wenidæ."—*Ibid.*

[2] The Danes, or Northmen, members of the great Scandinavian family, and second migratory wave which rolled over Europe from the East, encountered them in the North of Europe, about the same time that the Saxons and Angles encountered the Celts in Britain.

The Median and Persian languages, that is to say the Low and High Iranian dialects, thus becoming fused, there resulted the mixed language, which constituted the speech of those Persians with whom the Greeks had so much to do, and the connexion of which with modern High German was long ago perceived.[1] If this be so, then to this mixed Iranian migration are due the High German, and High Celtic languages. The former is divided into three classes, the Old, Middle, and New High German, the latter of which is now the written language of all Germany, and owes its position to the influence of Luther, who was from Upper Germany. The New or High Celtic comprises

> Welsh.
> Cornish.
> Breton Idioms.

Such is an extremely rough outline of the parentage of those languages boasting a pure descent, and of their family connexions with each other, which are now spoken in Europe. It may seem strange to some, that even so rough an outline as this should refuse to pay the slightest regard to the classic languages of Greece and Rome. Yet such is undoubtedly the case, and we are, therefore, left to conclude, that these languages must either have presented no affinity with the Indo-European family, or, otherwise, they have forfeited their claim to be considered as the pure descendants of any one branch. The influence of these two languages has been so great, not only, as we have already had occasion to see, on our own English, but also on the languages of Southern Europe, where the Latin, in conjunction with the primæval dialect, has given birth to that important family called

---

[1] *New Crat.* p. 87. "It was to one of the tribes of the Persians, the Γερμάνιοι, mentioned by Herodotus, I. 25, that the Germans owe their name."

[2] *Ibid.* p. 80.

the Romance tongues,[1] that a short time occupied in considering them cannot we think be mispent. Proudly as they stand aloof from the great representatives of the Indo-European family, they are yet no heaven-born offspring, and though, as it were in disdain, they refuse to disclose, or disclose only by obscure fable and shadowy legend, the manner of their birth, and their family connexions, yet Philology refuses to be hoodwinked, and lays bare with unsparing hand the secrets of their formation.

There is an opinion, which has long been, and, for aught we know, is still widely prevalent; an opinion which dates at least from the time, and has no less authority than that of Mr. Horne Tooke, that "the bulk and foundation of the Latin language is Greek."[2] Yet in spite of such high authority, it appears we must now learn to look upon this opinion as erroneous. Other and better Scholars and Philologers than Mr. Tooke take now a different view of the subject. Dr. Donaldson considers (for his intellect still lives) that the Latin is of at least equal antiquity with the Greek, and not derived from it; that the similarity existing between them, which has caused us to think so, is fully accounted for by the same people, the Pelasgians, probably of the Sclavonic stock, settling simultaneously in Italy and Greece; while the difference, which afterwards sprung up, and caused

A.D.

[1] Namely: 1. The Provençal, established at the Court of Bozon, King of Arles, ... 877—887

2. The Langue d'Oil, or d'Oui, Romance Wallon, or Norman French, from the mixture of which with the Anglo-Saxon has resulted our own English, at the Court of William Lonque-Epee, the son of Rollo duke of Normandy, between the years .... 917—943

3. The Castilian, in the reign of Ferdinand the Great.... 1037—1065

4. The Portuguese, under Henry the founder of the Monarchy .... 1095—1112

5. The Italian, under Roger I. King of Sicily .... 1129—1154

[2] "Diversions of Purley." p. 402. 1857.

Latin and Greek to be regarded as separate languages, or connected only by descent, was due to the difference of those lingual elements, which were hereafter superimposed and amalgamated with the original and common base.

Our own opinion, we are quoting the words of the same writer, drawn purely from philological and geographical considerations, is, that the first population of both Italy and Greece, was Erse, or Low Celtic. After them came the Sclavonian (Pelasgian) element in each country, and then a Lithuanian element was added in Italy, and a Persian, High German, High Celtic, or to speak generally, High Iranian in Greece.[1]

He founds thus much of his argument on the facts, that the Sclavonian, the most widely extended branch of the Low Iranian family, may be traced to the immediate neighbourhood of Greece and Italy, as there are singular coincidences between Latin and the oldest, or Æolian Greek, on the one hand, and even the modern Sclavonian languages on the other; and, as the Greek traditions point to the Hyperborean regions, we may safely call the Pelasgians by a name which, though now restricted, properly describes all those Low Iranian tribes, that came into immediate contact with the people of whom we are speaking.[2]

From what has been said, then, it should appear probable, that Latin and Greek possess two elements in common, namely, the Celtic and the Sclavonian, or Pelasgian; and, therefore, that the difference which has since sprung up between them was caused by the supervention of a Persian or High German dialect in Greece, and a Low German, probably Lithuanian, in Italy. But this

---

[1] *New Crat.* p. 90.

[2] "That the Pelasgians were of Sclavonic origin is pretty clear (not to speak of historic probability) from the agreement of even modern Sclavonic with Latin, and the oldest element of Greek. The resemblance of Russian to the Latin is so striking, that a modern traveller has not hesitated to assert *that the founders of Rome spoke the Russian language.*"—*New Crat.* p. 91.

theory, though probably true in its general outline, is still only a very rough approximation towards the ascertaining of the real constitution of these languages. Much, as it seems to us, is still left for the investigation of modern scholars; much that nothing but great versatility in modern languages, as they are sometimes called, can hope to elucidate. That the Latin language bears evident traces of Low German influence, it is impossible for a moment to deny; for the merest tyro in Latin and Anglo Saxon cannot fail to perceive them. The question rather is, what was the exact nature,—the particular dialect—of this Low German element, and in what relative order to the other components of the Latin tongue was its agency felt? The similarity which exists between many Anglo Saxon and Latin words, and, in many cases, the identity of the radicle, seems to point, if not to the Saxon itself, at least to a dialect closely akin to the Saxon, and not improbably the Gothic. We, however, must content ourselves at present with calling the attention of others to the striking similarity which exists between a large body of Anglo Saxon and Latin words. Not, indeed, that we wish to pride ourselves on this, as a new discovery, but simply, because it seems, that we have here a vein which has by no means been worked out. Nor will this investigation be altogether an easy one, or free from biassing influences. For instance, the ecclesiastical subjection of this country to Rome, which took place at a comparatively short period after the settlement of the various German tribes in this island, had, no doubt, the effect of introducing many Latin words, particularly ecclesiastical words into the Saxon of this country. Five, says the venerable Bede, was the number of languages spoken in this island in his day, the Angle, the British, the Scottish, (Lowland Scotch) the Pictish, and the Latin, which *by the study of the Scriptures has become common to all the rest*.[1]   And, as a natural

---

[1] Hæc in præsenti, juxta numerum librorum quibus lex divina scripta est, quinque gentium linguis unam eandemque summæ veritatis et veræ

consequence, nearly all the ecclesiastical words in Anglo Saxon are of Latin or Greek formation. As for instance, the Greek ἐπίσκοπος, *An Overseer,* which became in the Latin *Episcopus,* and when transferred to French soil assumed the form *Évesque,* and finally, *Évêque,* took up its position in this country as a Saxon word, under the form Biscop. So the Latin *Clericus* produced the Saxon *Cleroc,* or *Clerc,* a clerk, that is a priest.[1]

Again, our word *Kirk,* or *Church,* is the Anglo Saxon Cyricea, most probably[2] formed from the Greek τὸ κυριακὸν, (Eccl.) the *Lord's house.* The Saxon word Sacred, *A priest,* is probably connected with (per metathesin) the Latin word *Sacerdos.* And the same remark applies to a number of other words, which have found a place in the Anglo Saxon, such as Discipul, *A disciple;* Diacon, *A deacon;* Canon, *A canon;* Biblioðece, *A library;* Capitul, *A chapter;* Cantic, *A song,* &c.

These and similar examples shew, that, in striking a comparison between Anglo Saxon and Latin words, care is requisite to avoid all such as are likely to have owed their existence in the Anglo Saxon to the influence of the ecclesiastical Latin, which, in the words of the venerable Bede, became common to the other tongues spoken in Great Britain, "meditatione scripturarum," by the study of the Scriptures.

Such examples of similitude, or resemblance, in the two languages prove nothing as to their prior relationship, or their relative antiquity. Nor, indeed, is there the least necessity to choose such words, for others exist in great

---

sublimitatis scientiam scrutatur et confitetur, Anglorum videlicet Brittonum, Scottorum, Pictorum, et Latinorum, quæ meditatione scripturarum, cæteris omnibus est facta communis.—*Hist. Eccl.* lib. I. c. 1.

[1] The use of *clerk,* in its modern acceptation of a writer, arose from the fact, that for a length of time during the middle ages the clergy, priests, or clerici, were nearly the only persons who possessed the power of writing.

[2] We say probably, because some have been pleased to look to the Saxon verb Ceósan, *To choose,* for the root of *Church.*

abundance against which no such objection as the above can be urged. A few such instances, which seem to be trustworthy, and point clearly to the close affinity which existed at some former time between the Latin, and, we do not say the Anglo Saxon precisely, but, at any rate, some Low German dialect, will be found collated in the Appendix to this page. One cannot see two such words as *Erian* and *Arare*, both answering to the same English verb *To plough*, without being satisfied, that both must have had a common origin. Again, the very names of man and woman are radically the same in both Latin and Anglo Saxon. In the latter they appear as *Vĕr* and *Fœmne*, while in the former, the Latin, they take the form almost unchanged of *Vir* and *Fœmina*.[1]

But it is no part of our intention to pursue this investigation here, and our object in alluding to it at all is merely to point out the true relationship existing between Latin and Anglo Saxon, and, as a necessary consequence, between Latin and our own English. There seems the greater necessity that this should be done, because there is prevalent a vicious method of referring English words to what are falsely called Latin roots, when in reality the root both of the English and Latin is to be found in some Low German dialect. After what has been said of the nature and composition of the Latin language, it is almost needless to add, that, in the pursuit of etymological enquiry, even with respect to our own language, the Latin occupies a mediate and subordinate position. It is itself a compound tongue whose elements will be found, so far as it is now possible to find them, in extraneous sources. There is considerable danger of confounding together, what we shall call the *ultimate* and *proximate* elements of

---

[1] The word in the old Scandinavian is *feima*: in Saxon *fĕhmĕa, fadmia*; in Frisian, *fámne, fómne, fóvne*. Ettmuller makes the following almost superfluous remark on the origin of the word:—"Vox *fœmne* ex Latina voce *fœmina*, an originem sumpserit, dubito; neque fàm et fœmne ad faþan referri posse videntur, etsi Sax. *Fadmia* et Anglo-Sax. Faðu, amita, cum verbo faþan (alere, amplecti) congruant."

a language.[1] No one will deny, that French is an element in the English language; or again, that Latin is an element in the French language; yet in neither of these cases have we an ultimate element. The French is formed by the amalgamation of the old Gallic Latin with the German, or Teutonic dialect spoken by the Franks, who invaded, and settled in northern France about the middle of the fifth century of this era; while the Latin, as we have seen, is also compounded of a Low German and some other element, whose exact nature is less easily defined. And thus it appears, that neither the French, nor the Latin, have any claim to be considered as themselves ultimate elements of our English. We have attempted, by the aid of the following rough chart, to illustrate the successive steps in that process, which have led to the formation of the English tongue; as also, to show in what relative order the various dialects of which it is composed entered into its composition.

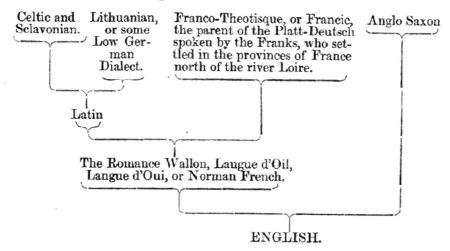

ENGLISH.

[1] If we may be pardoned for borrowing a simile from the laboratory in illustration of the meaning of *ultimate* and *proximate*, we would say, that, while albumen, casein, and fibrin are the *proximate* elements of food, because they approximate nearest to those substances which our digestive organs can receive and operate upon; the ultimate elements are those, of which albumen, casein, fibrin, are themselves compounded, namely, carbon, oxygen, hydrogen, and nitrogen.

Such appears to be the pedigree of the English language. Of its nearest relation, and that to which it still bears the strongest family likeness, we will not speak particularly here, but a word, or two, respecting those diverse elements, which have entered into its composition through the French side, may not perhaps be superfluous. With regard to the assumed constitution of the Latin it will at once be seen, that we have followed Dr. Donaldson. Of the exact nature of the old Francic, the combination of which with the Latin gave rise to the Romance Wallon, but little is known. It presents a closer affinity to High German, than either the Old Saxon, the Anglo Saxon, the Dutch, or the Frisian. Its original locality, and that from which it spread, by means of the conquests of the Carlovingian Franks through a large extent of Germany and France, were the parts on the Lower and Middle Rhine about Cologne. The written language of Germany, and the language of literature, at this day, is High German. Yet it is remarkable, that the districts, where the Highest German is spoken, are Hanover and Brunswick, Platt-Deutsch districts.[1] For some length of time after the subjugation of Northern France by the Franks, both the old Latin, spoken by the Gauls, who affected the name of Romans, and the Francisque existed as separate tongues. The settlement of the Franks in upper Gaul took place about the middle of the fifth century; yet the historian tells us, that Charlemagne, who was declared Emperor of the West in the year A.D. 800, or three centuries and a half later, still spoke the " patrium sermonem," or language of his ancestors. The fact is, that no less than three languages were in use during this period; for while the Francisque, or German, continued to be employed in the court, in conversation and in martial and historic poems, the Latin was still the written language, and the rustic population spoke a kind of *patois* which partook, more, or less, of the nature of both the German and the Latin. As time advanced, however,

[1] Dr. Latham's " *English Language.*" Vol. i pp. 135- 137.

this compound of the Latin and German gained ground amongst the people, until at last its existence became formally rocognized by the Council of Tours A.D. 813, which directed, that the Bishops should translate their homilies into the two languages of the people, the Romance and the Theotisque, or German,[1] instead of delivering them in Latin as had heretofore been the case.[2] It was not, however, until a century later that this new tongue received its full developement and recognition. Rollo, the Dane, acquired the Dukedom of Normandy in the year A.D. 912, and, strange though it may seem, William Longue-Epee, his immediate descendant, by adopting and introducing it at his court, gave to it a status and stability which, otherwise, it might never have possessed in his province.

While the inhabitants of southern France prided themselves on their nearer connexion with Rome, and called themselves *Romans Provençaux*, that is, Romans of the Province, and their language the Provincial Roman, or Romance Provençal; the Celtic population of the north were known to the Franks by the name of Waelchs,[3]

[1] Sismondi's "Literature of the South of Europe," Vol. I. p. 188.

[2] This historic fact is worthy of notice, because it shows that the Romish Church in the earlier period of its existence, never contemplated the monstrous imposition of administering her religious ordinances in a tongue which the common people could not understand.

[3] So in England, the Celtic population were called *Wealhas*, (a word signifying *foreigners*), modern Welsh, though the name was applied, not to the Welsh only, but also to the British inhabitants of Wessex, and those who took refuge in *Cornwall.* Had we not known from other sources, that the conquered Britons sought and found an asylum in this corner of the country, the name alone, which it bore amongst the Saxons, would have afforded a sufficient indication of the fact. It was called by them *Cornwealas*, a name, which might be freely translated "*the Welsh of Corn.*" As to the meaning of this word *Corn*, in the absence of any other hypothesis known to us, we feel inclined by a somewhat ambiguous remark of Thierry's in his "Norman Conquest," Vol. I. p. 16, and Note (2) thereto, to consider it a contraction of the Latin word *Cornu*, a Horn. Thierry says, that *Cornu Galliæ* is the same name with that of the westernmost county of England, Cornwall. It seems, indeed, probable enough, that the first syllable *Corn* is

or Walloons, and their language by that of the *Romance Wallon*. And such was the language introduced into this country by William the Conqueror, and such its composition. It is thus, that the Latin occupies the important position it does in the English language. To the other, the Francisque element, little attention has hitherto been directed in this country. In its nature it bears a somewhat close resemblance to the other Low German element and main constituent of our tongue, the Anglo Saxon. We have had occasion in a former part of this book to notice English words, which may be traced to Germany, either through Anglo Saxon, or the Francisque. In some cases a word will be found to have existed in both, and yet to have transmitted no offspring, or representative, to our English. The Anglo Saxon *Orgel*, and the modern French *Orgueil*, both signifying *Pride*, is an example to the point. It might perhaps too be considered a debatable question, whether the word *Trouble* has any just claim to be considered a German word on the Francic side. Mr. Horne Tooke, indeed, would make it one on the Anglo Saxon; carelessly assuming, that because *Trouble* is an English word, and the Anglo Saxon verb *Tribul-an*, sounds very like it, the former must necessarily be the offspring of the latter; never stopping for a moment to ask, whether such a substantive as *Trouble* or its like, ever existed in the Anglo Saxon. Dean Trench, if we recollect rightly, considers it as nothing more than the old Latin word *Tribulum*, a kind of threshing machine, or roller with which the ancients beat out their corn, used in a metaphorical sense; and, therefore, to this extent a new word. This hypothesis seems far the most likely; for although in the old Francic there may have been, not only a verb corresponding to the Anglo Saxon *Tribulan* (doubtless connected with the Latin *Tribulo Tero*, &c.) but also, that

a contraction of the Latin *Cornu*, but, if Thierry's remark implies further, that the second syllable, -*wall*, is a contraction, or rather a corruption, of *Galliæ*, then we must decline to acquiesce, since the Saxon termination *Wealas* seems to us decisive on this point.

which in the Anglo Saxon is wanting, a substantive answering to *Trouble*; yet, in the absence of any proof of this, it is far more probable, and credible, that the French and consequently the English word *Trouble* (for it never was Anglo Saxon) is the easily modified form of the Latin *Tribulum* used figuratively.

This is a digression, yet it may perhaps serve the purpose of impressing on the mind, that, besides the Latin, another German element, of which we will not say more, than that it closely resembled and was ultimately connected with the Anglo Saxon, crept into our language along with the French. Both Saxons and Franks left the homes in which we first find them,—and those homes not far remote from each other—not more so than the rivers Elbe and Rhine—about the same time; and it is by no means certain, that the Germans, who settled in Kent, were not, to some extent at least, of Frankish origin.

Thus it appears, that at the Norman invasion, there was another accession of the German element to our language, along with the Latin which had absorbed it. True, that element occupies but a subordinate place in the composition of the French language, pretty much the same, indeed, as the French itself does in the composition of the English; yet, nevertheless, it exercised a very decided influence on the character of the Latin language, which had previously been spoken in France. And this, too, in a manner precisely similar to that in which the Norman French affected the Saxon; namely, in destroying the pre-existent organization of the national tongue, and leaving it in that condition, without making any attempts to restore the devastation it caused. The resemblance of the present French verbal conjugation to the Latin, is perhaps, more minute and striking, than that of the English to the Saxon; yet the inflexions of Nouns Substantive, the comparison of Adjectives and Adverbs, and, perhaps generally, the useful conventionalities of language have been every whit as severely dealt with in the old Latin as in our old Saxon.

Still, as in English, the character and bulk of the language is Saxon, so in French the character and bulk is Latin.[1]

So far, then, as relates to our own language and the fresh constituents which have had access to it through the French, we may confine our attention generally speaking to two only, the Latin and the Anglo Saxon, or rather the Anglo Saxon and Latin, for the former has in several respects prior claims to our own consideration. These claims are founded; first on the ground of the intrinsic linguistic importance of the Anglo Saxon—its great antiquity and its freedom from adulteration; secondly, on the ground of its relative importance to us as the only descendants of those whose language it formerly was.

On these grounds the claims of Anglo Saxon far exceed those of the Latin language. It seems, that our long continued connexion with Rome, whether that connexion have been of a military, ecclesiastic, or literary nature, has had the effect of concealing this great fact from our eyes and leading us almost unconsciously to assign to her language a position of importance, which is due from us rather to the Anglo Saxon. We wish it to be clearly understood, that we are speaking of Latin, not as a medium of literature, not as it has been adorned by men of the greatest genius, and refined by writers the most brilliant, and orators the most eloquent that the world has ever seen; but we are speaking of Latin as a language, and in its relation to the other members of the great European family. So much of Latin etymology has been lost, or, if not lost, has, at least, not yet been investigated; the process and *rationale* of its construction is so obscure; that it can occupy but a secondary position in the rank of those languages, which are fitted to throw light on the earliest operations of the mind as they developed themselves in the form of speech.

Nor need we be surprised at this.

Cast but a pebble on the smooth surface of the brook and the trembling agitation is borne in a thousand concen-

---

[1] See Appendix to this page.

tric annulations to the surrounding waters; cast in another, and immediately the pleasing regularity is lost, and a hopeless confusion succeeds. Or, watch the waves of the ocean as they break in regular succession on the shingly beach of some sheltered bay, and then ascend some beetling crag which overlooks the seething caldron fathoms below. Watch those furious waves as they rush on like crested warriors to storm the rock-bound coast, watch how they lash its basement, leap up its sides for a moment, and then repulsed return but to carry confusion amongst their yet advancing comrades.

And the history of the population of the world, as it has been accomplished by successive waves of migration transmitted apparently from one common centre, seems but to find a parallel in the above simile.

CHAPTER XI.

THE VALUE OF ANGLO SAXON—FIRST, AS ILLUSTRATING
THE FORMATION OF LANGUAGE GENERALLY, AND OF
ENGLISH IN PARTICULAR;—SECONDLY, AS DISCOVER-
ING THE TRUE MEANING OF ENGLISH WORDS.—
EXAMPLES.—CONCLUSION.

The Sanscrit is a language which admits of complete
analysis, the most perfect and symmetrical of any now in
existence. The reason why it is so is obviously because no
ulterior circumstances have occurred to disarrange those
forms of thought in which the human mind at first
disposed itself. And doubtless the fewer the causes which
at any past time have tended to disturb the original shape
and disposition of a language, the more correctly will that
language register the history of its formation. Of course
this amounts to the same thing as saying, that the purer
the descent the clearer will be the insight afforded into the
logic of the formation of language. In this respect the
Anglo Saxon has pre-eminently the advantage over both
Latin and Greek. Its descent is much purer, and consequently its antiquity is greater. Like the Sanscrit it has
had fewer catastrophes to modify, or destroy its primæval
articulation, and it, therefore, more clearly reveals the successive processes of human thought engaged in its construction. It admits of a very tolerable analysis, too, which has
not, perhaps, even yet been pushed to its extreme limits.
Give us the monosyllabic portion of the language, two, or
three, primary verbs; tell us the meaning of a few terminal forms—these probably will turn out to have been,
or to be, monosyllabic substantives too—and we may be
said to possess the materials out of which the language has
been formed.

We can do little more than call attention to this
remarkable characteristic in the construction of the Anglo

Saxon language; a characteristic, which, while it creates a broad line of distinction between the Saxon and those other languages with which Englishmen usually come in contact, does at the same time exalt it far beyond them in point of illustrating the principles on which language generally, and our own in particular, has been constructed. At the risk of being thought tedious, however, we will, by way of illustrating this position make a few extracts, principally from Dr. Bosworth's larger Anglo Saxon grammar, to the chapters on the Verb and Noun in which we must refer the reader, if he wish to see the subject more fully discussed.

ANGLO SAXON NOUNS SUBSTANTIVE.

We start, then, from the Noun, or Noun Substantive, the most important and essential part of speech.

Anglo Saxon Substantives are of two kinds, *Simple* and *Compound*. The former, as their name would imply, are monosyllabic in form; the latter are formed by combining two, or more, of the simple Substantives together. Thus, from Ac, *An oak*, and Corn, *Corn*, is formed the substantive Acorn, *An acorn*; from Wig, *An idol*, or *temple*, and Cræft, *An art*, is formed *Wigcræft, Witchcraft*, &c.

Besides the casual combination of substantives, there are other terminal syllables, which either are, or have been independent substantives. The following are some of these together with their real, or supposed, signification, and the English forms they have bequeathed to us.

Dóm, *Judgement, Power*, surviving in the English *Doom*, and -*dom*. As from Cyne, *A king*, by the addition of this syllable, is formed the substantive *Cynedom*, a kingdom; from Freo, *A lord*, or *Freeman*, the substantive -Freodom, *Freedom*, &c.

Ríce, *Power, Dominion*. Example: Bisceop-ríce, *A bishopric, i. e.* the dominion of a Bishop.[1]

---

[1] Though this is the only compound of Ríce, which seems to have survived to our time, in the "Vision of Piers Ploughman," we find *Kyng-ryche,* and *Herene-riche.*

Hád, *A person, habit, sex, state, order, degree.* This substantive survives in the English termination *-hood;* or, as it is generally written by Chaucer, *-hade,* a form still more closely resembling the Saxon model. Examples: Broðor-hád, *Brotherhood;* Mæden-hád, *Maidenhood;* Man-hád, *Manhood;* Preost-hád, *Priesthood,* &c.

Scir, *A share, or part cut off, A shire, or district.* Examples: Preost-scy're, the *Priest's shire,* or *Parish,*[1] Scir-gerifa, *A shire-reeve; i. e.* by contraction *A sheriff.*

---

[1] The attempt has been made, as it seems to me without sufficient grounds, to derive the word *parish* from the Anglo Saxon preost-sc'yre, by contraction. If it is so derived, then the contraction is at least an extraordinary one. But, indeed, the earlier forms in which the word occurs, as for instance in "the Vision of Piers Ploughman," and in Chaucer, seem to point rather to a Norman, than a Saxon origin, as the following quotations will show :—

> "And yvele (*evil*) in this y-holde
> In *parisshes* of Engelonde;
> For persons (*parsons*) and parish-preestes
> That sholde the people shryve,
> Ben curatours (*Curates*) called,
> To know and to hele
> All that ben hir *parisshens,*
> Penaunce to enjoigne."   *Lines* 14483—14490.

And again, in Chaucer's graphic description of the Persone, one of the guests at "the Tabard," who contributed various homilies on religious and moral subjects for the edification of his fellow pilgrims, and as his share towards their mutual divertisement.

> "A good man there was of religioun,
> That was a poure persone of a toune
> But rich he was of holy thought and werk,
> He was also a lerned man, a clerk,
> That Cristes gospel trewely wolde preche.
> His *parishens* (parishioners) devoutly wolde he teche.
> Benigne he was and wonder diligent,
> And in adversite full patient:
> And swiche he was ypreved often sithes,
> Ful loth were him to cursen for his tithes,
> But rather wolde he yeven out of doute,
> Unto his pour parishens about,
> Of his offring, and eke of his substance.
> He coude in litel thing have suffisance.
> Wide was his *parish,* and houses fer asonder,
> But he ne left nought for no rain ne thonder
> In sikenesse and in mischief to visite
> The ferrest in his *parish,* moche and lite,
> Upon his fete, and in his hand a staf."
> *Prologue to Cant. Tales, line* 469.

If *parish* had been contracted from the Saxon preost-sc'yre, these early

Scip, *A shape, form, state, dignity*, answering to the English termination -*ship*. Examples : Freond-scip, *Friendship ;* Weorð-scip, *Worship.*

-*er*, or -*ere*, from the Saxon Wér, *A man*, corresponding to our termination -*er*. As, for example : Writ-ere (*i. e.* Writ-wér) *A man who writes, A writer*. Fiscere (*i. e.* Fisc-wér) *A man who fishes ; A fisherman*.

Such are some of the terminating syllables and their meanings. Others there are besides, whose signification is more obscure; such are -*ing*, -*ling*, -*incle*, -*els*, -*el*, -*a*, &c.

But we must pass on to take a hasty glimpse at the construction of the Saxon verbs.

SAXON VERBAL FORMATION.

The mental operation, which has been engaged in the formation of the next important part of speech, the Verb, is, if we assume the truth of the theory propounded by the best Anglo Saxon scholars, and in itself highly probable on account of its simplicity, no less conspicuous, than that in the formation of the compound substantives.

Indeed, the process seems little more, than converting Substantives into Verbs by the simplest method possible,— that of affixing to them one of the three " almost primitive" verbs Unnan, or An, *To give*, Gangan, or Gan, *To go*, and Agan, *To have*, or *possess*.

By the aid of these transforming elements the vast class of Saxon verbs has been constructed out of the Substantives. What could be more simple ? there is here no fresh

---

forms of it would have exhibited a closer resemblance to the Saxon than they do. But the resemblance of *parish* and *parishens* to the French forms *paroisse* and *paroissien*, seem to us conclusive, that at least no Saxon root is involved. Whence comes the French *paroisse* we cannot now stop to enquire.

call for ingenuity, or invention, and no waste of intellectual resource.[1]

The meaning of the verb varies slightly, according as the substantive is verbalized by one or other of these primary verbs.

The following examples will sufficiently illustrate the method of verbal formation.

The verb Unnan, or An, *To give*, affixed to the substantives :

Cnott, *A knot,*		Cnytt-an,	*To give a knot, To knit.*
Coss, *A kiss,*	produces the verbs	Coss-an,	*To give a kiss, To kiss.*
Dæl, *A part,*		Dæl-an,	*To give a part, To deal, or divide.*
&c.		&c.	

The verb Gan, *To go*, affixed to the substantives

Bæð, *A bath,*		Bæð-ian,	*To go to a bath, To wash.*
Bidde, *A prayer,*	produces the verbs	Bidd-an,	*To go to Prayer, To pray.*
Cíd, *A quarrel,*		Cíd-an,	*To go to a quarrel, To quarrel.*

The verb Agan, *To have, possess, acquire*, affixed to the substantives

[1] The following is part of Dr. Bosworth's note on the formation of verbs, p. 134:—

"*Anan*, which in its simplest form is *An*, makes *end, and*, &c., for *anend* (in the present participle); *and, ad, od*, &c. for *anad*: *gangan*, which is only *gan* doubled, makes *gend, gand*, &c., and *ged, gad*, &c. for *gangend*, and *gangad*."

[2] It may seem that the verbs compounded of *Gan* terminate the same as those of *An*, and that, therefore, the distinction is fanciful rather than real. It is not so, however; for the older forms of verbs compounded of Gan, *To go*, end in -*gan* and not -*an*. The earlier forms of the examples above given were Bæð-gan, Bidde-gan, Cíd-gan. See "*Bosworth's Anglo Saxon Grammar*," p. 135, *note*.

O

Blostm,	*A flower,*		Blostm-ian,[1]	*To have a flower, to blossom.*
Car,	*Care,*	produces the verbs	Car-ian,	*To have care.*
Luf,	*Love,*		Luf-ian,	*To have love, to love.*

Sometimes, however, the substantive, which forms the hypothecate of the verb, has disappeared from the language in which its existence has been perpetuated by that verb, and must be sought for in some kindred tongue. Amongst this class Dr. Bosworth would write the Anglo Saxon verbs :—

Bér-an,	*To bear,*	derived from	Bar, (Franco Theotisc),	*Fruit.*
Writ-an,	*To write,*		Writs, (Gothic),	*A letter.*
Cunn-an,	*To know,*		Can, (Keltic),	*A head.*
Cenn-an,	*To procreate,*		Con, (Icelandic),	*A woman.*

When words had been formed to express *action* of various kinds, nothing is easier to conceive, than that those parts of the verb which express the continuation, or state of action, and the completion, or effect of action, which parts are the 3rd person singular of the indefinite, or present tense, and the past participle (probably, little else than the past participle of one of the three primary verbs above noticed, affixed to the radicle or substantive portion of the verb), should in turn be used to designate; first, *agents,* or *objects,* in which the main idea of the verb is prevalent; secondly, *things,* which are the result of the completed action of the verb; and thirdly, *states, conditions, qualities,* &c., which are intimated to us by such action.

Hence we arrive, by means of the verb, at the three following classes of words :

1st.   At a class of Substantives ending in the Anglo Saxon in -ð, and in English in -*th*, examples of which, as *filth, health, wealth,* &c., may be found on page 49.

---

[1] Earlier forms—Blostm-agan, Car-agan, Luf-igan.

2nd. At another class of Substantives, formed from the past participle ending in *-d, -t,* or *-n,* in examples of which, such as *bread, head, weft, haft, welkin, yarn,* &c., the whole language is sufficiently abundant.

3rd. At a class of adjective words, descriptive of *state, condition,* or *quality,* ending, as in the last class, in *-d, -t,* or *-n;* examples of which are *lost, own, forlorn, afeard,*[1] &c.

So much for the Verb, its formation and the functions it discharged in enriching and furnishing language. The third class of verbal derivatives naturally leads us to the consideration of *descriptive,* or *adjective* words generally, and the methods by which the want of such words, in any but the most barbarous societies of men, was supplied.

ADJECTIVAL FORMATION.

The first form in which we meet with the Adjective is the same as that of the Substantive; that is, the same word was used to express, not only a substance, or thing, but also the nature, or quality of that substance, or thing. Thus, the same word, both in Anglo Saxon and English is used to express both the Substantive *Light,* and the quality or nature of *Light.* So also with the word *Deep,* or *The deep,* the same word expressed both.

The next step in the formation of Adjectives was to append to the monosyllabic Substantives, whether those Substantives appear as the roots of Verbs, or otherwise, one of the terminations *-ed, -en, end,* or *-ig.* The former three of these terminations are Participles past and present of the verb Unnan, *To give,* or *To add;* the latter *-ig,* is from Ican, *To increase* or *add,* and in meaning, therefore,

---

[1] Though we have given examples in English only, the originals in all cases are to be found in the Anglo Saxon.

closely resembling the others, -ed and -en. The termination -end answers to the English present participle in -ing, as Anglo Saxon Lufig-end, *Loving*, &c. The termination -ig has been merged into the English termination -y; as Blod-ig, *Bloody*, Æn-ig, *Any*, Cræft-ig, *Crafty*, &c.

The syllables -en, -ed, in conjunction with Substantives proper, appear in the words :—

Bece,	*beech*..............	Búcene,	*beech-en.*
Bræs,	*brass*..............	Bræsen,	*braz-en.*
Wulle,	*wool*	Wull-en,	*wooll-en.*[1]
Gold,	*gold*	Gy´ld-en,	*gold-en.*
Ly´n,	*flax*	Lin-en,	*linen.*
&c.		&c.	
Ecge,	*edge*	Ecg-ed,	*edg-ed.*
Sceo´,	*a shoe*	Ge-sceod,	*shod.*
Hyrne,	*a horn*	Hyrn-ed,	*horn-ed.*
&c.		&c.	

The meaning of these syllables, which convert the original monosyllabic Substantives into Adjectives, (as before, by the aid of the primitive Verbs, they were converted into Verbs), is simply that of *addition* to some other Substantive, whose nature and quality it is thus intended to subjoin. A "linen shirt," then, only means, if we thoroughly analyze the construction, "flax add shirt;" "brazen goblets," "brass add goblets;" &c.

But, besides these verbal terminations, there are also substantive terminations, which, when affixed to other Substantives, are made to denote quality, and thus produce *Adjective Words*. Such for instance are the Substantives Líc, *A form, figure, body*, (English -*ly*); Sum, *A part, or portion of a thing*; Fyll (*plenitudo*), *The fill, plenty* (English -*full*).

Examples,

God, *God*.................God-lic, *Godlike.*
Freó, *A Lord* ....Freo-líc, *free.*

---

[1] I question the propriety of doubling the final consonant in this and similar words.

Wynne, *pleasure* .... Winsum,   *pleasing.*
Woh,   *woe* .... Woh-full,   *injurious.*
Tung,   *tongue*........... Tung-full,   *loquacious.*
Weorc, *work* .... Weorc-sum, *worksome,* i. e. *irksome.*
Bug-an, *To bow* .... Boc-sum, *flexible, obedient, buxom.*

Other terminations, too, there were used by the Anglo Saxon, which, as they have transmitted no descendants to us, we need not stop to mention here.[1]

Of course the method of analysis, or synthesis we rather ought to say, which we have briefly applied to the construction of the Substantive, the Verb, and the Adjective, is capable of a much more extended application. But we have pursued this subject far enough for our present purpose. We are making no new discoveries. All we have said, and very much more we might say, has been known for years.

Our object is simply to afford some insight into the constructive principles of the Anglo Saxon, and thence, as a necessary consequence, of the English Language. And there are two characteristics which seem to us particularly striking in the formative processes we have been considering.

These two characteristics are *œconomy* and *intelligence.* Starting with nothing more than a few monosyllabic roots, and two, or three, primitive verbs, we have seen how the mind of man has raised a superstructure of Substantive, Verb, and Adjective ; and formed a surface, as it were, capable of receiving every impress, and registering the most varied conceptions of which that mind was capable. When we see for ourselves how replete with meaning, how full of life and individuality words become when

---

[1] The Saxon termination -fæst, has, however, transmitted two which have been already noticed. They are Staþol-fæst, *steadfast*, and Scam-fæst, *shamefast.*

considered from this primæval point of view, it is no
longer difficult to credit the assertion, that there is
not in language,—that is in language where the plastic
moulding of the mind has not been defaced by subsequent catastrophe,—that there is not in such language
anything arbitrary, or any such thing as capricious usage.
Yet who dare assert this of our own language, or indeed of
half the languages of southern Europe? Would the English of to day, bear the rigid test which the Anglo Saxon
will sustain with such unflinching firmness? Certainly
not. Yet still it is possible, by recurring to the source
whence so many of our words and terminations have sprung,
to restore to them some portion of the life and vitality they
have now lost. And be it observed, that the Anglo Saxon
is the only source whence we can derive information
on these and kindred points; and be it further observed,
that when once words and terminations have lost the intelligent spirit, which at first called into being and animated them, from that time forth, the tie which coupled
them with, and, when pronounced, recalled a particular
emotion of the mind, is dissevered; henceforth they become, to all intents and purposes, mere arbitrary sounds,
significant indeed to the ear, and, for a while it may be,
suggestive of the same emotion as before to the mind, but
fluctuating in their character, and uncertain in their meaning, because the clue which alone could conduct us aright
has been dropped. The immense majority of Saxon words
in the English language has been referred to *ad nauseam,*
and it may perhaps be considered superfluous to call attention to those few unhappy remnants of Inflexion and Syntax
to which we are still pleased to assign the name of English
Grammar. If we do so, it is merely to point out, that
these remains are of a strictly Anglo Saxon character.
Indeed, it seems a remarkable fact, that when our language was swarming with French words, and our country
with Frenchmen—no not Frenchmen—that our English
should be so remarkably free from French inflexion, or
construction; so free, indeed, that we cannot call to mind
a single instance of either.

After the complaint of Robert Holcot, that it was the custom for children in those days[1] first to learn French, and from the French the Latin language, this seems very strange. Yet it is no more strange than true. And here we have a strong argument too in favour of the Anglo Saxon over every other language; because it gives us the key to our own Syntax and Grammatical construction, and affords us a full and entire view of that symmetrical structure, of which the English Language can only be considered the decayed and dismantled ruins. Neither French, nor Latin are of any assistance to us in this respect; German, it is true, is much more so, though the claims of German are not to be compared with those of the Anglo Saxon. Consider for a moment the words *Then, There, When, Where, Wherefore,* &c. Will French, or Latin (or even the German directly) assist us at all in investigating the nature and meaning of these words? And what say our Grammarians? Oh! they call them Adverbs of time, or place; or Interrogatives, or something else equally vague, but equally useful and effective in concealing their own ignorance. While the fact is, that these words are as definite in their nature, and concise in their meaning, as the Latin correlatives *Eo*, here, In that place; *Quâ*, (sc. parte) Where; *Quare*, Wherefore; &c.

There, is nothing more than the regular dative of the Article, or relative pronoun, we have already had

---

[1] Namely, at the beginning of the Reign of Edward III. the following passage, on the education of children in England, is taken from Trevisa's Translation of "Hygden's Polychronicon:"

"Children in Scole against the usage and maner of all other nations beeth compelled for to leve hire owne langage and for to construe hir lessons, and hire thynges in Frenche: and so they have sethe Normans came first into Engelond. Also gentilemen children beeth taught to speke Frensche from the time that they bith rokked in hire cradell and kunneth speke and play with a childes broche. And uplondissche men will likne himself to gentylmen, and fondeth with greet besynesse for to speke Frensche to be told of. This manner was moche used to for first deth (time) and is sith some dele changed. So that now the year of our Lord a thousand thre hundred and four score and five, and of the seoond Kyng Richard after the Conquest nyne and in alle grammere scoles in England children lereth Frensche and construeth."

occasion to notice in the chapter on THAN, and was originally used, not alone, but in conjunction with the substantive Stowe, *A place*, just as the Latin *Eo* was with *Loco*. And "þære stowe" exactly corresponded to the Latin *Eo loco*, in that place. Then, when by frequent use and for the sake of brevity, the *Stowe* in the former, and the *Loco* in the latter were dropped, we have left the two Relative Pronouns "þære" in the Saxon (*There*, English,) and *Eo* in the Latin. And so, had we time, it would be easy to show, that the other words of this class are equally definite in their meaning and construction.[1]

But, indeed, it is not one class of words alone but the whole language, more or less, which has suffered, and still suffers from our neglect. Words are but the paintings of the mind, and like other paintings they are liable to become obscured by neglect and time. Yet, to take down these pictures from the dark corners where they have been too long suspended, to brush away the cobwebs, to remove from them some of the dust and dirt of ages, and bid them stand out from the canvass with somewhat of their old expression and vivacity, seems to be one of the highest aims of practical philology.

For the sake of illustration, we have gathered a few miscellaneous words together, whose meaning seems to receive fresh light by referring them to their Anglo Saxon sources.

---

[1] It is more than probable, that what we are now compelled to call the definite Article, in such constructions as "the more *the* merrier," is in reality the Ablative, or Instrumental case of the same pronoun Se, Seo, þæt, and corresponds exactly to the use of *quo....eo* in similar constructions.

"The second condition of veray confession is, that it be hastily done: for certes, if a man hadde a dedly wound ever the lenger that he taried to warishe himself, the more wold it corrupt and haste him to his deth, and also the wound wold be the werse for to hele."

The Persones Tale.

A. S. Wíf,[1] *a Woman, a Female, Wife.*

This word in the Anglo Saxon had a much wider application than it has in English. It was in fact a feminine affix, used to denote the female gender. Accordingly, we find

> Wífcild, *i. e. A female child, a girl,*
> Wífcynn, *The female kind,*
> Wíflác, *Matrimony,*

as well as Wífmann; *i. e. A female specimen of the Human species, (Fœmina homo)* whence by contraction comes the word *Woman.* In the Anglo Saxon, however, Wífmann signified, not only *A woman,* but also a *Lay Person* who was permitted to marry.

A. S. Wér, (Lat. *Vir*), *a Man,*

still enters into the composition of the following words :—

> *Canterbury, i. e.* A. S. Cantwaraburh, The town of the men of Kent.
> *Wer-wolf,* The man-wolf, or devil.
> *World,* The world,[1] An age, or generation of men.

A. S. Row-an, *To row.*
Roðer, *An oar.*

From the latter of these comes the word *Rudder,* that part by which a ship is steered. How it has come to have this signification is fully explained by its own ety-

---

[1] Some of the German writers on Anglo Saxon ignore the letter *W*, and write *V* in its place. Yet, it should seem they are scarcely justified in doing so, unless, indeed, as is not likely, they pronounce the *V* like our *W*. We cannot but think, that the pronunciation of our provincial English must be a surer guide to the pronunciation of Anglo Saxon, than that of the present High German spoken on the continent.

[1] Qui cum *viro* aliquo unâ eodem tempore vivunt.—Ettmuller, sub voce.

mology, and by the fact, that the earliest method of steering ships was by means of the oars (for I believe there were two) placed near the stern of the vessel.

A. S. Stíg, *A way, A path.*
Stíg-an,[1] *To ascend.*

Hence are derived,

Stair or *Stairs*, from Anglo Saxon Stæ'ger, *A step, degree.*
Stee, the provincial word for, *A ladder.*
Stile, Anglo Saxon Stigel, *A step, a ladder.*
Stirrup, from the combination of the above root Stíg with the Anglo Saxon Ràp, *a rope.* A stirrup, therefore, is nothing more than a *Stee-rope*, or ladder of rope, for the purpose of ascending the saddle. But, indeed, there is no occasion to go so far back as the Anglo Saxon Stíg-ràp. In the "Romance of King Richard," the word occurs in a form but slightly different:

> "In his shield verament
> Was paynted a serpent,
> Wyth the spere that Richard held.
> He bare him thorugh under his shelde,
> Non of hys armour might him last,
> Brydell and peytrell all to-braste,
> Hys gyrthes and his *steropes* also.
> Hys mare to ground whent tho."

A. S. Georn, *Eager, anxious.*
Geornian, *To desire.*

Hence have descended to us,

Earnest, which is merely the Saxon Geornest, that is, the superlative of the above Adjective; and the verb *To yearn,* or *long for.*

A. S. Gise, Gese, *Yes.*

According to Ettmuller, this particle of affirmation is composed of the Anglo Saxon Gea, *Even so,* and Si, *Let*

---

[1] See also "Tooke's Diversions of Purley," p. 509.

it be. *Yes,* therefore, implies assent, not from any arbitrary usage, or conventional signification, but because it contains within itself the true condition of assent.

A. S. Ceósan, *To choose.*

Corn, Anglo Saxon Corn, *i.e.* the Past Participle of the above Verb Coren, *Chosen.* *Corn,* therefore implies by its very name that part of the plant which is *chosen,* or separated from the straw and chaff.

Cyrnel, is probably a verbal derivative from the same source and with the same meaning as *Corn.*

A. S. Fangan or Fo'n, *To take, Seize, Receive, Undertake.*

The following important words seem undoubtedly connected with Fangan, or Fo'n, *To take:*

Finger, Anglo Saxon Finger; that is, the part which *takes* or *receives a thing.*

Fang, Anglo Saxon Fang, *A taking,* or *grasp.* This word, however, may perhaps be the root of the verb itself.

Although one feels strongly inclined to look to this verb as that from which we have derived the word *faith,* we fear the objections against such a derivation are too strong to be overcome. Mr. Horne Tooke, indeed, attempted long ago to set the matter at rest, but his theory, though plausible enough, in outward appearance, will be found to fail when put to the test. He says "*Faith,* Anglo Saxon Fægð—That which one covenanteth or engageth. It is the third person singular of the indicative of Fægan, Pangere, Pagere, *To engage, To covenant, To contract.*" Unfortunately for Mr. Tooke the only meaning of Fægð, or Fæhð, (for it is written in both ways) in the Anglo Saxon is *A feud*, or *quarrel*, and is a derivative, not of the verb Fægan,[1] *To plant, To fix*, but of

Fian, *To hate*,

which is also, as Mr Tooke has shown, connected with *Fiend*, Anglo Saxon Feónd, and *Foe*, Anglo Saxon Fáh, the former being the Present Participle, the latter the Past Tense of the same verb.

Indeed, the verb Fægan has not produced any verbal substantive in -ð. And the same objection lies against looking for a solution to the verb Fo'n, *To take ;* because neither has thus transmitted a Substantive, which, either in sound or meaning, could possibly have given birth to the word *Faith*. If the Anglo Saxon Fæhð, *Strife, Contention*, be in reality the same word, then we require to know how, in passing from Saxon to English, its meaning has become so seriously modified. That it was unknown as a Saxon word in its present acceptation seems pretty certain, for we find the word Geleafa, *Belief*, constantly used where we should now expect to find *Faith*.[2] The question, therefore, seems at present an open one.

A. S. Hindan, (*Capere*) *To take*.

As *Finger* is connected with, and owes its name to, the verb Fangan, *To receive*, because it is that which apprehends, or receives a thing, so in like manner, *Hand* (A. S. Hand) is for the same reason connected with the verb Hindan, *To take ;* as also

---

[1] Indeed, it seems not improbable, that Mr Tooke was carried away by the meaning of the Latin *Pango*, or *Pago*, which better suited his purpose, and acquired a wider signification with the Latins than the cognate form, *Fægan*, possessed with the Saxons.

[2] "We habbað gesæced embe þæt Pater noster, nu we wyllað secgan eow þone *geleafan* þe on þam Credan stent, swa swa se wisa Augustinus, be þære Halgan þrynnysse trahtnode."

Homilies of Ælfric. De fide Catholicá.

Handle, (A. S. handel), that by which a thing is *handled*.

Hunter, (A. S. hunta), verbal substantive in *-a*, (signifying *An agent*, or *actor*), one who *takes* prey by pursuit. For the same reason,

Hound, (A. S. hund), *a dog* which takes prey by running it down, is so called.[1]

A. S. Here, *An army*.

We have already had occasion to notice this word as entering into the composition of

Harbour, and
Harbinger.

Besides these, however, and another of its compounds, Herepath, (A. S. Herepæð, *An army-path*), which survives only as a family name, there is another interesting little word which hence derives its origin.

---

[1] Although we can quote no authorities in favour of such an hypothesis it seems far from improbable that the Anglo Saxon and Mæso-Gothic HUND, *A hundred*, is also connected with this family of words. And what seems rather to make in favour of this supposition, is the peculiar use of the word in Anglo Saxon and Gothic computations. The Saxons prefixed this word HUND to numerals, from 70 to 120. The Goths postfixed the same word. Thus, after sixtig, *sixty*, the Saxons wrote HUND-seofontig, *seventy*, &c. up to HUNDtwelftig, *a hundred and twenty*. Both Junius and Ettmuller think the word HUND a mere expletive, yet may it not rather indicate the method by which the Saxons performed their arithmetical calculations, namely, by their *hands* and fingers? The number *ten* of the fingers (for the thumb, if our derivation be correct, is also a *finger*) is generally allowed to account for the universal prevalence of the denary scale of notation, we surely, then, cannot be surprised if we find the word HAND occurring also. If we suppose the *hand* to have been closed when the first *ten* was completed, and as indeed its probable Etymology from A. S. Ty'nan, *To shut*, or *close*, renders it easy to do, and a finger of the other open hand to have been successively bent to denote each successive *ten*, and then this *hand* itself to have been entirely closed to denote the last, or seventh ten, (or some similar process adopted), we shall then perhaps, be better able to understand why HUND was prefixed to numerals from 70 to 120, and also why *hundred* (100) being the tens marked, or reckoned by the closing of the five digits on both hand. is so called. But of course this is hypothetical.

The *Herring* is only the Anglo Saxon Hering,[1] that is, the *Shoal*, or *Army fish*, because it is accustomed to swim in large shoals. Here then we may learn a lesson in Natural History, as well as in Etymology.

Lîsan, To trace, To apprehend, To know.

(Secutus, Consecutus sum, Accepi Scio.[2])

The past participle of this verb, *Lisen*, by the change of *s* into *r* becomes *liren*. Hence we have obtained the following words:

Lore, A. S. Lâr, *doctrine, instruction ; Last, A cobbler's last*, (A. S. Lást, *A trace, A footstep*).

So, then, even the cobbler's *Last* has a meaning of its own, and is not without reason applied to denote the foot-model so necessary to the shoe-maker. Indeed, the very name of shoe-maker in the Anglo Saxon is *Last-wyrhta*, i.e. *Last-worker*. Often as we had heard of the cobbler's *last* we are not ashamed to confess, that it was a mere sound, whose very object was unknown to us, until it sprung into life an Anglo Saxon word. Are we alone in this respect?

There is another old Verb which may properly come under our notice here. It is now obsolete, and would, perhaps, be scarcely deserving of notice were it not that another Verb, still in common use, is, or rather has been, liable to be confounded with it. We mean the verb *To lere*, (Anglo Saxon Lær-an, *To teach*). This verb, being formed regularly, according, to the law of Saxon verbal formation, as already indicated, namely, from Lár, *Doctrine, Instruction*, and one of the primitive verbs, must and did in the Saxon signify *To give instruction, To teach*. The root of the second verb Leorn-ian, which enters also into the composition of Leorn-ere, *A learner*, or *scholar*, and Leornung, *Learning*, is undoubtedly connected with Lár, *Doctrine*,

---

[1] The aptitude of the name must at once commend itself to anyone, who has had the good fortune of being out at sea, when the herrings were on the water.

[2] These are the meanings which Ettmüller attaches to the word. It is somewhat difficult to render them accurately and yet intelligibly in English.

Instruction ; but the Verb Leorn-ian, which is formed from it, signifies the act of *obtaining instruction,* in contradistinction to that of *imparting* it. Even in Chaucer's time, both these verbs were used, though it should seem indifferently, and without a just appreciation of their different meanings, as the following passage will show :—

> "This cursed craft whoso wol exercise,
> He shal no good have, that him may suffice,
> For all the good he spendeth thereaboute
> He lesen shal, therof have I no doute.
> Whoso that listeth uttren his folie,
> Let him come forth and *lernen* multiplie:
> And every man that hath ought in his cofre,
> Let him appere and wex a philosophre,
> Ascaunce that craft is so light to *lere.*
> Nay, nay, God wot, al be he monk or frere,
> Preest, or chanon, or any other wight,
> Though he sit at his book both day and night
> In *lerning* of this elvish nice lore,
> All is in vain, and parde mochel more
> To *lerne* a lewed man this subtiltee."
>
> *The Chanon Yemannes Tale.*

In this short quotation, the verb *To learn,* seems used for both *To learn,* and *To teach ;* and not only so, but the Verb *To lere* seems to have dropped its true signification of *teaching,* and to be used in the same loose way as the verb *To learn.*[1]

In the "Vision of Piers Ploughman," however, the distinction between the two verbs *To lere,* and *To learn,* is somewhat more carefully preserved; though even at this early date the Verb *To learn,* seems to have been used to signify either *To lere,* (i. e. *To teach*), or *To learn.* Thus, in the following passage :—

> "'I shal cessen of my sowyng,' quod Piers,
> And swynke noght so harde
> Ne about my bely joye,
> So bisy be na-more;
> And but if Luc lye,

---

[1] Cf. in French the use of *Apprendre. Apprenez-vous le Français?* Do you *learn* French? *Il m' apprend à lire.* He teaches (learns) me to read. Though *Enseigner* is more correct and usual than *Apprendre* in the latter sense. H. N.

He *lereth* us by foweles;[1]
We sholde noght be to bisy
About the worldes blisse;

*   *   *   *

'What,' quod the preest to Perkyn,
'Peter! as me thynketh,
Thou art lettred a litel:—
Who *lerned* thee on boke?'"

Piers tells us how Grace gave each man some gift to guide himself wherewith, "That ydelnesse encombre hym noght, envye ne pride." He says:

"And some he *lered* to laboure,
A lele[2] life and a trewe;
And some he taughte to tilie,
To dyche and to thecche,
To wynne with her[3] liflode
Bi loore[4] of his techynye."

"And some he *lered* to lyve
In longynge to ben hennes;[5]
In poverte and in penaunce,
To preie for alle Cristene,
And all he *lered* to be lele,
And ech a craft love oother."

But the verb *To lere,* is now entirely obsolete, and probably, has been so for a great length of time. The use of its survivor, the verb *To learn,* is now pretty clearly defined, though it would appear that it has only recently become so.

In the Prayer Book version of the Psalms, it frequently occurs in the sense of teaching. Thus, in Psalm xxv. 8, "Such as are gentle them shall he learn his way." Psalm cxix. 66, "O learn me true understanding and knowledge."[6]

---

[1] The fowles of the air.

[2] Loyal.   [3] Their.   [4] Lore.   [5] Hence.

[6] I have not found any instances of this usage in our authorized Version; so that it would appear the error was discovered and rectified previous to the publication of that Version about the year A.D. 1611.

Hornet is the A. S. Hyrnet, *i. e.* Hyrn-ed, *The horned one.*

Beech, book. Both these words spring from the same Anglo Saxon root Bôce or Béce, *A beech tree.* Here again Philology becomes our instructor, not in natural history this time, but in the manners and customs of our early ancestors. It teaches us in a word, that the first *Book* was the *Beech Tree;* that on its bark, or on tablets made out of its trunk, our ancestors were in the habit of incising their rude *Staves* or *Runes,* long before the letters of Greece and Rome became known to them, or, perhaps, even before those letters were invented. The simple connection of these two words is sufficient to tell us all this, even had we no other direct testimony, and even had not the Danish historian, Saxo Grammaticus, who flourished about the 12th century of this era, spoken of " letters carved on wood."[1]

Threshold. Anglo Saxon þærsc-wald (Wald, or Weald, *Wood.*) It is less easy to discover not the meaning, but the *rationale* of the word *Threshold.* What is the story of its formation, and why is it so called?

Assuming the above Etymology to be correct, what should it indicate or imply? The Saxon Verb þærsc-an signifies *To beat, To strike, To thrash, To knock at.* Does the *Thresh-old,* the *Thrash-wood,* then, mean the wood which must be knocked at in order to obtain admission into the house? If not, what does it mean?

Yule is the Geól, or *Merry Feast* of our Saxon ancestors, so called from Gál, *merry, pleasant,* &c. The same word, slightly modified, was used by them to denote the months answering to our December and January. The former was called, " Se æ'ra Geola," *The first Yule ;* the latter, " Se æftera Geolu," *The after,* or *second Yule.*

---

[1] " Literas ligno insculptas secum portarunt." *Sax. Gramm.* III. p. 52.

P

Wedlock. I much doubt whether the composition and meaning of this word are understood by half who use it. As the Saxon Wed-lác, compounded of the Substantives Wed, *A pledge, promise,* or *agreement,* and Lác, *A gift,* it signified first, and literally, *A pledge-gift* (pignus fœderis) and was used, not in the narrow and contracted way it now is, to designate the *matrimonial pledge,* but any *plight* or *treaty.* So says Chaucer in the "Knightes Tale :"

    "Let him beware his nekke lieth to *wedde.*"

That is if Arcite were found, "ever in his lif, by day or night o stound in any countrie of this Theseus" his nekke would be forfeited in consequence.

Farm. Here we have a word so simple and so common, that we should be ashamed to notice it, were it not that its original signification, and the reason of its present application seem to have been forgotten. *Farm* is the Anglo Saxon Feorm,[1] *food, provision.* The Saxon verb, Feormian, whence comes our verb *To farm,* signified *To procure food, To feed, To support, To entertain.* From this its original signification it is easy to conceive how its second arose ;—how, from being used to denote *food, support,* &c., it afterwards came to denote *An establishment* on which food of various kinds is raised.

Welkin. We have a faint recollection of reading somewhere in Lucretius how that the term *Universe* first came to designate the heaven with all its starry multitude, from the supposition, that by one turn, or revolution, every point in it was successively brought before the gaze of the observer. If so, then the word *welkin* is very similar in its construction to the word *Universe.*

The Saxon Wealc, signifies *A revolving,* or *revolution of the heavenly bodies,* and the verb Wealcan, making the past participle Wealcen, signifies *To turn, revolve, roll.*

---

[1] Connected probably with Anglo Saxon Feorh, *life.*

Welkin (Anglo Saxon *wolken*), therefore, simply means, that which is rolled over our heads, whether as applied to the clouds only, or, more generally, to the whole visible area of heaven.

Such are a few of the words we have stumbled across, whose early history and true meaning seem to have become buried in oblivion. We forbear to pursue the enquiry further, not because examples and instances are wanting,—for our whole language abounds with them,— but because our object is simply to call attention to the importance of this subject, to illustrate it further by a few examples to the point, but by no means to exhaust the subject, or to diminish either the obligation, or the interest attaching to a personal investigation.

When a people, who have once possessed a language of their own, and that language too, as was the case with the Anglo Saxons, of a very early type and pure origin, are called to pass through an ordeal so severe as that which it was the lot of this country to pass through, in consequence of the Norman Invasion, it can excite but little astonishment that results of the most vital importance, both to the people and their language, ensue.

And the case before us forms no exception to this general rule. As regards the people, history speaks in a voice of thrilling interest, in tones which cannot fail to excite in the breast of every impartial man amongst us, be he Norman, or Saxon, an agony of sympathy for the sufferers, and of indignation at the profound injustice and inhuman barbarity of their oppressors—whom it were shame to call conquerors. And, as regards their language, there needs not the testimony of history to inform us, for itself is its own chronicler. The effect of that terrible ordeal was as it were to ossify, or convert it to stone. As it entered, so, indeed, in the main as to external form did it emerge. But how changed in other respects! Its vitality destroyed, its animation suspended, its delicate machinery broken and deranged; in a word, the spirit had fled from the body it had formerly quickened, and left it deserted and lifeless. Words which before had been instinct with life, nay, glowing with their early force of meaning, were now mere sounds, depending for their very existence and meaning on the thin superficial soil of diurnal usage. And so have they continued even up to our own time. No satisfactory attempt has as yet been made to catch up again the clue which has so long lain unheeded at our feet, or to restore to the body of our language that intelligent spirit by which it was formerly animated. Yet the body is there, and the limbs are there, only the soul is wanting to quicken and make them live again.

Surely it is not the part of an intelligent people to treat this subject any longer with such apathetic indifference;—a people who, like ourselves, have been called by Eternal Providence to occupy so high a place in the scale of nations, and discharge so many a heaven-sent task in civilizing and christianizing the world;—a people endowed with energy, which has carried them to the frozen north and the torrid belt, and, whithersoever it has carried them, has earned for them a name of glory and renown, until at length their home may be said to be not so much England as the world at large. If, indeed, "the welfare of the coming world is now the proper care of the Anglo Saxon race,"[1] then at least the duty is incumbent on us to make the language of the coming world our proper care also. We must not forget, that still to the old mother country will the eyes of our children in every foreign land be turned for their patterns of excellence and truth in speaking and writing the English language. Surely, then, we cannot be too jealous of its integrity, nor bestow too much pains in increasing its intelligence and preserving its force and accuracy. There seems to us but one way in which this can be effectually and certainly done, and that way is by keeping our eyes steadily fixed on the great model of our language, the Anglo Saxon.

---

[1] "The West Indies and the Spanish Main." By *Anthony Trollope*, p. 85.

But, if after all the importance of this subject fail to receive public recognition, and be left as heretofore to the regard of private and adult individuals only, then all hope of national progress must for the present be abandoned. The time, we feel assured, will come, sooner or later, when we shall look back with wonder and with shame on the hollow disregard wherewith we are now treating our own language.

If on the contrary the time has now arrived, when we are prepared to admit the national importance of increased attention to the study of Anglo Saxon, not so much, perhaps, on its own account as on its intimate bearing on the language we speak and write, then the plan we would humbly advocate is, *that the study of Anglo Saxon be introduced into our public and private schools as soon as possible ;* that there, it should form the *first* language, after the rudiments of English are acquired, to which the attention of pupils is directed.

It should be looked upon not as a fresh study, nor yet the study of a foreign language, but as a continuation of the study of English, and as the means—the only means—whereby a sound and accurate knowledge of the same may be obtained. It should be allowed to take the precedence, not only of the modern languages, which are so called, but also, as by its antiquity, the peculiar nature of its constitution and the purity of its origin it is so well calculated to do, of the languages of Greece and Rome. Its inflections being more perfectly developed than in the English, it admits of a more perfectly organized syntax, and a greater choice in arrangement than is the case with English composition.

In these respects, too, which it may be observed are merely supplemental to its grand object, it is admirably adapted to form a stepping stone—to abridge the wide chasm—between English and the still more elaborate and complicated structures of the Latin and Greek languages.

APPENDICES.

Page 34. *Verbal Substantives.*

VERBAL Substantives are of two kinds, those formed from the third person singular of the present, or indefinite tense of the Indicative Mood, and those from the past participle. Anglo Saxon verbs have but two tenses, the Indefinite and the Definite. The Indefinite, as the name implies, does not define any particular time, whether present, or future, but may refer to either; accordingly, there is no future tense in the Anglo Saxon, nor is there any, properly speaking, in English verbs, though we have got into the habit of supposing there is. "*I will love,*" is nothing more than "*I wish to love,*" *I will,* being the first person singular Indefinite, or Present Indicative of the Saxon verb *Willan,* To Wish, or Will, which makes its definite or past tense *Wolde,* thus also giving us the auxiliary *would,* as in "*I would love.*" So also the forms *shall, should,* are nothing more than the Indefinite, or present, and the Definite, or past, tenses of the Saxon verb Sceal, *I must, I ought, I am obliged,* frequently followed by an Infinitive Mood, which in English escapes our notice when *To,* the only *sign* which distinguishes the Infinitive from the Indicative Mood, is omitted, as it frequently is. "*I shall love,*" is simply "*I must love.*"

Neither was there a Passive Voice in Anglo Saxon any more than there is in English at the present day. The Anglo Saxons wrote "*he is lufod.*" But *he is* is only the Indicative Mood Indefinite tense of the neuter verb Wesan, *To be,* and Lufod is the past participle of the active verb Lufian, *To love.* It may be very convenient to say, that "*I may be loved*" is the Potential Mood Passive Voice of the verb "*to be loved*"; but it is nothing of the kind. The Saxons would have written it thus "Ic mæg beon lufod," where "Ic mæg," *I may,* would be properly referred to the verb Magan, *To be able,* (making its past tense Mihte, *might*); Beon would be the Infinitive Mood governed by Mæg, and Lufod, as before, the past participle of the verb Lufian, *To love.*

The Definite Tense defines past time.

Anglo Saxon Verbs, though they might almost be called English, are divided into two classes, Regular and Irregular.

The Regular verbs form the past tense and the past participle in the same manner as our own regular verbs, such as *To love,* which makes the past tense and the past participle *loved.*

The Irregular verbs form the past tense by a change in the vowel of the root; and the past participle of these verbs end in *en* instead of *ed;* as Sing-an, (root, *sing.*), past tense Sang; past participle Gesung-en; or, in English, *sing, sang, sung.*

With regard to the personal terminations of Anglo Saxon verbs it will be sufficient for our present purpose to say, that generally speaking, the third person singular of the Present or Indefinite Tense ends in ð: and hence are supposed to arise that large class of Anglo Saxon and English Substantives, which like *mirth, birth, filth,* are of such constant use.

Scarcely less numerous, or important, are those substantives which have been derived from the various forms of the past participle. I have collected a few of them by way of example only, as it would occupy far too much space to attempt to do more.

Bread.   Broth.   Cloth.

The Saxon verb Breowan, or Briwan, *To brew,* gives us from the third person Singular of the Indefinite Indicative the Anglo Saxon Substantive Broð,[1] English *Broth;* and from the past participle (though not the regular past participle, which is *Browen,* but with participial ending *ed*) the Anglo Saxon Substantive Bread, English, *Bread.*

It is strange that, while Mr. Horne Tooke derives *Broth* from this verb, of Bread he says "it is the past participle of the verb to Bray (French, *Broyer*), i. e. *To pound,* or *To beat to pieces:* and the subaudition is *corn,* or *grain,* or any other similar substances, such as *chestnuts, acorns,* &c." But this is both absurd and incorrect. It is absurd, because we know that the Anglo Saxon word *Bread* could not be derived from the verb *To Bray,* (French, *Broyer*), *To pound,* inasmuch as the word *Bread* was in existence in England, long before *To bray* was an English verb; and being absurd, it must be incorrect. Indeed, the verb *To bray,* coming to us as it does through the French *Broyer,* has a Celtic origin, and it is a sheer impossibility that the Anglo Saxon word *Bread* can be referred to it. Mr. Tooke's very ingenuity is too much for him, and frequently, instead of assisting, only betrays him into error. Surely he could not have known, or, if he knew, could not have thought of the Saxon word (for such we may call it) *Bread,* when he made this wonderful discovery. For had he known it, he must have seen, that the onus of his task still rested upon him.

[1] Cf. with *Broth* and *Malt* the word *meltith* in the following passage:

" If ye be thinking of the wreck wood that the callants brought in yesterday, there was six unces of it gaed to boil your parritch this morning, though I trow a carefu' man wad have ta'en drammock, if breakfast he behoved to have, rather than waste baith *meltith* and fuel in the same morning."

The Pirate, vol. I. p. 95.

In nothing is speculation more unsafe and deceptive than in Etymology. True, the temptation is sometimes a strong one to connect words together, and thence to seek an explanation, on the ground of mere similarity of sound. Yet the principle is a false one, and will generally lead to false results, or, at best, results on which no real dependence can be placed.

In Etymological, as in every other branch of investigation, there are certain rules to regulate the enquiry, which can on no account be violated without fatal consequences.

In many of his derivations Mr. Tooke appears to ignore the fact, though it is he himself who asserts it, that English is essentially and substantially Anglo Saxon, and to have prosecuted his labours, the great value of which no one can for a moment deny, too much under the impression that English dates only from the time it has been spoken.

I shall give one more example by way of illustration, for the subject is one extensive enough to fill a whole volume, and this I shall take from the Anglo Saxon Verb Hlid-an, *To cover.* This Verb, of which the root is Anglo Saxon Hlid,[1] *A lid,* or *Cover,* makes the past participle Gehlidàd, or Gehlyd, *Covered.* This word, slightly altered in spelling (Gehleod), signified in Anglo Saxon, *A vault as of the heavens,* from which, with some slight alteration of meaning, perhaps might come the English word *Cloud.* Mr. Tooke, indeed, would derive, not *Cloud* only, but those similarly sounding words, *Glade, Blot, Lot,* also, from this Verb, Hlidan, or its compounds. Without absolutely denying that such is really the case, we would say, that Mr. Tooke brings forward nothing to support his hypothesis beyond mere conjecture. While he was on the subject, he might as well have included *Blood* amongst the rest (for it is at least probable that *Blot* and *Blood* were the same word originally), and we could as readily have believed him. With the exception of *Lid* and *Lot,* which really were Anglo Saxon words with the same meaning as they now bear, there is not an iota of evidence to show that these words are derived from the Anglo Saxon Hlidan, *To cover;* and it is by no means certain even that the Anglo Saxon word Hlot (*sors*), English *Lot,* is so derived.

But there is another Anglo Saxon word Gehlíð, *A covering,* which is unquestionably a derivative from this Verb, Hlidan, *To cover.* And this word it was, I suspect, which the Saxons afterwards contracted into the monosyllable Clað, which is nothing more nor less than our English *Cloth.* So then, following out the analogy of Verbal Substantives in ð (th), *Cloth* is no arbitrary word, with a mere conventional and usual meaning, but one

---

[1] A compound of this word Hlid, amongst the Saxons, was Hlid-geát, *A postern-gate, A back-door.* — Query: Is *Ludgate* a corruption of this compound?

for whose formation the very best of reasons can be given; namely, that it essentially denotes that which *clotheth*, or *covereth*, the body. But, indeed, the Verb, Hlidan, might almost be called an English word, since it occurs so late at any rate as the 14th Century. In Adam Davie's "Life of Alexander," unless we are mistaken, a corrupt form of the Anglo Saxon Verb, *Hlidan*, occurs:

> "Hire yalewe har (hair) was fayre attired,
> Mid rich strenge of golde wyred (twisted),
> It *helyd* hire abouten al
> To hire gentil myddle smal.
> Bright and shine was hir face
> Everie fairehede in her was."

In this charming description of Dame Olympias, *helyd* is certainly to be referred to the above Verb, Hlidan, or else to the Anglo Saxon Verb with the same meaning, Hélan, *To cover*, from which also have descended such a numerous progeny. Let us consider for a moment what words this Anglo Saxon Verb, Helan, *To hide*, or *cover*, has bequeathed to us. This Verb, then, produced:

(*a*) A. S. Helm, Something that *covers*. Hence we have obtained,
    1. *Helm*, or *helmet*, That which *covers* the head. Again, as applied to trees, the A. S. Helm, signified the foliage, or covering. Hence, I suppose,
    2. *Haulm*, or *Halm;* and
    3. The *Holme*, or evergreen oak.

(*b*) A. S. Hol, A *hiding* place, cavern, den; whence descend
    4. *Hole* and *Hollow*.

(*c*) A. S. Holt, A *covered* place. Hence,
    5. *Holt*, as Osier holt.

(*d*) A. S. Heolster, A *hiding* place, a cave. Hence,
    6. *Holster*, A cover, or case for a horseman's pistol.

(*e*) A. S. Hule, The husk, or covering of anything, as of corn. Hence,
    7. *Hull* (of a vessel).

(*f*) A. S. Hell, A *concealed* place; also, used by the Anglo Saxons to denote, The *grave*. Hence,
    8. *Hell*.

Berne, Barn.[1] Page 36.

Earlier forms of this word are Beren, Berern, that is Bere-ern. Now Bere-ern is an Anglo Saxon word, compounded of Bere, *Barley*, and Ern, or Ærn, *A place, A closet*.

---

[1] I forget whether Mr. Tooke's derivation of *Barn* from Bar-en, (the p. p. of the Verb *To Bar*) i. e. *A place barred up to keep thieves, &c. out*, has been noticed. Of course it is quite unnecessary to offer any comment upon it.

Bere[1], or *Barley*, was a grain much grown by our Saxon Ancestors in England: we read of the Bere-hláf, or *Barley-loaf*, but not of *Wheat-loaf*. And I suspect its evident connexion with the Anglo Saxon verb Béran, *To produce, To bear* (and afterwards) *To excel*, is to be traced to the fact, that *Bere*, or *Barley*, was that produce of the earth on which our Ancestors mainly depended for their sustenance.

It makes no essential difference to our present investigation, whether we assume the above word Bere, or with Dr. Bosworth the Franco-Theotisc Bar, *Fruit, Any produce of the earth*, to be the root of the Anglo-Saxon verb Béran. Undoubtedly, if Bere and Bar be not the same word, one of them is the root, and it matters not which. The following words, then, Anglo Saxon and English, constitute the members of this family.

(*a*) Verbal Derivatives from the Anglo Saxon verb Bér-an, *To bear, produce, carry.*

1. *Birth*, Anglo Saxon Berð, third person Singular, *A bringing forth.*
2. *Bearn*,[2] Anglo Saxon Bearn, *One born, A child.* From this word according to Wachter is derived
3. *Baron.*
4. *Barm*, or *Yeast;* that which is *borne* up, Anglo Saxon *Bearme.*
5. *Bier*, Anglo Saxon Bær, *A portable* bed.
6. *Bird*,[3] (perhaps). Anglo Saxon Brid, the young of any animal.

(*b*) Anglo Saxon and English words connected with Bere, *Barley.*

1. *Barn*, Anglo Saxon Bern, *i. e.* Bere-ærn, *A storehouse*, or receptacle for Barley; Ærn, signifying *A place.*
2. *Barton*, Anglo Saxon Bere-tún, in connexion with Anglo Saxon Tún, *An enclosure;* similarly we have Berwic in connexion with Wíc, *A dwelling.*
3. *Beer*, Anglo Saxon Beor,
4. *Berry*, Anglo Saxon Berie.

---

[1] "Now good be gracious to us," said Triptolemus, as he sate thumbing his old school copy of Virgil, "here is a pure day for the *bear* seed."

Pirate, vol. I. p. 83.

[2] Also written "Bern." Thus in the "Pirate," "He remarked moreover that the *bern* preferred home-brewed ale to Scotch twopenny, and never quitted hold of the tankard with so much reluctance as when there had been by some manœuvre of Jasper's own device, a double straik of malt allowed to the brewing, &c."

Vol. I. p. 67.

[3] This is Dr. Bosworth's derivation, but, if *Bird* and *Brood* were originally the same word, then we must refer both, as *Breed* also, to the verb Brœden, *To hatch.*

[4] Though there are several towns in England of this name, there is one on the south shore of the Humber in North Lincolnshire, through which the great North Street passes, famous to this day as a corn growing district.

The Anglo Saxon word Ærn, of which together with Bere *Barn* is compounded, enters into the composition of a few other words. *Dom-ern,* with the Anglo Saxons, signified *A place of Judgment;* Carc-ern, *A prison,* or *place of care,*[1] i. e. *trouble* and *labour.* It is supposed to survive in the English words *Northern, Southern,* &c., with the signification of *towards* the *North, South,* &c.

Strong, Strength.   Page 46.

Neither is *Strong* the past participle, nor is *Strength* the third singular of the Verb, *To string.* This method of deriving Saxon words from English Verbs, is highly reprehensible. It cannot be denied that the Verb *To string,* did at one time make its past participle *Strong,* which is only another form of *Strung;* but from this mere outward resemblance, to assert, that hence is derived the Adjective *Strong,* is simply childish. If the Adjective *Strong* is the past participle of the Verb, *To string,* to what must the Saxon word Streng, *Strong,* be referred? similarly with regard to *Strength,* and Anglo Saxon Strengð?

The Anglo Saxon Substantive Streng, or String, *A string,* produced the Verb String-an, *To compress,* or *bind together;* thence *To make strong.* This Verb makes the past tense *Strang,* and past participle *Strungen.* From the former of these arose the Anglo Saxon Adjective *Strang,* or *Strong,* which is our English Adjective *Strong;* while *Strength* is simply Anglo Saxon Strengð, the verbal Substantive formed from the third person Singular of the same verb.

Mould, Mouldy.   Page 53.

The question of the parentage, whether Saxon, or Norman, is not very easy to decide. Mr. Tooke so rudely shakes the faith we might otherwise be inclined to repose in him, by his preposterous derivation of *Malt,*[2] that it is impossible for any further remarks of his on this subject to have the weight of a straw in influencing our decision.

Mr. Tyrwhitt says the word is Saxon, as it occurs in the following passages of Chaucer:—

"But ike am old; me list not play for age;
Gras time is done, my foddre is now forage.
This white top writeth min olde yeres;
Min herte is also *mouled* as min heres."
                    The Reves Prologue.

---

[1] *Carc* is the Anglo Saxon word for *care;* hence the expression "*carking-care,*" is simply a tautology.

[2] See page 52.

"Let us not *moulen* thus in idlenesse."
The Man of Lawes Prologue.

Mr. Thomas Wright, on the contrary, calls the word Anglo Norman; though on what grounds we do not know. The following passages, assuming as I think we may do, that the same root is contained both in *moled* and *moles*, would certainly point us to the Anglo Saxon Substantive Mál, *A mole, spot, mark, blot.*

"I tooke good kepe, by Crist!
And Conscience bothe,
Of Hankyn the actif man,
And how he was y-clothed.
He hadde a cote of Cristendom,
As holy kirke bileveth;
And it was *moled* in many places
With many sondry plottes."

Then shortly after in speaking of this self-same coat—

"By Crist!" quod Conscience tho,
Thi beste cote Hankyn
Hath many *moles* and spottes,
It moste ben y-wasshe."

Yard of Beef. Page 96.

"I did purpose to have fasted this morning, as well to save victuals as on a religious score; but the blessings of the saints must not be slighted.—Sir Cook, let me have half a *yard* or so of broiled beef presently; bid the pantler send me a manchet, and the butler a cup of wine. I will take a running fast on the western battlements."*

* "Old Henry Jenkins, in his recollections of the Abbacies before their dissolution has preserved the fact, that roast beef was delivered out to the guests, not by weight, but by measure."
The Betrothed. Page 124 and Note.

Gome. Page 106.

Gome is clearly the Anglo Saxon word Guma, *A man.* But whence comes the word *Groom*, so much resembling it? Mr. Tooke thinks that *Groom* is simply a corruption of *Gome*; yet, if it be, it must have been a very early one, since both the words, both *Gome* and *Grom*, occur in the "Vision of Piers Ploughman," as early as the fourteenth century:

"I Gloton, quod the *grom*,
Gilty me yelde
That I have trespassed with my tonge
I can noght telle how ofte."
Lines, 3221—3224.

It is difficult to account for the insertion of the letter *r*, as it does not appear either in the Anglo Saxon, or in any of the cognate languages—the Gothic, German, Dutch, Danish, or Swedish—where we should have expected, or not have been surprised, to find it. The Anglo Saxon word corresponding to, if not identical with, the word *Bride-groom*, is Bry'd-guma.

Aught.   Page 113.

The Substantive *Aught*, is the Anglo Saxon A'ht, *Aught, Anything, Something.* The question then resolves itself into this; what is the Anglo Saxon A'ht? That this also is a derivative from the Verb A'gan, *To Own*, or *Possess*, is highly probable, not only because it is literally the past tense of that Verb, A'ht, but also from the further consideration of this perfect, which in the 3rd person singular is written Æhte, appearing again as the Substantive A'ht, with a signification to all intents and purposes the same as that of Æ'ht, *Aught*, namely, *Property* of any kind, *Lands, Goods, Riches, Cattle*, &c. Of course *Naught* is the Anglo Saxon Naht, *i. e.* Na-a'ht, N-a'ht, *Nothing*.

Another example of the old meaning of the verb *Aught* will be found in "Red Gauntlet," Vol. II. p. 62.

"God forbid Mr. Fairford! I who have done and suffered in the forty-five! I reckon the Highlandmen did me damage to the amount of £100. Scots, forby all they ate and drunk.—No, no, Sir; I stand beyond challenge; but as for plaguing myself with county business, 'let them that *aught* the mare shoe the mare.'"

Than.   Pages 138, 146.

There is no difference between THAN and THEN, except that which usage and convention have begotten. We might gather thus much even from the ambiguous usage of the two words in the Breeches Bible, and when we ascend still higher to the Anglo Saxon, the question is settled at once by their entire coincidence. The following, according to Ettmüller, are the various meanings in which this Relative Pronoun was used by the Anglo Saxons:—

1. Adverb. Tunc, Tum, *Then*.

    Example : "And þonne com þu siððan and bring þinu lác :" And *then* come thou afterwards and bring thy gift.

2. Conjunction:

    (*a*) Quam, *Than*, after a comparative.

    Example : "Soðlice ic secge eow. Buton eower rihtwisnys mare sy þonne þæra writera and sundor-halgena. Na ga ge on heofenan rice." *Matth.* v. 20. "Truly, I say to you, unless your righteousness be more *than* (that) of the Scribes and Pharisees," &c.

(*b*) Ergo, Antem, Igitur, *Therefore.*
    Example: "Hu mæg þonne his rice standan." How *therefore* may his kingdom stand." *Matth.* xv. 26.

(*c*) Nam, *For.*

(*d*) *Then,* in introducing a conclusion.

(*e*) Si, *If.*

(*f*) Quando, *When.*
    Example: " Se móna hwîl-tidum þonne he full byð."

(*g*) Quam si, *Than if.*
    Example: "Hwelc is wyrsa wôl oððe æninum men mâre darn, þonne he hæbbe feónd on freóndes anlîcnesse." "What is a greater calamity or more mischievous to any man, *than if* he have an enemy in the disguise of a friend ?"

Such were the meanings and uses of the word þonne, or þenne, or þænne, for, though spelt in all these different ways, it is still the same word amongst the Saxons. But it is more particularly its function in enabling us to compare one thing with another which we have now to consider, and the arguments which may be adduced from the analogy of other languages in defence of the theory we have already laid down. We will begin, then, by asking what is the verdict of Latin? What is the word *Quam*, that word which is precisely analogous to the þænne in the Anglo Saxon? What is *Quam*, but the same case of the same Relative Pronoun; that is, the corresponding Relative Pronoun in the Latin Tongue? The only difference seems to be, that instead of taking the masculine gender, as was the case in the Anglo Saxon, the Latins have taken the feminine gender; simply, no doubt, because with them the original Substantive which was afterwards dropped, was of the feminine gender.

Again, is the method of instituting comparisons in the Greek language likely to assist us at all? True, it is impossible to speak with the same certainty of the nature and origin of the comparative particle ἤ, as we can of the corresponding particles *Quam* and *Than*, in Latin and English. Yet, is it highly improbable, that even the Greek particle ἤ, should have been, in the early period of the language, a relative Pronoun? On this point, however, we do not insist, but pass on to consider another peculiarity in the construction of comparative clauses in Latin and Greek, and even English too. Every schoolboy knows, that in the former two a comparison may be expressed by using one of the particles, *Quam*, or ἤ, as the case may be, or, otherwise, by placing the second Substantive, that with which the principal Substantive is compared, in the Ablative Case in Latin, or in the Genitive case in Greek. Now what are these but Genitives, or Ablatives absolute? Tacitus says,

"Res prosperæ acriore stimulo animos explorant quam adversæ; quia miseriæ tolerantur felicitate corrumpimur."

which we may render for the sake of comparison "Prosperity tries the disposition with a keener probe than adversity; because the latter is endured, by the former we are corrupted."

Here it will be observed, that *quam adversæ*, exactly corresponds to *than adversity*, and, were we to supply, or complete the ellipsis, we should read, " *Quem* (for *Quam*) *stimulum*"—"þonne (for þone) gád,"—" *Which probe*"—*Adversity tries the disposition with.* Where " *Quem stimulum*," "þonne (i. e. þone) gúd," and " *Which probe*" are ungoverned accusatives, introduced, not as Agents, but, if we may so speak, as dummies for the purpose of comparing something else with them. But the comparison, in the Latin, might have been otherwise expressed, instead of by *quam adversæ*, by *adversis*. And in that case what would *adversis* be but an *Ablative Absolute*, standing by implication for "*adversis rebus acri stimulo animos explorantibus.*" Which, in reality, is only another method of introducing the dummy. And similarly, in the Greek the particle ἤ, might have been replaced by the *Genitive Absolute*.

Of course it is useless to apply to the Romance Languages for further information, as they would only dimly reflect the light already borrowed from the Latin. We may, however, observe that the Dutch *Dan*, and the German *Denn* (the Accusative Masculine of the Article, or Relative *Der, Die, Das*, just as þonne is of *Se, Seo, þæt*) afford additional strength to our arguments.

It is true, there are other particles for expressing comparison, both in German and English, which, like angry creditors will not accede to the terms of our composition. Such are the German *Als*, and the provincial English (I scarce know how to spell the word) *Nor :* " He is no better *nor* he ought to be." What the word *nor* may be, and why it is thus used, I have hitherto been unable to ascertain.

Anglo Saxon and Latin Words indicating original connexion.
Page 181.

The following examples, which seem to point clearly to the connexion between, and in some sort the common origin of, the Anglo Saxon and Latin languages, have been selected from amongst many others, and it is hoped are examples against which no objection can be urged on the score of Latin influence on Anglo Saxon, posterior to the introduction of the latter into this country. We have but to remind the reader of that important principle in Phonetics, we might almost call it, which is so important an agent in diversifying, though in reality of shewing the connexion between apparently different dialects, or even languages. We refer, of course, to the interchange amongst themselves respectively of the consonants which form the three principal classes of sound; namely, the *k, p,* and *t* sounds. The consonants pronounced with the throat, and therefore called *Gutterals*, or *k* (*c* hard) sounds are *c, g, h* (*x*); those with the tongue, and therefore called *Linguals*, or *t* sounds, are *t, d, th* (þ, ð) and (*z*); lastly, those with the lips, hence called *Labials*, or *p* sounds, are *p, b, f*. As a simple illustration of this interchange, take the English word *Seven*. In the Gothic it appears as *Sibun*; in the Anglo Saxon as *Seofon*; in the Latin as *Septem*; and in the English (from the Saxon) *Seven*.

Other phonetical laws, and scarcely less important than this for the influence they have had in modifying the external appearance—the dress of a language, so to speak, without destroying the generic characteristics, we must not stop, nor is this the place, to consider.

The following, then, are the examples we have selected :—

Anglo Saxon.		*Latin.*
Fefer,	*A Fever*	Febris, Ferveo.
Feorm,	*Food*	Frumentum.
Brucan,	*To Use, Enjoy*	Fruor.
Metan,	*To Measure*	Metior.
Midde,	*Middle*	Medius.
Micg-an,	*To Water*	Ming-cre.
Misc-an,	*To Mix*	Misc-cre.
Tribul-an,	*To Beat, Pound*	Tribulo.
Grada,	*A Step*	Gradus.
Gcot-an,	*To pour* ⎫	⎧ Gutta.
Geota,	*A Pourer* ⎬	⎨ Guttur.
Gyte,	*A Pourinp* ⎭	⎩ Guttus.
Sæl,	*Health*	Salus.
Spiw-an,	*To Spue*	Spu-erc.
Man-ian,	*To Advise*	Mon-ere.
Mynd,	(Gothic, *Munds*) *Mind*	Mens.
Cyste,	*Virtue* ⎫	Castus.
Cost,	*Approved* ⎭	
Ange,	*Trouble, Anguish*	Angor, Anxius.
Sitt-an,	*To Sit*	Sed-eo.
Eorre,	*Anger*	Ira.
Cear,	*Care*	Cura.
Tihtle,	*An Accusation,* from ⎫	⎧ Titulus.
Teón,	*To Say, To Point to* ⎭	⎨ Titulo.
Pín,	*Pin, Punishment*	Pœna.
Suc-an, ⎫ Sug-an, ⎭	*To Suck*	Sug-ere.
Scort,	*Short*	Curtus.
Widewe,	*A Widow*	Viduus.
&c.		&c.

Q

Romance Wallon. Page 187.

"Frankes spech is cald Romance
So say clerkes and men of France"
Robert de Brunne.

As in studying the English language, the nearer we approach the times of Saxon domination, the closer does the resemblance of English to the Anglo Saxon tongue become; so in the French, the greater the antiquity, within certain limits, the more closely does the Romance Wallon resemble the Latin. As English tends towards, and is finally merged into Anglo Saxon, so does French tend towards, and finally coincide with Latin Of course, this Latin was not the language of Classic Rome, but rather the barbarous and corrupted dialect of the far distant provinces of Gaul. Still, it was Latin; the vocabulary Latin, the inflexion Latin. It would be quite impossible, as well as out of place, to attempt to give any detailed account here of the rise and progress of this language. Those who are desirous of such information, we may confidently refer to Chapters VII. and VIII. of "Sismondi's Literature of the South of Europe," Vol. I., and for an account of its connexion and influence with the Anglo Saxon, whence in the course of time the English Language sprang, we may as confidently refer the reader to Dr. Wharton's "History of English Poetry," Vol. I., where he will find the whole subject most fully and ably discussed. There is, however, one leading fact, which cannot fail to attract the attention of the most superficial student of these times, on account of the paramount influence it must have had in modifying the Saxon, and so giving birth to the English. We refer to the prevalence of the French metrical Romances in this country during the earlier period of the Norman sway. By means of these metrical Romances, and the English Translations which were presently made of them, we apprehend, the Romance Wallon must mainly have made its influence felt.

Had the Norman Conquest been only, what it was, the successful subjugation of a stubborn people to a foreign yoke, the Saxon language would never have yielded to external influence, even to the extent it did. But the Conquest was not merely such a subjugation; and the Norman Kings, in inviting over from Normandy the composers of the Metrical Romances and the Gestours, adopted, perhaps unconsciously, the very surest means of giving to the Romance Language a footing in this country. And how nearly these measures had succeeded we may have some idea from the facts, that Gower, the English Poet, wrote some of his earlier works in French, and that Chaucer was the first who had the courage "to emancipate the muse from the trammels of French in which at his time it was the prevailing fashion to write." In some copies of Bishop Grosthead's French Romance, called "*Chateau d' Amour*," there is the following apology for the poem being written in French: "And although the Romance Tongue is looked upon with distaste by the learned, yet, for the sake of the laity, who are less educated, the work has been written in that Tongue.[1]

"It was undoubtedly," says Dr. Wharton, "a great impediment to the cultivation and progressive improvement of the English language, at these early periods, that the best authors chose to write in French."

Beyond a few ballads, which were sung, or recited, by strolling minstrels, at the village ale-bench, or the country manor-house, we meet with no original productions in English for some centuries after the Conquest. Those who alone had the power of cultivating and rewarding the muse, as well as of enjoying and appreciating her during these troublesome times, were of Norman extraction; they spoke the Norman Tongue, and affected to despise the manly, though less sweetly flowing, accents of the Anglo Saxon. When at length time burnt out from the minds of the Saxon population the bitter recollection of past suffering and degradation, and they began to awake to the consciousness, that life had still its blandishments to offer them, they emulated the example of their Norman Masters, and sought and found recreation in the recital of those same metrical Romances, not indeed in the original Romance dialect, but *translated* into their own tongue. Nearly all the tales of Adventure and Knight-Errantry with which our language presently swarmed were nothing more than translations from the French: and there can be no doubt, it was mainly through the means of these translations, that the Saxon became impregnated with so vast a mass of Norman, that is, French words.

[1] "Et quamvis lingua Romana coram clericis saporem suavitatis non habeat, tamen pro laicis qui minus intelligunt, opusculum illud aptum est." The reader will observe that the textual rendering is not altogether literal.

FINIS.